lonely planet

Dubai & Abu Dhabi

Dubai Marina & Palm Jumeirah p103
Jumeirah p89
Bur Dubai p61
Deira p49
Downtown Dubai & Business Bay p75
South Dubai p117

Christabel Lobo, Hayley Skirka, Natasha Amar, Sarah Hedley Hymers

Yas Waterworld (p175), Abu Dhabi

CONTENTS

Plan Your Trip

The Journey Begins Here ... 4
Our Picks ... 6
Perfect Days in Dubai ... 22
Perfect Days in Abu Dhabi ... 24
When to Go ... 26
Get Prepared for Dubai & Abu Dhabi ... 28
Dining Out ... 30
Bar Open ... 32
Showtime ... 34
Treasure Hunt ... 36
How to Navigate Dubai Mall ... 38
Fine Dining in the UAE ... 40

Abu Dhabi Falcon Hospital (p159)

The Guide: Dubai

Neighbourhoods at a Glance: Dubai ... 46
Deira ... 49
Bur Dubai ... 61
Downtown Dubai & Business Bay ... 75
Jumeirah ... 89
Dubai Marina & Palm Jumeirah ... 103
South Dubai ... 117

The Guide: Abu Dhabi

Neighbourhoods at a Glance: Abu Dhabi ... 126
Downtown Abu Dhabi ... 128
Breakwater & Around ... 136
Al Zahiyah, Al Maryah Island & Al Reem Island ... 146
Sheikh Zayed Grand Mosque & Around ... 152
Al Mina & Saadiyat Island ... 162
Yas Island & Around ... 172
Day Trips from Dubai & Abu Dhabi & Around ... 180

Dubai Garden Glow (p68)

Toolkit

Arriving ... 196
Getting Around ... 197
Money ... 198
Nuts & Bolts ... 199
Accommodation ... 200
Food, Drink & Nightlife ... 202
Family Travel ... 204
Accessible Travel ... 205
Responsible Travel ... 206
Health & Safe Travel ... 208
Language ... 210
Travelling to the UAE During Ramadan ... 212
How to Visit a Mosque ... 213
How to Visit the Desert ... 214

Storybook

A History of Dubai & Abu Dhabi in 15 Places ... 218
Street Food & the City ... 222
Building Narratives ... 224
Pearls, Petrol & Progress ... 226
The Canvas of a Nation ... 228

FROM LEFT: VLADIMIR ZHOGA/SHUTTERSTOCK ©, KIRILL NEIEZHMAKOV/SHUTTERSTOCK ©, EILEEN_10/SHUTTERSTOCK ©

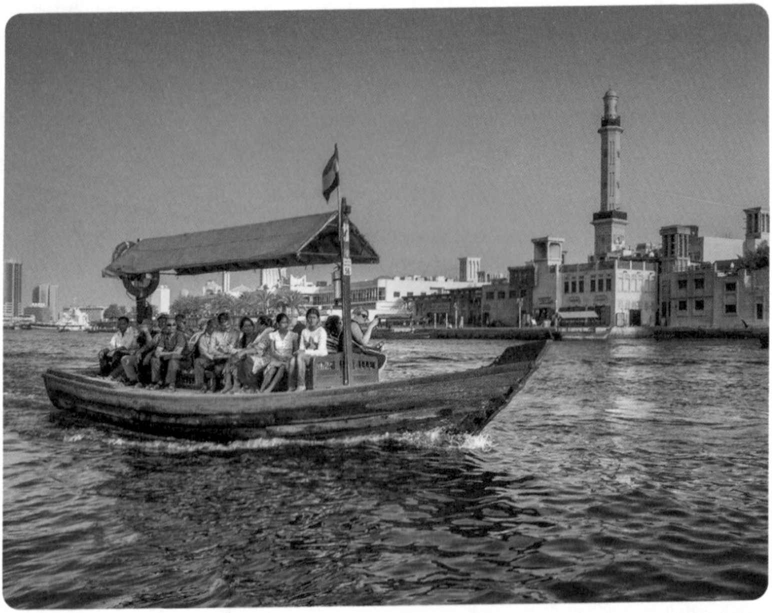

ALEXANDR VLASSYUK/SHUTTERSTOCK ©

Abra, Dubai Creek (p57)

DUBAI & ABU DHABI

THE JOURNEY BEGINS HERE

The United Arab Emirates comprises seven emirates, but two, in particular, garner the most attention. Like brothers, the neighbouring emirates of Abu Dhabi and Dubai bear a striking resemblance to one another, their chiselled features encompassing dramatic high-rise skylines, towering dunes, rugged mountains and sunny, sandy shores. Born of the same Bedouin drifters and pearl divers, the discovery of oil fuelled their ambition, but the pair went on to pursue very different futures. The more conservative Abu Dhabi pledged to preserve and present art and culture, opening the Middle East's first Louvre (p166), and commissioning more world-class museums to come. Hedonistic Dubai set its sights on the future (the theme of its most famous museum), becoming a playground for celebrities and the subject of reality TV shows, all of which serves its key goal: to become the world's most popular tourist destination. As these emirates realise their ambitions, there's never been a better time to visit.

Sarah Hedley Hymers

@hedleyhymers

Sarah is a TV presenter, editor and author specialising in travel. She has lived in the UAE for more than 15 years.

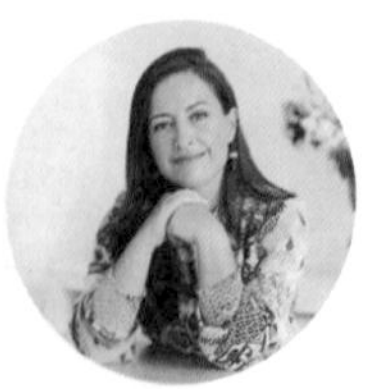

My favourite experience is crossing Dubai Creek (p57) in a traditional wooden abra. A ride in these taxi boats feels like travelling back in time.

WHO GOES WHERE

Our writers and experts choose the places that, for them, define Dubau & Abu Dhabi.

MATTEO COLOMBO/GETTY IMAGES ©

Dubai is one of the world's most vibrant, stimulating cities and offers a staggering number of singular pleasures, from the classic to the cutting-edge. It's famed for its ambitious futuristic vision and is inlaid with a deep sense of history and tradition, as felt in places like Bur Dubai Souq (pictured; p70).

Hayley Skirka

@hayleyscottie

Scottish-born and UAE-based, Hayley is a professional travel writer.

KARIM SAHIB/AFP/GETTY IMAGES ©

In Abu Dhabi, there's a strong sense of being connected to the UAE's heritage almost everywhere you go. The cultural scene in the city is phenomenal, and for nature lovers, Abu Dhabi is a dream to explore, with mangroves, parks, and the stunning landscapes of the desert and oases in Liwa (pictured; p181).

Natasha Amar

@thebohochica

Natasha is a Dubai-based writer, photographer and blogger.

M7KK/SHUTTERSTOCK ©

Step on the grounds of Qasr Al Hosn (pictured; p130) for a stunning glimpse of the UAE's storied past it's home to the city's oldest stone structure, a stunning Bauhaus-style Cultural Foundation, and Al Musallah, a, cave-like prayer hall that doubles as a serene urban park.

Christabel Lobo

@whereschristabel

Christabel is a freelance food and travel writer and journalist based in Abu Dhabi.

ART & SOUL

Jorge Marin's *Wings of Mexico* statue is an Instagram-famous example of the UAE's alfresco art. Follow its public art trails and make stops at emerging galleries to discover more. In Abu Dhabi, the scene is centred on Saadiyat Island, while Al Quoz industrial estate is its beating heart of art in Dubai. Smaller galleries aimed at investors can be found in Dubai International Financial Centre (DIFC), alongside the lucrative auction houses of Sotheby's and Christie's.

LEFT TO RIGHT: PLAZA © LOUVRE ABU DHABI - PHOTOGRAPHY ROLAND HALBE, KARIM SAHIB/AFP VIA GETTY IMAGES ©, LOUVRE ABU DHABI'S EXTERIOR © LOUVRE ABU DHABI, PHOTOGRAPHY: MOHAMED SOMJI

Capital of Culture

Abu Dhabi is set on being the UAE's cultural capital, with a Guggenheim and National History Museum soon to join Louvre Abu Dhabi (pictured) on Saadiyat Island.

Dubai on Display

Find Dubai's best art inside and out, from sculpture trails around Downtown to the galleries of DIFC, Al Jaddaf and Al Quoz.

Fair Attraction

The best time for enthusiasts to visit is during Art Dubai and Abu Dhabi Art Fair (pictured), which take place in March and November respectively.

BEST ART EXPERIENCES

Admire the ethereal architecture of ❶ **Louvre Abu Dhabi** (p166) as well as its compelling exhibits spanning human history.

Discover emerging local artists as well as international contemporary exhibitions and independent film screenings at ❷ **Manarat Al Saadiyat** (p169).

Explore Emirati culture through the lens of contemporary art at creative community space ❸ **421** (p170).

Wander through the cool galleries of Al Jaddaf Waterfront's ❹ **Jameel Arts Centre** (p68), which presents enthralling exhibitions and is home to Michelin-green-starred Teible.

Find many of Dubai's best galleries at ❺ **Alserkal Avenue** (p97) in the repurposed industrial warehouses of Al Quoz.

Skydiving over Palm Jumeirah (p107)

SKY-HIGH THRILLS

With record-breaking architecture, the UAE demands to be admired from every angle. Facilitating this, there's a dizzying array of ways for you to get your head in the clouds, from swimming in rooftop pools and gliding between skyscrapers on ziplines to jumping out of planes. The question is: how brave are you feeling?

Making a Splash

Near-vertical slides form the vertiginous summits of waterparks, and rooftop pool choices include the highest one ever built, perched above Palm Jumeirah.

Head for Heights

Bird's-eye views can be found in transparent tunnels wrapped around glass towers as well as from the observation deck of the world's tallest building.

BEST SKY-HIGH EXPERIENCES

Swim breathtaking laps around the world's highest 360-degree infinity pool, ❶ **Aura Skypool** (p109).

Experience a tandem parachute jump over Palm Jumeirah with a ❷ **SkyDive Dubai** (p107) instructor strapped to your back.

Fly down the world's longest urban zipline, ❸ **XLine Dubai** (p102), which descends from the top of a Dubai Marina skyscraper.

Take sightseeing to new heights on the 148th-floor observatory of ❹ **Burj Khalifa** (p78), the world's tallest building.

Shoot down the ❺ **Sky Slide** (p81), a glass tunnel attached to the top of the Address Sky View hotel.

Kite Beach (p91)

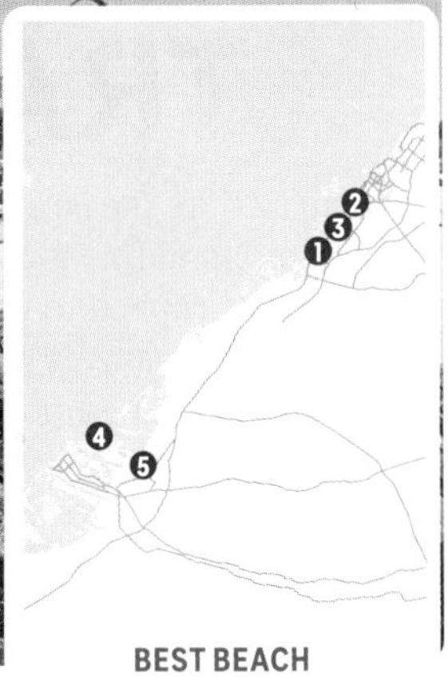

A SHORE THING

With year-round sunshine, the UAE is a sure bet for sun-, sea- and sand-seekers. The warm salty waters of the Arabian Gulf form a playground. Jet skiers and wakesurfers weave between boat parties cruising past Instagram-friendly landmarks on the shore. Below the surface, look out for sea turtles, rays and the odd whale shark.

Barefoot Bliss

Between the mainland and its many islands, the UAE has miles of coastline fringed with soft sandy shores divided into public and private beaches.

Beach Clubs

A shoreline this vast and picturesque is a breeding groun for glamorous beach clubs, complete with trendy cabanas flamingo-shaped inflatables an cool cocktail bars.

BEST BEACH EXPERIENCES

Experience ❶ **The Beach, JBR** (p111), which boasts the world's largest inflatable waterpark, as well as restaurants and changing rooms.

Enjoy water sports and early-morning walks at ❷ **Kite Beach** (p91), named after the kitesurfers who frolic in its waters.

Take ubiquitous Burj Al Arab holiday snaps at Jumeirah Al Naseem's slick ❸ **Summersalt Beach Club** (p114).

Enjoy live music, a pool bar, restaurants, spa, gym and padel courts at the Blue Flag sands of ❹ **Saadiyat Beach Club** (p170).

Play a game of volleyball at upbeat ❺ **Yas Beach** (p175), a hive of barefoot activity, which also has air-conditioned chalets for rent.

WELLNESS TRAVEL

Hammams are the cornerstone of UAE spa menus. In steaming marble tombs, tourists are laid out on slabs and scrubbed to within a millimetre of their epidermis. Massages with ever-more ludicrously luxurious and exotic local ingredients follow. Alongside next-level spa experiences, there's a packed schedule of fitness classes, including yoga sessions on the observation deck of Burj Khalifa and free outdoor circuit training, offered during autumn's Dubai Fitness Challenge.

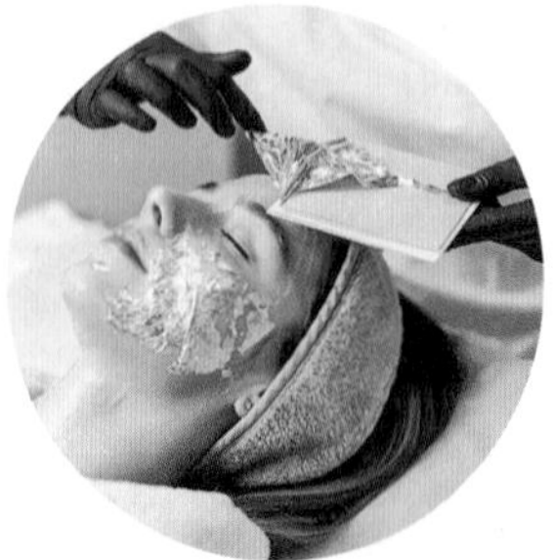

LEFT TO RIGHT: LANABENDINA/SHUTTERSTOCK ©, ABIE DAVIES/SHUTTERSTOCK ©, CRISTINA BERNARDO/SHUTTERSTOCK ©

Hammam Hype

Are gold and diamonds good for the skin? Find out at the UAE's five-star hotel spas, where they're used as decadent massage ingredients.

Dubai Fitness Challenge

From late October, the 30-day Dubai Fitness Challenge (pictured) sees the emirate overtaken by all kinds of fitness events, including free exercise classes. Join in!

Arabian Ingredients

Locally sourced spa ingredients include frankincense oil used in aromatherapy, desert sand employed as an exfoliant and cleansing rose water applied as a skin toner.

Aura Skypool (p109)

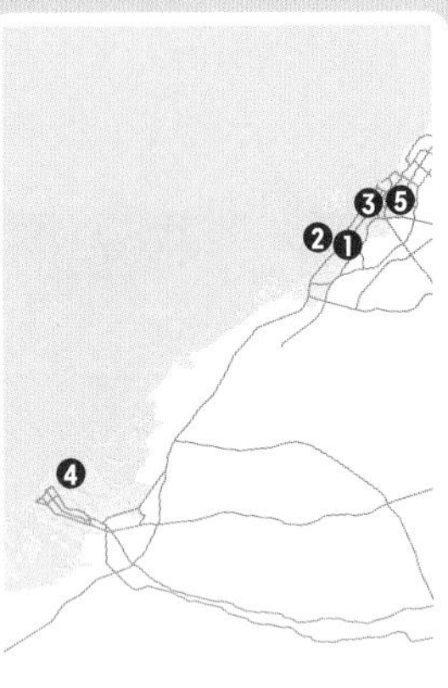

BEST WELLNESS EXPERIENCES

Relax at leading local spa brand ❶ **Talise** (p101), with on-site facilities including thalassotherapy pools, plus week-long wellness programs.

Look for pop-up yoga sessions at landmarks such as ❷ **Aura Skypool** (p109), one of the tourist attractions hosting winter classes.

Eat plant-based food at villa-based cafe and wellness centre ❸ **Seva** (p96), which also sells wellness products and hosts meditation and healing sessions.

Treat yourself to the Royal Hammam at st Regis Saadiyat Island's ❹ **Iridium Spa** (p171), which incorporates a honey and royal jelly mask.

Experience a diamond and gold royal hammam journey at ❺ **Palazzo Versace** (p101), which includes a massage using oil infused with real crushed diamonds!

ALEXEY STIOP/SHUTTERSTOCK ©

Dubai Miracle Garden (p87)

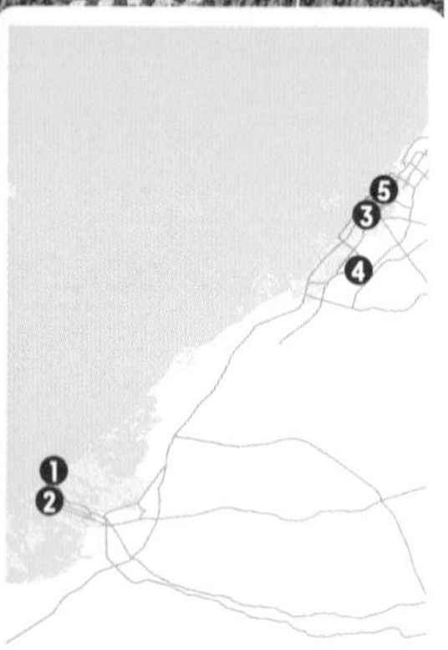

PARK LIFE

The UAE is known for its deserts and beaches, but there's more to this warm and pleasant land than sand. In between the dunes and shores, there's a plethora of surprising parks and gardens. Some are frequented by residents jogging, walking dogs and gossiping over lattes; others attract busloads of tourists on day trips.

Gardens of Plenty

Gardens come in all shapes and sizes in the UAE, but Dubai Miracle Garden has broken the mould with its record-breaking floral sculptures and butterfly pavilions.

Common Grounds

The country's mix of urban and coastal parks offers public places to relax, picnic and attend community events, from food fairs to fashion shows.

BEST GREEN EXPERIENCES

Make a picturesque pit stop on Abu Dhabi's Corniche at ❶ **Lake Park** (p134), whose centrepiece features a 15m jet fountain, surrounded by manicured lawns.

Get a free workout at the outdoor gym at neighbouring ❷ **Formal Park** (p134), which is looped by an exercise track.

Enjoy Dubai Fountain shows and attend pop-up events at ❸ **Burj Park** (p82), in the shadow of Burj Khalifa.

Walk among the butterflies at Dubai Miracle Garden's neighbour, ❹ **Butterfly Garden** (p87), home to more than 15,000 butterflies.

See optical illusions at Magic Park and life-size animatronic dinosaurs at Dino Park, along with electric flower displays at ❺ **Dubai Garden Glow** (p68).

Yas Links (p178)

GREAT OUTDOORS

Famous for its skyscraper cities, the UAE is also home to vast swathes of outdoor space dedicated to preserving wildlife, enjoying nature and having fun. Pursuits run the gamut from kayaking through mangroves to floating over the dunes in hot air balloons. Mountain hiking and golf have become hot post-pandemic trends, too.

Desert Safaris

If you have time for only one excursion, make it a desert safari, which typically encompasses dune-bashing, camel rides, henna tattoos and campsite banquets.

Mountain Highs

Al Hajar Mountains, the highest in the UAE, are home to Hatta Wadi Hub, an adventure playground with zorbs and rope courses, and lodges for sleepovers.

BEST OUTDOOR EXPERIENCES

Take the 30-minute hike from ❶ **Hatta Wadi Hub** (p186) to the Hollywood-style Hatta sign in the hills.

Go on a luxurious desert safari with ❷ **Platinum Heritage** (p101), with the option to ride in vintage jeeps.

Kayak through mangroves in ❸ **Eastern Mangrove National Park** (p159), a hot spot for biodiversity.

See wild oryx and gazelles roam through ❹ **Al Marmoom Desert Conservation Reserve** (p122), which covers 10% of Dubai.

Swing like a pro at ❺ **Yas Links** (p178), billed as the Middle East's only true links course.

THEME PARKS

In Abu Dhabi, Yas Island is home to a concentration of theme parks guaranteed to get pulses racing: Ferrari World Abu Dhabi, Yas Waterworld and Warner Bros World Abu Dhabi all vie for attention. In Dubai, the amusements stretch from Downtown Dubai to Jebel Ali, with a similar mix of weatherproof indoor and outdoor offerings, from IMG Worlds of Adventure to Dubai Parks and Resorts, a trio of theme parks with a Neon Galaxy.

Record-Breaking Rides

The UAE is hell-bent on breaking records, ensuring visitors have access to the tallest, fastest and scariest rides in the world.

Cool Waterparks

When you break a sweat, it's time to dive into one of the UAE's many waterparks. Yas Waterworld (pictured above), Aquaventure and Wild Wadi are super-cool.

Virtual Reality

Arena Games and Play DXB are among the parks offering VR adventures. Ride off into a fantasy world on a VR-powered motorbike or chase down zombies in an augmented reality.

LEFT TO RIGHT: KRITSANA LAROQUE/SHUTTERSTOCK ©, VLADIMIR ZHOGA/SHUTTERSTOCK ©, KIEVVICTOR/SHUTTERSTOCK ©

Atlantis Aquaventure Waterpark (p112)

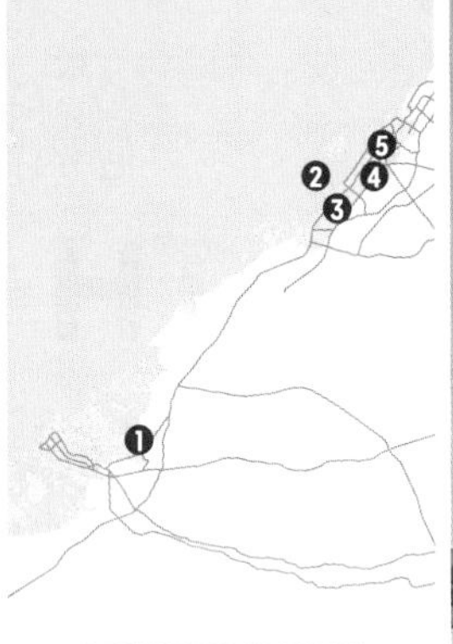

BEST THEME PARK EXPERIENCES

At ❶ **Ferrari World** (p176), strap in on Formula Rossa (pictured far left), the world's fastest roller coaster, going from 0 to 240kph in under five seconds.

Experience Aquaventure's near-vertical ❷ **Blackout** (p108) ride, said to be even scarier than its Leap of Faith slide.

Visit Legoland, Legoland Water Park, Motiongate and Neon Galaxy Indoor Playworld, which make up the multi-themed ❸ **Dubai Parks and Resorts** (p119).

Enjoy ❹ **Global Village** (p86), a world unto itself, with stunt shows, fairground rides and country-themed pavilions selling refreshments and souvenirs.

Tackle the coaster wearing a headset that takes you to scenes of devastation at ❺ **Play DXB** (p82), the world's biggest indoor virtual reality zone.

WITH KIDS

Family-oriented Emiratis have created one of the most child-friendly destinations on the planet, spoiling kids with exciting theme parks, adventure playgrounds and cutting-edge attractions designed to broaden their minds. Hotels cater to the little ones with fun facilities and tailored services, such as kids' spa treatments and mini check-in desks. Add to that affordable childcare, engaging kids clubs and family-friendly restaurants without curfews and it's understandable that so many cherubs want to return.

Playground Attraction

There are designated children's play areas in malls and parks, and on beaches and walks. Dubai's 19m steel Downtown Slide (pictured) is just one fun example.

Centres of Attention

Little travellers are spoilt for choice with so many attractions dedicated exclusively to them, from KidZania 'edutainment' centres (pictured) to the Children's Museum.

Summer Camps

During the school holidays, some child-focused attractions, such as Play DXB and Ski Dubai, host summer camps for kids, keeping them occupied all day.

BEST KIDS' EXPERIENCES

Hit the slopes at ❶ **Ski Dubai** (p91), the UAE's snow-covered indoor ski park.

Dress up and perform creative roleplay at ❷ **KidZania** (p86), a surreal world in miniature.

Experience zookeeping and overnight camping at ❸ **Green Planet** (p83), an indoor rainforest home to sloths, anteaters and armadillos.

Choose from more than 5500 varieties of sweets at ❹ **Candylicious** (p85), the Middle East's biggest confectionary shop.

Be transported to other worlds through the immersive exhibitions at the ❺ **Children's Museum** (p167) at Louvre Abu Dhabi.

FOR FREE

The UAE has a reputation for being eye-wateringly expensive, and it can be – but it's equally possible to enjoy the country on a budget. In fact, some of its most raved-about attractions are free, from the capital's gleaming marble Sheikh Zayed Grand Mosque to the dancing Dubai Fountain, which has been known to move tourists to tears. Dine at famously affordable restaurants such as beloved Ravi's and your dirhams will go a very long way.

LEFT TO RIGHT: VICTOR JIANG/SHUTTERSTOCK ©, M7KK/SHUTTERSTOCK ©, THE CONSTELLATION BY RALPH HELMICK. MDXB/SHUTTERSTOCK ©

Religious Encounters

To help promote the country's philosophy of tolerance of all faiths, certain mosques, including Jumeirah Grand Mosque (p95; pictured), offer free tours and you can even visit a synagogue and a church.

Fountains & Memorials

Public spaces are centred on water features and commemorative masterpieces that are worthy of admiration, like the Founder's Memorial (pictured).

Shoreline on a Shoestring

The UAE has generously furnished miles of coastline with free toilets, changing rooms and showers, along with outdoor gyms and running tracks.

Dubai Fountain (p79)

BEST FREE EXPERIENCES

Marvel at ❶ **Dubai Fountain** (p79), at the base of Burj Khalifa, which dances with music and lights every 30 minutes from 6pm to 11pm.

Visit the UAE's landmark ❷ **Sheikh Zayed Grand Mosque** (p156) and take a free guided tour.

Enjoy free tours of a church, a mosque and a synagogue in one day at the ❸ **Abrahamic Family House** (p165) complex symbolising tolerance.

Don't miss the ❹ **Founder's Memorial** (pictured left; p139), a three-dimensional portrait of UAE founder best viewed as day turns to night.

Spend lazy days on ❺ **free beaches**, from Corniche Beach (p144) to The Beach, JBR (p111), complete with showers and changing rooms.

UNDER THE RADAR

The UAE is a hive of hidden attractions – and we're not just talking about Hatta's Honeybee Garden. Once you've collected memories at all of the landmarks reimagined as fridge magnets, make time for the country's lesser-known gems. Look far and wide enough and you'll find drone-friendly lakes, arthouse theatre productions, and spree-worthy shops at container parks and out-of-town outlet malls. Spend your evenings at secretive boutique hotels, steeped in Arabian history.

LEFT TO RIGHT: GIUSEPPE CACACE/GETTY IMAGES ©, MOATASSEM/SHUTTERSTOCK ©, AGEFOTOSTOCK/ALAMY STOCK PHOTO ©

Underground Arts Scene

Dig deeper for culture fixes, from the exciting little gallery at XVA Art Hotel to Alserkal Avenue's cosy arthouse Cinema Akil (pictured), furnished with vintage cinema seats.

Retail Therapy

Grab some bargains at Dubai Outlet Mall and the Outlet Village (pictured), discount shopping centres housing fashion brands including Birkenstock, Coach, Mango and Tommy Hilfiger.

Unnatural Wonders

From meticulously manicured residential parks to a series of striking constructed lakes in all shapes and sizes decorating the desert, there are hidden oases everywhere.

XVA Art Hotel (p66)

BEST UNDER THE RADAR EXPERIENCES

Stay at the ❶ **XVA Art Hotel** (p66), set in a historical courtyard home.

Get a masterclass in beekeeping at ❷ **Hatta Honeybee Garden** (p188), the UAE's first queen-bee-rearing facility.

Take the kids to ❸ **Children's City** (p52), Deira's overlooked entertainment centre featuring a planetarium, park and library.

Picnic at Al Marmoom Desert Conservation Reserve's constructed ❹ **Al Qudra Lakes** (p122) – there's even one shaped like a heart.

Get cut-price sunglasses from the likes of Burberry and Oakley at Al Jaber Optical at the ❺ **Outlet Village** (p121).

Perfect Days in Dubai

From traditional wind towers to the world's tallest tower, Dubai's storied past and futuristic present can be traced in a few days, leaving plenty of time for award-winning food.

Dubai Mall Waterfall (p39)

DAY 1

Bur Dubai

Begin your day in the alleyways of 'Old Dubai'. **Al Fahidi Historical Neighbourhood** (p66) is a maze of dusty lanes lined with traditional wind tower houses. Originally homes for the aristocracy, today they're museums, hotels and cafes. Visit the **Coffee Museum** (p72) to learn drinking customs and pick up a coffee ice pop from the shop.

Lunch Savour plant-based creations at the **XVA Cafe** (p66), set in a traditional courtyard.

Bur Dubai

Next, sail between the **Textile Souq** and **Spice Souq** (p51), both favourites for souvenirs. Souq-hopping is more fun when you cross **Dubai Creek** (p57) by abra. These old wooden taxi boats are Dubai's most-loved attraction. Late afternoon, head to Downtown Dubai to marvel at the size of **Burj Khalifa** (p78). Stick around until 6pm when **Dubai Fountain** (p79) erupts in the first of its nightly performances, which run every half-hour until 11pm.

Dinner Enjoy front-row seats to Dubai Fountain at romantic and authentic Thai restaurant **Thiptara** (p85).

Downtown Dubai & Business Bay

After dinner, catch a show at **Dubai Opera** (p80) or head to **Dubai Mall** (p38) for late-night shopping, or to visit the resident Dubai Dino, a full-size skeleton of a Brachiosaurus dinosaur, located in the Grand Atrium.

DAY 2

Dubai Marina & Palm Jumeirah

Get an early morning start at **The Beach, JBR** (p111) before the crowds arrive. The shower and changing-room facilities are free. Feeling energetic? Tackle the assault course at sea that is **AquaFun** (p111), the world's largest inflatable park just off the shoreline. It's not as easy as it looks!

Lunch Grab a trendy stacked burger and some Instagram shots at **Bounty Beets** (p31).

Dubai Marina & Palm Jumeirah

After lunch, head to nearby **Jungle Bay** (p109) waterpark within the Le Meridien Mina Seyahi complex. The name doesn't fit the venue at all: this pretty water park looks more like an Aegean seaside village. Next, visit Palm Jumeirah's **Nakheel Mall** (p104), home to high-street shops, Depachika food hall, a cinema and a trampoline park. Sunsets are best enjoyed sipping cocktails in the world's highest 360-degree infinity pool at **Aura Skypool** (p109), 50 floors above the mall.

Dinner Experience a sublime two-Michelin-star Indian tasting menu at **Trèsind Studio** (p115).

Dubai Marina & Palm Jumeirah

Party the night away in the same tower at **Soho Garden Palm Jumeirah** (p104) cocktail bar and terrace or head down to **Palm West Beach** (p105) where the rooftop bars and beach clubs rock until the small hours.

DAY 3

Jumeirah

Start the day with an early-morning stroll along **Kite Beach** (p91). Famous for kitesurfing, other popular pursuits here include beach tennis, volleyball and taking selfies with the landmark Burj Al Arab hotel in the background.

Lunch The best way to see inside **Burj Al Arab** (p92) without booking a room is to eat there. Go casual at **Sal** or fancy at **Al Muntaha** (p92).

Jumeirah

Avoid the heat and take cover on a guided tour of **Jumeirah Grand Mosque** (p95; available 2pm Saturday to Thursday), where you can learn about the Islamic faith at one of the UAE's few mosques open to non-Muslims. Next, visit Jumeirah's other most significant landmark, the faithfully restored **Union House** (p94) where tribal leaders signed the declaration to form the UAE in 1971. The site is signposted by its towering flagpole, while the neighbouring new-build **Etihad Museum** (p94) tells the story of the union.

Dinner Delight in modern Middle Eastern creations at **Orfali Bros** (p42), named after the wonderful Syrian brothers who run it.

Al Quoz

After dinner, head to **Alserkal Avenue** (p97) art district, a hive of galleries, concept stores and hipster coffee bars. Check listings for late-night exhibitions, performances and screenings.

Perfect Days in Abu Dhabi

Thumb through the chapters of Abu Dhabi's rich history on foot, taste its culinary traditions and shop like a local with our engaging itineraries that hit all the highlights.

Cycling, Corniche Beach (p144)

MASSIMO BORCHI/ATLANTIDE PHOTOTRAVEL/GETTY IMAGES ©

DAY 1

Sheikh Zayed Grand Mosque & Around

Dress modestly for a free guided tour of **Sheikh Zayed Grand Mosque** (p156), famous for its marble domes and gold minarets. The external arcades are supported by more than 1000 columns featuring floral designs inlaid with amethyst, lapis lazuli, red agate, mother-of-pearl and abalone shell. A 10-minute drive from the mosque you'll find the **Eastern Mangrove National Park** (p159). Kayak through its intertidal forest of mottled crabs, turtles and herons.

Lunch Experience Emirati cuisine at **Al Mrzab Traditional Restaurant** (p155).

Yas Island & Around

After lunch, walk off some calories at the vast **Louvre Abu Dhabi** (p166). The building itself is as impressive as the art collection it holds. Next, hop to theme-park-filled Yas Island and ride the world's fastest roller coaster at **Ferrari World Abu Dhabi** (p176).

Dinner Fill up on maki rolls, dim sum and robata grills at Yas Bay's exotic **Asia Asia** (p177).

Yas Island & Around

Check out listings for **Etihad Arena** (p177). From *Hamilton* to music by the likes of Maroon 5, Backstreet Boys and Sting, there's a year-round lineup of entertainment. Alternatively, end the night at award-winning **Café del Mar** (p177), a Yas Bay waterfront beach club and restaurant with Ibiza vibes.

DAY 2

Downtown Abu Dhabi

Start your day exploring the 8km-long **Corniche Beach** (p144), boasting sandy beaches, beautiful parks, a cycling track and promenade. Free beach A'l Bahar, at the western end, is home to AquaDhabi waterpark. Loungers, kayaks and paddleboards are available to rent.

Lunch Head to Conrad Abu Dhabi Etihad Towers for **Li Beirut** (p143), a restaurant that delivers on the name.

Breakwater & Around

The Presidential Palace, **Qasr Al Watan** (p140), is a dramatic mass of arabesque archways, domes and landscaped gardens. Take a tour to learn about the UAE's diplomatic relations, heritage and culture of tolerance. At sunset, make your way to the **Founder's Memorial** (p139). The captivating three-dimensional portrait of the UAE's founding father, Sheikh Zayed bin Sultan Al Nahyan, transforms from day to night, lighting up as a reminder of his vision.

Dinner Feast on mixed grills, including camel, at **Patron Meat House** (p143) on A'l Bahar Beach.

Breakwater & Corniche

After dinner, stroll around the grandeur of **Emirates Palace, Mandarin Oriental** (p144), a hotel patronised by film stars and dignitaries, and see how many of its 1002 crystal chandeliers you can count. Private tours can be arranged. End the night back at the Corniche, stopping for a digestif at boho-chic West Bay Lounge.

DAY 3

Downtown Abu Dhabi

Discover the past at the **Qasr Al Hosn** (p130), a palace and fortress complex. A museum since 2018, it's home to Abu Dhabi's oldest structure, a watchtower dating back to 1793, and exhibits of furniture and clothing that help visitors imagine the lives of the previous occupants, the ruling family. Opposite, the **Cultural Foundation** (p131 is dedicated to the creation and appreciation of Emirati arts.

Lunch Sample the region's favourite kebab, the shawarma, available with chicken or beef, at **Bait El Khetyar** (p134).

Al Mina & Saadiyat Island

Capture atmospheric photos of the wooden dhow boats at **Mina Zayed** (p168) and experience the hustle and bustle of the colourful **Mina Markets** (p168). Head to the **Dates Market** to pick up some homegrown souvenirs, then visit the nearby **Carpet Souk**, on Mina Rd, for an authentic Arabian rug.

Dinner Enjoy the fresh catch of the day with Lebanese wine at **Em Sherif Cafe** (p149).

Al Maryah Island

After dinner, wander the marble avenues of **Galleria Al Maryah Island** (p148), filled with designer boutiques, then catch the latest movie at the on-site cinema. Afterwards, enjoy a stroll along the 5.4km waterfront **Al Maryah Island Promenade** (p146).

WHEN TO GO

Keep your cool in the more costly, crowded winter months or grab some hot deals in the summer.

November to April is peak season. Temperatures drop to a comfortable level, and all the big outdoor sporting events take place, along with a calendar of food and art fairs. Residents and visitors enjoy lazy days on the water, long leisurely walks by the beach and sunset soirees in rooftop cocktail bars.

Christmas and New Year are the busiest times, with festive brunches and fireworks attracting holidaymakers in their droves. It's also an ideal time to go hiking in the mountains or camping in the desert.

Temperatures start to climb again from May. Some rooftop bars and beach clubs may close for summer, but indoor theme parks, museums and malls offer air-conditioned sanctuary.

The Rise & Fall of Hotel Rates

Hotel rates rise and fall in opposition to the weather. The higher the temperature, the more the cost of accommodation falls. Grab the biggest bargains in July and August.

I LIVE HERE

SUMMER DINING

Food blogger **Courtney Brandt** relishes the greater availability of seats in restaurants and reduced traffic during summer @_courtneybrandt_

Dubai in the summer is so much better than you think! As a long-time resident of the city, I look forward to the less hectic sunny months. While many restaurants in Europe close during August, I find that Dubai's restaurants are more accessible. I'm able to book wherever I like and get around my ever-growing list of restaurants to visit without the hassle of traffic jams.

Abu Dhabi Grand Prix

RARE RAINS

Don't be surprised to see locals enjoying the rain. It's a novelty, albeit one that shows up every year between December and March. Avoid the roads in downpours. A lack of drainage systems can lead to flooding.

Weather Through the Year

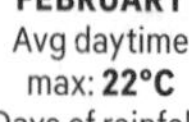

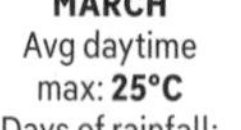

JANUARY
Avg daytime max: **21°C**
Days of rainfall: **6**

FEBRUARY
Avg daytime max: **22°C**
Days of rainfall: **4**

MARCH
Avg daytime max: **25°C**
Days of rainfall: **6**

APRIL
Avg daytime max: **29°C**
Days of rainfall: **2**

MAY
Avg daytime max: **33°C**
Days of rainfall: **0**

JUNE
Avg daytime max: **35°C**
Days of rainfall: **0**

SANDSTORMS

When winter transitions into spring and during the rising temperatures of summer, strong winds can cause sandstorms across the UAE. The storms carry pollutants as well as sand, so stay indoors should one hit during your holiday.

Religious Festivals

The UAE's calendar shifts to accommodate **Ramadan**, which moves forward by 10 or 11 days each year subject to moon sightings and the Islamic calendar. Throughout the Holy Month, Muslims fast during daylight hours and certain rules are observed. It's forbidden for anyone to eat, drink water or chew gum in public. Restaurant and bar opening times may be reduced. After sunset, hotels serve *iftar* buffets groaning under the weight of dates, Arabic meze and roast meats, such as lamb *ouzi*.

Eid al Fitr, 'festival of the breaking of the fast', runs for two to three days and marks the end of Ramadan.

A second slightly longer holiday, **Eid Al Adha**, 'festival of sacrifice', follows a couple of months later. Hotels don't skip a beat, but private and public sector businesses close for the holidays.

I LIVE HERE

WINTER HIKING

When temperatures drop, photographer and avid hiker **Ausra Osipaviciute** climbs the UAE's magnificent mountains. @theroadreel

When the rest of the world is covered in snow, winter in UAE is the perfect time for hiking the Hajar Mountains. Some of my favourite well-marked hiking trails of varying difficulty start from Hatta. For a more challenging route, I head to Jebel Hafeet in Al Ain in Abu Dhabi. Hafeet's ancient beehive-shaped tombs date back 5000 years.

Hajar Mountains (p185)

Sporting Highlights

Previous winner Rory McIlroy is among the golfing legends to have played the **Dubai Desert Classic European Tour** golf tournament, which takes place on the sun-defying green grass of the Majlis course at Emirates Golf Club. **January**

Serena and Venus Williams, Novak Djokovic, Rafael Nadal and Roger Federer have all battled it out at the **Dubai Duty Free Tennis Championships**. **February-March**

The world's richest horse race, the **Dubai World Cup**, gives punters an excuse to buy a hat. Before the thoroughbreds race for the $12m purse, guests compete for the best-dressed awards. **March**

Abu Dhabi Grand Prix sets pulses racing every year. The striking Yas Island track is straddled by a W hotel and the adjoining marina is loaded with superyachts where after-parties take place. **November**

COOL HEIGHTS

When temperatures begin to rise, many residents beat a path up the mountains. The temperature on Ras Al Khaimah's Jebel Jais, the highest peak in the UAE, can be as much as 10°C cooler than temperatures at sea level.

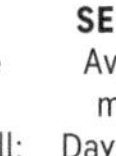

JULY	AUGUST	SEPTEMBER	OCTOBER	NOVEMBER	DECEMBER
Avg daytime max: **37°C**	Avg daytime max: **37°C**	Avg daytime max: **35°C**	Avg daytime max: **32°C**	Avg daytime max: **27°C**	Avg daytime max: **23°C**
Days of rainfall: **0**	Days of rainfall: **0**	Days of rainfall: **0**	Days of rainfall: **0**	Days of rainfall: **1**	Days of rainfall: **4**

Palace Downtown (p39), Dubai

GET PREPARED FOR DUBAI & ABU DHABI

Useful things to load in your bag, your ears and your brain

Clothes

Comfortable shoes You're going to need these to get around those mega malls. In the winter, you might even want to pack hiking boots to explore the country's majestic mountains.

Hats and sunglasses There's rarely a grey day in this sun-drenched desert land.

Layers While outdoor temperatures may soar from around 20°C (68°F) to more than double that, the UAE is armed with efficient air-conditioning systems. Indoor venues can be chilled to as low as 17°C (63°F). Pack a light jacket, or at least a cardigan, even in the summer.

Modest attire Tolerance is a cornerstone of the UAE's multicultural society, but expats and tourists are guests in a country where respect can be shown through modest dress. Keep bikinis and other revealing Lycra items on the beach, and off the streets.

Manners

Lewd conduct is an offence. Rude hand gestures and aggressive swearing can land you in serious trouble.

Don't photograph people without their consent. Posting pictures of others on social media without their permission is an offence.

Refrain from PDAs. Public displays of affection, such as kissing or groping, are not permitted, regardless of whether you're straight, gay, married or just mucking about.

READ

Arabian Sands (Wilfred Thesiger; 1959) An explorer's journey through Arabia's Empty Quarter in the '40s.

From Rags to Riches (Mohammed Al Fahim; 1995) A tale tracing a path from barefoot Bedouin to well-healed Emirati citizen after the UAE struck oil.

The Sand Fish: A Novel from Dubai (Maha Gargash; 2009) Insightful memoir about living through the country's epic transformation.

Rigged (Ben Mezrich; 2007) The 'mostly true story' of a Wall Street broker who helped shape the region's oil trade.

Words

Be polite in any language. With 200 different nationalities calling the UAE home, you're as likely to encounter residents speaking Tagalog as you are to hear Arabic. Folks on the hospitality front line are impressively adept at switching between multiple languages, but English is the most widely spoken. Road signs, shop names and menus are all typically written in English, too. If you want to get your tongue around Arabic, a few choice words and phrases can help break the ice with the locals.

'As salam alaykum' is a common greeting, meaning 'peace be upon you'. *'Wa alaykum as-salaam'* – 'and peace be upon you too' – is the typical response. *'Salam'* means 'peace', and in a casual encounter, *salam* can stand alone as a way to say hello or goodbye.

'Ahlan' is another way to say hello.

'Inshallah', which means 'God willing', is used like the word 'hopefully'. It can be a source of frustration when trying to ascertain definitive information. For example, 'Will the bus be leaving on time?' might be answered with *'Inshallah'*.

'Yalla!' is a word often overheard with several connotations. It can mean 'let's go', 'hurry up', 'come on' and even 'alrighty!'.

'Habibti' frequently follows *'yalla'*, softening the urgency of it with a term of endearment that means 'my love', 'my dear' or 'my darling'.

'Shukran' is used in all Arabic-speaking countries, in both formal and informal settings, meaning 'thank you'.

WATCH

Mission: Impossible – Ghost Protocol (Brad Bird; 2011) Agent Ethan Hunt climbs Burj Khalifa (pictured).

City of Life (Ali F Mostafa; 2009) The fates of three Dubai residents – an Indian taxi driver, a Romanian flight attendant and a rich Arab – collide.

Star Wars: The Force Awakens (JJ Abrams; 2015) In a galaxy far, far away floats planet Jakku, depicted in part by the UAE's Empty Quarter.

Dubai Bling (Netflix; 2022) Reality TV series following the lavish lifestyles of Dubai's biggest influencers.

LISTEN

Deep Fried A podcast series by Frying Pan Adventures, Dubai's favourite food tour company, detailing its best finds.

Afternoons with Helen Farmer Radio show and podcast dissecting UAE life, with guest experts sharing tips on fun stuff to do.

Inspiring UAE Women A podcast dedicated to the UAE's pioneering female business leaders.

The People of Dubai Podcasters Annie and Hollie interview the everyday folk of Dubai, getting under the skin of the emirate.

Lamb *ouzi*

DINING OUT

The UAE's diverse and delicious culinary landscape reflects the 200 nationalities that live here.

Foodies visiting the UAE should aim to experience both a Michelin-starred restaurant and **Ravi's**. This authentic and affordable Pakistani restaurant with plastic tablecloths has been serving curries to expats and Emiratis, rich and poor alike, since the '70s. The flagship brand of this family-run institution is in Al Satwa, where you'll also find cheap and cheerful Filipino eateries offering a taste of home, from adobo stews to pancit noodles.

More multi-ethnic meals, created from the passed-down recipes of the expat diasporas, can be found in the streets of Bur Dhabi, known as Old Dubai, Al Karama (infamous for the sale of counterfeit handbags), and Deira, north of Dubai Creek. In Abu Dhabi, check out Madinat Zayed, which hosts a street-food night market, and Al Khalidiya, where you can find hole-in-the-wall cafes serving popular Indian paratha wraps and sweet *karak* tea.

Michelin-starred restaurants, reflecting a similar mix of cuisines, from Syrian to Portuguese, are mostly located within five-star hotels.

Emirati Cuisine

With so many cuisines to choose between, Emirati food can sometimes fall between the cracks. Be sure to seek it out. With branches across the UAE, **Al Fanar** is a chain restaurant that offers faithful Emirati dishes in a traditional setting. Some of the pudding recipes come from the owner's mother.

Best Emirati Dishes

CHEBAB
Fluffy pancakes, best smothered in date syrup.

RIGAG BREAD
A thin and crispy crêpe, typically served with triangles of processed cheese.

DANGO
Basic but delicious side dish of chickpeas boiled with red chillies.

LAMB OUZI
Traditionally baked in sandpits by Bedouins, lamb remains a staple of Emirati banquets.

Emirati cuisine is heavily influenced by neighbouring countries, dominant expat diasporas and locally sourced ingredients: dates, spices, goat, lamb, camel milk and hamour fish. It's not the best destination for vegans. Beyond specialist Indian vegetarian eateries, most places offering plant-based food are billed as 'vegan-friendly' and serve meat and fish, too.

Savoury Emirati dishes are flavoured with *baharat* – the local equivalent of Indian masala, a mix of spices – and the combination of spices used by each Emirati mother is a family secret. Signature desserts almost always feature dates, baked, blended, mashed or as a syrup.

Halal food is readily available; pork, less so. Restaurateurs must apply for a pork licence the same way they apply for an alcohol licence. Don't be surprised to see beef bacon and chicken sausages at breakfast buffets.

Supper Clubs

In Dubai, beyond the restaurants, there's a growing supper club trend. It all started with A Story of Food, a ramen-focused home-based dining experience created by Neha Mishra, the noodle queen who went on to open her own Japanese restaurant, Kinoya (p43). Another supper club, **Hawkerboi**, followed suit, taking up permanent residence in Dubai's JLT neighbourhood where it serves modern Asian street food.

Inspired by these success stories, more supper clubs have been cooked up, from the **Haus of Vo**, where 'Madame Vo' prepares nine-course menus that draw on her Asian and German roots, to **Girl and the Goose**, helmed by self-taught Nicaragua chef Gabriela Chamorro. Make enquiries via their Instagram pages at @hausofvo and @girl.and.the.goose.

Al Fanar

BEST PLANT-BASED RESTAURANTS

Avatara (avatara.ae) Chef Rahul Rana offers an elevated fine-dining Indian degustation menu at this exclusively vegetarian Michelin-starred restaurant (p115).

XVA Cafe (xvahotel.com/cafe) Browse the on-site art gallery after a colourful 'Creek Salad' of watermelon, mint and feta, or an 'XVA Thali' of chickpea curry and paratha (p66).

Bounty Beets (bountybeets.com) Tuck into vegan burgers, avo toast and açai bowls at this Instagram-savvy cafe (p109) with peacock and wing murals on the walls.

Wild & the Moon (wildandthemoon.ae) From its orange blossom pancakes to its veg tacos, this raw-centric cafe is fully and proudly vegan. The golden turmeric lattes are divine.

Raw Place (therawplace.com) Get vegan power bowls, superfood soups, nut milks and organic juices served in the cafe or delivered to your door.

Luqaimat

MACHBOOS
The Emirati version of biriyani, spiced rice with fish or meat.

CAMEL MILK ICE CREAM
Richer and creamier than standard ice cream due to the milk's high fat content.

UMM ALI
Fabled bread-and-butter pudding once made by 'hungry Ali's poor mum from scraps'.

LUQAIMAT
Light and spongey deep-fried dough balls drizzled in date syrup.

Siddharta Lounge by Buddha Bar (p178)

BAR OPEN

Whatever your preferred tipple – international beers, wines and bubbles, potent cocktails, molten chocolate or invigorating coffee – you'll be well fuelled in the UAE.

Fashionable nightclubs share postcodes with sticky-floored sports bars and terminally hip coffee houses. Whatever your vibe, there's a bar stool with your name on it in the UAE.

With confusion regarding alcohol laws, some visitors to the UAE wonder whether they can drink at all. In fact, they can. Across the emirates, with the exception of Sharjah, alcohol is sold to tourists aged 21 and over in licensed hotels, restaurants, bars and clubs. In Dubai, tourists can also get a temporary liquor licence from the high-street shops of the country's official distributors, A&E and MMI, to buy and drink alcohol within their private quarters.

As many of the expat communities that occupy the country choose not to drink, both hot chocolate and coffee bars are thriving. You'll find a glut of hot chocolate specialists in malls, where alcohol sales are forbidden and shoppers fuel 10,000-step sprees with cups of calorie-rich molten cocoa. As the signature drink of Arabia, coffee can be found everywhere.

Coffee Society

With its history steeped in coffee and an entire museum dedicated to the stuff, it's no wonder the UAE is home to so many artisanal coffee shops. Some of the most sought-after arabica beans in the world – among them Jamaica Blue Mountain and Geisha – can

Lonely Planet's Top Bars

SIDDHARTA LOUNGE BY BUDDHA-BAR
Med-Asian nibbles, classy cocktails and views of Yas Bay. (p178)

LOCK, STOCK & BARREL
Happy hours are multiplied by four at this Instagram-friendly chain. (p178)

LOCA UAE
Feel the fiesta at this bar-restaurant with beer taps in tables. (p92)

be found at Dubai's Mokha 1450, a temple of coffee worship located on Palm Jumeirah.

Dubai's original urban roastery, the Raw Coffee Company in Al Quoz, sources the best arabica coffee from farms in the 'Bean Belt', the area between the tropics, 1000m above sea level, and supplies local cafes, as well as selling coffee by the cup and bag.

Themed coffee shops are emerging. Petrol heads should race to motorbike-inspired Café Rider in Al Quoz or Abu Dhabi's motor-car-gallery-cum-cafe DRVN Coffee (p161).

Budget Beverages

When drinking alcohol, long opening hours and high prices can pinch budgets, so it's prudent to capitalise on the UAE's drinks promotions, such as happy hours, which generally run between 4pm to 7pm, and ladies' nights, which historically took place on Tuesday but now land any night of the week. Listings are available online.

Club Land

The UAE club scene is alive and kicking. Dubai veterans will wax lyrical as they recall late-night sessions in Ramee Rose Hotel's unpretentious Rock Bottom – one of Dubai's first nightclubs, opened in the '90s and still going strong, though the eponymous rock music is more likely to be R'n'B these days.

At the other end of the scale, the Penthouse Dubai at Five Palm Jumeirah is an example of an uber-glam rooftop nightclub where waiters weave through writhing crowds balancing trays loaded with sparkler-topped bottles of champagne.

In the capital, head to White Abu Dhabi in Yas Bay for a high-tech mega club setting with twerking podium dancers. Its Friday ladies' night deal offers entry and three drinks for just Dhs100.

***Gahwa* (Arabic coffee)**

NEED TO KNOW

Opening Times

Opening times vary widely, with some of the more popular bars serving from 9am to 3am, and late-night clubs closing at 4am.

Prices

Import taxes and markup on alcohol are high in the UAE. Outside of promotional periods, such as happy hours and ladies' nights, expect to pay in the region of Dhs40 for a pint of beer or a glass of wine, while champagne starts from around Dhs100 per flute.

Alcohol Laws

Alcohol rules vary between emirates. It's a punishable offence under UAE law to drink or be under the influence of alcohol in public, but alcohol can be consumed by those aged 21 and over in moderation and within private, licensed premises in all emirates other than Sharjah, where it is illegal to possess or consume alcohol anywhere.

FOLLY	ABOVE ELEVEN	ATTIKO DUBAI	IRISH VILLAGE	GOLDEN LION
A Madinat Jumeirah favourite, famous for prosecco popsicle cocktails. (p115)	West Beach rooftop bar with palm plants and dance acts. (p115)	The crowning glory of W Dubai Mina Seyahi, serving chic cocktails. (p115)	The original Irish pub. Expect a party vibe and live music.	Your chance to sup a pint on the retired QE2 ocean liner. (p73)

FEROZ KHAN/ALAMY LIVE NEWS ©

Dubai Desert Classic

SHOWTIME

From the world's richest horse race to the celebrity-filled boat parties that accompany the Grand Prix, the UAE injects as much glamour into its spectator sports as it does into its concerts and shows. While standard tickets are available, VIP packages push the boat out – and by boat, they usually mean private yacht.

Abu Dhabi's entertainment scene is centred on Yas Island's Etihad Arena and Etihad Park, offering a packed program of big-ticket spectator sports, stand-up comedy gigs, concerts and shows. Dubai's stages are scattered throughout the emirate and offer an eclectic mix of performances, from acrobatics at La Perle by Dragone to motivational talks by the likes of Tony Robbins at City Walk's Coco-Cola Arena.

Spectator Sports

The UAE is a hive of spectator sports, catering to residents who don't need an excuse to dress up. International jet-setters join in at world-famous events in the global sporting calendar. Among them are the Dubai Duty Free Tennis Championships, the Dubai Desert Classic and DP World Tour Championship golf tournaments, and Abu Dhabi Showdown Week presenting Ultimate Fighting Championship battles.

The Emirates Airline Dubai Rugby Sevens is the one to book if you're a fan of fancy dress, while the top-billing events (that see nearby hotels charging five-digit-dirham figures for their penthouse suites) are the Abu Dhabi Grand Prix, held during the last weekend of November, and the Dubai World Cup, the richest horse race in the world, held at the end of March, featuring the finest thoroughbreds on the planet racing for a $12 million prize.

Comedy & Concerts

Surprisingly risqué comedians (Michael McIntyre is a regular) headline at Dubai's Coca-Cola Arena and Abu Dhabi's Etihad Arena. When it comes to musicians who have graced UAE stages, it would be easier to ask who hasn't? Beyoncé, Coldplay, Jennifer Lopez, Robbie Williams and Lady Gaga have all wowed crowds. Mega stars often perform at sporting events, particularly the Grand Prix and the Dubai World Cup, so guests enjoy two spectacles in one night.

Theatres

From Tony prize-winning musicals, such as *Hamilton* and *Westside Story* to *Disney on Ice*, famous productions tend to make their way to Etihad Arena and Dubai Opera. Independent theatre can be enjoyed on the fringes, and the dinner-and-a-show trend is raging in Dubai.

LONELY PLANET'S TOP...

Dinner-and-a-Show Experiences

Billionaire Dubai (billionairesociety.com/dubai) With branches in Monaco and Italy, this upmarket cabaret in Business Bay's Taj Dubai hotel attracts napkin-swirling celebrities.

Dream (dreamdxb.com) Vegas-style chorus rows, podium dancers and singers blur the line between fantasy and reality at Address Beach Resort in Dubai Marina.

Krasota (krasota.art) With cuisine by Vladimir Mukhin, scenography by Boris Zarkov and visual art by Anton Nenashev, this Address Downtown storytelling restaurant is a hit.

Sublimotion Dubai (mandarinoriental.com/en/dubai/jumeira-beach) Augmented reality features in this seasonal sensory soiree at Mandarin Oriental Jumeira.

Tabū (tabudubai.com) Entertainment at this show-driven restaurant at St Regis Hotel Downtown Dubai stretches from dancing to sumo wrestling!

ENTERTAINMENT BY NEIGHBOURHOOD

Al Habtoor City	Unless you're staying at one of the three hotels at Al Habtoor City, you might pass it by, but it would be a shame to miss the spectacular water-theatre production *La Perle* by Dragone – that's Franco Dragone, the legendary art director known for his work with Cirque du Soleil.
Al Quoz	The Dubai industrial estate has been repurposed by the creative community. Among the art galleries, there's Cinema Akil showing arthouse films, and the 70-seat Courtyard Playhouse hosting improv shows and live screenings from London's National Theatre.
Al Wasl	Dominated by the 17,000-capacity Coca-Cola Arena, City Walk also has ample bars and restaurants where you can arrange to meet friends before a show.
Downtown Dubai & Business Bay	Besides Dubai Opera, Dubai Fountain delivers performances every 30 minutes from 6pm to 11pm. Spectators have been rendered spellbound as its lasers and jets reach for the skies in time to the ballads of the likes of Whitney Houston and Andrea Bocelli. Most of the city's best dinner-and-a-show concepts can also be found in these neighbourhoods.
Yas Island & Around	Alongside a roster of headliners at Etihad Arena, Yas Marina Circuit is also used to host gigs. The Yasalam After-Race Concerts held here are legendary.

LEFT: ZHUKOV OLEG/SHUTTERSTOCK ©, RIGHT: HEMIS/ALAMY STOCK PHOTO ©

Dubai Gold Souq (p50)

TREASURE HUNT

Shopping is a national pastime in the UAE. There are more than 25 malls and 3500 retailers in Abu Dhabi alone. The biggest malls in the capital include Yas Mall, stretching across 230,000 sq m and stocking more than 400 brands, and Al Wahda Mall (named after the local football club, which has its stadium next door), spanning 310,000 sq m and housing more than 350 shops.

In neighbouring Dubai, Mall of the Emirates is perhaps best known for its snow-covered indoor ski slope, but it's also home to more than 500 shops. A sprawling complex in the shadow of record-breaking Burj Khalifa, world-famous Dubai Mall has more than double that number of shops and its own indoor ice rink.

In truth, some might find smaller malls more manageable, like Abu Dhabi Mall, with its 200 or so shops, or Dubai Marina Mall, with just under 120. Even modest-sized shopping centres like these feature cinemas and eateries galore.

Beyond the malls, souqs attract crowds looking for more authentic Arabian retail experiences.

Souqs Appeal

Visit Arabian souqs for fresh food, spices, jewellery, fragrances, *oud* burners and textiles, from abayas (the cloaks worn by Emirati women) to striped *majlis*-style cushions.

Dubai's most popular souqs – the Gold Souq, Spice Souq, Textile Souq and Al Seef Heritage Souq – are clustered on either side of Deira Creek, making them easy to navigate in a single day. Traditional abra boat stations line the creek's banks and you can sail across for just Dhs1.

The capital's souqs are more spaced out, and they range from modern interpretations of markets, such as the souq at the World Trade Center mall, to the traditional souqs of Al Ain, a 90-minute drive from the city.

Shopping Festivals

The UAE hosts festivals dedicated to the pursuit of bargains. Abu Dhabi's **Summer Shopping Season** was launched to entice international shoppers in the hotter months, from June to September, with the allure of air-conditioned malls, prize raffles and juicy discounts. **Dubai Summer Surprises** does the same. The **Dubai Shopping Festival** follows, running from December to January, offering Christmas shopping trips and end-of-year sales. A program of entertainment for children accompanies the festivals. Expect life-sized cartoon characters roaming the malls.

Arabian Souvenirs

Dubai has been dubbed the City of Gold and great quantities of the commodity are traded here. One of the most popular souvenirs is a personalised necklace featuring the wearer's name written in Arabic. Get yours at Dubai's Gold Souq or Gold & Diamond Park, or Abu Dhabi's Madinat Zayed Gold Centre (p133), also referred to as the Gold Souq.

Arabian perfumes and incense are potent. Hit the souqs for a demonstration on how to burn fragrant oud and layer scents like a local.

Popular edibles include dates and Arabian coffee (a winning combination that is the cornerstone of hospitality in UAE homes) and camel milk products, such as chocolate, though it's also used to make soap.

LONELY PLANET'S TOP...

Independent Shops

Lighthouse Part cafe, part concept store, fully loaded with on-trend souvenirs.

Sneaker District Wall-to-wall footwear from the likes of Nike and Adidas for 'sneaker freaks'.

Sauce Beloved UAE-born fashion chain with boutiques in both Dubai and Abu Dhabi.

Mirzam Chocolate Makers Bars, bonbons and truffles with Arabian flavours.

Edit Oo La Lab Blend your own bespoke fragrances in arty Alserkal Avenue.

Odd Piece Dubai's treasure trove of original and restored antique furniture.

Flip Side Vinyl records of every musical genre, plus DJ workshops.

Comptoir 102 Boho boutique selling fashion and homeware, alongside snacks from the cafe.

Sauce (p85), Dubai

SHOPPING BY NEIGHBOURHOOD

Downtown Dubai & Business Bay	The Dubai Mall joins forces with Souq Al Bahar to offer visitors an overwhelming selection of shops.
Jumeirah	Mall of the Emirates dominates Al Barsha with a dizzying array of fashion and household shops.
Al Quoz	At Alserkal Avenue, once a humble Dubai industrial estate, the warehouses have been converted into galleries and boutiques selling everything from art to kimonos.
Al Zahiya, Al Maryah Island & Al Reem Island	High-end Galleria Mall is the retail gem on Al Maryah Island, with fashion giants such as Hermès, Zadig & Voltaire and Bauhaus rubbing shoulders with trendy cafes.
Al Mina & Saadiyat Island	The markets around Abu Dhabi's Mina Zayed, the port named after the country's founding father, are where to pick up fresh produce, including local dates.

SYLVAIN SONNET/GETTY IMAGES ©

Dubai Aquarium & Underwater Zoo (p79)

HOW TO... Navigate Dubai Mall

The Dubai Mall is one of the world's biggest shopping destinations. Navigating it can be overwhelming and it's impossible to see all of it in one day – but with forward planning, you can avoid the pitfalls and map out the most rewarding mall day for you.

Getting There

In the heart of Downtown Dubai, the mall is open from 10am until 11pm from Sunday to Tuesday, and until midnight from Wednesday to Saturday. There are strictly designated taxi drop-off and pick-up points. Cabs aren't allowed to stop outside of these, so don't try hailing one from just any exit. The nearest metro station is the Burj Khalifa/Dubai Mall, and the mall is a five-minute walk from the station via the air-conditioned Metro Link Bridge.

Plan Ahead

Wear comfortable walking shoes and take a bottle of water. Divide time spent on your feet with breaks for refreshments or a visit to Reel Cinemas. Don't overload your day. Identify your priorities. Which shops and attractions do you most want to see? See full listings at thedubaimall.com, which also features an interactive map, or download the Dubai Mall app. Inside the mall, you'll have access to free wi-fi. You can also pick up a map from any of the eight guest service desks dotted throughout the mall.

Shop Selection

There are more than 1200 shops, spanning high-street and high-end fashion and accessories, food and drinks, beauty and grooming, homewares, electronics and toys. Most visitors like to ogle at Fashion Avenue, lined with the world's most admired designer boutiques, from Cartier to Christian Louboutin.

MIND YOUR MANNERS

Mall etiquette is a serious business. Security guards are at liberty to issue warnings to visitors who overstep the country's cultural and religious boundaries. Refrain from public displays of affection. Holding hands doesn't raise eyebrows these days, but kissing is not a good idea. Visitors should dress respectfully. Save bikinis and cover-ups for the beach. Low-cut, cleavage-revealing tops, short shorts and see-through fabrics are not suitable attire in this family-friendly space.

Top Attractions

You can dive at **Dubai Aquarium & Underwater Zoo**; skate at Olympic-sized **Dubai Ice Rink**; get spooked at **Hysteria**, a haunted house experience; ride an indoor augmented-reality roller coaster at Play DXB (p82), and let the little ones loose at KidZania, a world in miniature designed for roleplay. Whatever you do, don't leave without seeing the Dubai Fountain (p79) in action. The water, light and music show takes place takes place every 30 minutes from 6pm to 11pm daily.

Where to Eat

With 200 dining options, deciding where to eat can be a daunting task. Food courts house all the usual globalised chain joints, but you can do much better than that.

Oozing French chic, luxury tearoom and patisserie **Angelina** is the place to get your cake fix in style. Impossibly pretty, it also serves a wide selection of savoury dishes, from steak frites to prawn risotto.

Galeries Lafayette Le Gourmet is a speciality grocery store, set out like a quaint European market, and a food hall of tasty concessions. Famous local chef Izu Ani's **Izu Bakery** is among its many treasures.

Eataly restaurant-cum-shop gathers an abundance of premium Italian food under one roof.

Across the promenade from Dubai Mall, Souk Al Bahar is where you'll find **Time Out Market Dubai**, a collection of the UAE's finest homegrown restaurant brands. Try the char-crust pizza at **Pitfire**, the stacked burgers and chicken tenders with secret spicy sauce at **Pickl**, and Reif Othman's Wagyu sando.

Where to Stay

If shopping is the sole purpose of your visit, get a room at the mall.

Address Dubai Mall hotel is decorated with display cases of designer items designed to entice and available to buy. Facilities include a spa, a gym, a club lounge and restaurants. Pool bar **Cabana** is a perfect spot for alfresco sundowners and Mediterranean nibbles, even if you're not staying at the hotel. You can reach the hotel on foot directly from the mall, slipping down the access corridor next to Bloomingdale's.

Palace Downtown hotel is connected to Souk Al Bahar, a madinat-style shopping centre a stone's throw from Dubai Mall. Among the dining options is the romantic Thai restaurant **Thiptara**, a prime spot for watching Dubai Fountain performances. The hotel spa features hammams, steam rooms, whirlpools and monsoon showers, and there's an outdoor infinity pool where you'll find trendy cabanas and Burj Khalifa views.

TOP DUBAI MALL ATTRACTIONS

Infinity Des Lumières Dubai A 2700-sq-metre exhibition space comprising 130 projectors, 58 speakers and 3000 moving images, this immersive art experience brings to life the works of the history's most famous artists, from Van Gogh to Kandinsky.

Hysteria Like a scary horror film house, this 'haunted attraction' invites guests to walk through its dimly lit corridors where ghosts and ghouls lie in wait. Even though you know they're just staff members, it's impossible not to get spooked.

Dubai Mall Waterfall Designed by architect Toh Sze Chong, the 24m-high Dubai Mall Waterfall features fibreglass sculptures of bodies plunging head-first, arms splayed, into the rushing water, honouring the region's early pearl divers.

LEFT: HORST FRIEDRICHS/ALAMY STOCK PHOTO ©; RIGHT: QUENTIN BARGATE/ALAMY STOCK PHOTO ©

Zuma (p42)

TRIP PLANNER

FINE DINING IN THE UAE

The UAE is undergoing a culinary revolution – and you're all invited. The dining scene has exploded in recent years, attracting global attention from the world's most prestigious restaurant awards and international gourmets. Those who travel specifically for food will be dazzled by the epicurean offerings now available. Don't forget to pack an elasticated belt.

Michelin Stardom

Michelin made its debut in the Middle East with the launch of its first-ever Dubai guide in May 2022. By 2023, the second edition held three two-star restaurants and 11 one-star restaurants. Michelin Guide Abu Dhabi quickly followed, launching in November 2022, awarding three restaurants a one-star rating.

At the same time, the World's 50 Best Restaurants awards established its first regional listing, Middle East and North Africa's 50 Best Restaurants, which the UAE dominated with 18 entries. This recognition accompanied by its newfound Michelin stardom elevated the UAE's position on the global culinary map, attracting more talent to the dining scene, which in turn has fuelled further advancement. Put simply, there's never been a better time to dine in the UAE.

Causing a Stir

The country's culinary scene never stops evolving. By the time you've ordered your aperitif, chances are another restaurant will have launched in the UAE. The upcoming openings currently causing a stir include **StreetXO** by Dabiz Muñoz at Dubai's new urban resort, One&Only One Za'abeel. By the ripe old age of 33, Muñoz's Madrid restaurant DiverXO had landed three Michelin stars, so all eyes are on his first-ever Middle East endeavour.

Other renowned chefs introducing establishments at the new One&Only One

CELEBRITY CHEFS IN THE UAE

Gordon Ramsay Get your Ramsay fix at Bread Street Kitchen at Atlantis, The Palm, and at Hell's Kitchen at Caesar's Palace Dubai.

Heston Blumenthal The Dubai outpost of Heston's Dinner restaurant won a Michelin star within months of opening.

Jason Atherton Spanning three floors at Dubai's Grosvenor House hotel, Atherton's three-in-one venue encompasses City Social restaurant and a chef's table experience.

José Avillez Portugal's most famous chef has brought dishes from his Michelin-starred restaurant in Lisbon to Tasca at Mandarin Oriental Jumeira, Dubai.

Massimo Bottura Often billed as the best chef in the world, Massimo is serving nostalgic pasta and pizza at Torno Subito.

Za'abeel include Anne-Sophie Pic, best known for her three-Michelin-star Maison Pic restaurant in Valence, France; TV chef Mehmet Gürs, whose Mikla restaurant in Istanbul has remained in the World's 50 Best Restaurants list since 2015, and Paco Morales, the man behind two-Michelin-star Noor in Cordoba.

In Atlantis, The Palm, **Studio Frantzén** has taken the space previously occupied by Nobu. While it's set to serve an à la carte menu, **FZN** (a take on Frantzén's surname) will offer elevated degustation menus in the new mezzanine level above the studio. Björn Frantzén's eponymous flagship restaurant is the only one in Stockholm to win three Michelin stars as well as ranking on the World's 50 Best Restaurants list. Eager foodies are champing at the bit.

At Dubai Marina's Grosvenor House hotel, Jason Atherton launched his **City Social** restaurant and **7 Tales** speakeasy bar before revealing the icing on the cake. His **Row on 45** degustation experience is set to compete with the most luxurious chef's tables in town.

Al Muntaha (p92)

Four-Hand Dinners

Coinciding with the UAE's rise to culinary fame, more and more award-winning chefs are flying in to collaborate with local Michelin-starred restaurants. Four-hand dinners give chefs the opportunity to share ideas, while guests get to experience a one-off menu in an atmosphere of heightened creativity.

SUSTAINABLE GREEN-STAR DINING

Conscientious diners keen to know their gourmet experiences are sustainable can take Michelin's green star rating as a guide. Green stars are awarded to establishments at the forefront of sustainable industry practices. In the UAE, just three restaurants hold a green star.

Boca Offers cheerful Mediterranean cuisine, while general manager Omar Shihab upholds an impressive sustainability ethos that includes using local produce, adopting conscious waste management and using renewable energy.

Lowe The first restaurant in the UAE to receive a green star, Lowe earned respect and admiration for serving farm-to-table fare. Dishes include grilled asparagus with white macadamia nuts and grapefruit butter.

Teible Housed within Jameel Arts Centre, artisan bakery Teible (pronounced 'table') focuses on seasonal ingredients sourced from nearby farms, creating fabulous dishes such as fermented hummus with sourdough.

Previous collaborations have seen Joan Roca of El Celler De Can Roca in Girona, widely considered one of the world's best chefs, join forces with Grégoire Berger at Dubai's one-star **Ossiano**, which hosts a series of four-hand dinners throughout the year.

Dubai's two-Michelin-star **Trèsind Studio**, helmed by chef Himanshu Saini, has hosted collaborations with the likes of Bangkok-based German twins Thomas and Mathias Sühring, whose self-named restaurant also holds two stars.

Meanwhile, **Hakkasan** celebrated its branches in Dubai and Abu Dhabi earning a star apiece by inviting the chefs from London's two one-star branches to the UAE for an eight-hand dinner!

Collaborations are typically announced on restaurants' Instagram pages, so keep a lookout ahead of your trip.

Ones to Watch

Chinese-Canadian chef Kelvin Cheung's flagship restaurant **Jun's**, located in Downtown Dubai, made its way to number 44

HEINRICH VAN TONDER/SHUTTERSTOCK ©

Orfali Bros Bistro

Best of the Rest

ZUMA
Popular Japanese restaurant with branches in Abu Dhabi and Dubai, where there's also an award-winning bar.

LPM
Abu Dhabi and Dubai diners adore this reliably good Mediterranean chain with tomatoes on tables as condiments.

ORFALI BROS BISTRO
The fabulous Orfali brothers bring Syrian flavours to their modern creations. Order the caviar bun.

on the Middle East and North Africa's 50 Best Restaurants list within a year of trading – and his dishes just keep on getting better. The XO sauce lobster spaghettini made with Cheung's homemade XO is unforgettable, and the charred rainbow heirloom carrots topped with smoked labneh, candied nuts and soy honey butter is gaining legendary status as one of Dubai's best plant-based dishes of all time.

A joint venture between sushi master chef Takashi Namekata and Wagyu master Hisao Ueda, **TakaHisa** is a lesser-known, high-end omakase restaurant. Pull up a bar stool at the counter and prepare to be seduced by seafood flown in from Tokyo's Toyosu Market and premium Japanese beef reared to order. Dishes include caviar-topped Kobe beef carpaccio and abalone straight from the shell.

Chez Wam – the slang French version of *'chez moi'* or 'at mine' – is a homey French restaurant in Dubai's St Regis Gardens on Palm Jumeirah run by chef Hadrien Villedieu, who previously worked for culinary kings Alain Passard and Joel Robuchon. Comfort food classics of baked Camembert, alongside vibrant dishes of charred tomatoes and nectarine with Yarah Valley goat's cheese and blueberry dressing, show Villedieu's mastery of flavours.

The grandest of brasseries in the capital, **Fouquet's** is another French restaurant drawing the favourable attention of local food critics. The original Fouquet's opened in 1899 on the Champs-Elysees; the UAE's branch is at the Louvre Abu Dhabi on Saadiyat Island. The setting is suitably striking, with chic white interiors punctuated by red leather chairs, and the dishes are refined. Think citrus Breton lobster with asparagus, cream and caviar, and dream sweets such as biscuit *soufflé au chocolat.*

MICHELIN-STARRED DINING

Dubai Two-star

Il Ristorante – Niko Romito Giacomo Amicucci creates Niko Romito's refined Italian fare.

Stay by Yannick Alléno Renaud Dutel serves Alléno's vision of haute French cuisine.

Trèsind Studio One of only two Indian two-Michelin-starred restaurants in the world.

Dubai One-star

11 Woodfire Akmal Anuar fires up a feast at this laid-back, alcohol-free grill restaurant.

Al Muntaha The best way to visit Burj Al Arab is by dining at this French-Italian treasure.

Armani Ristorante A decadent Italian restaurant in the world's tallest tower.

Avatara The only vegetarian fine dining in the UAE, spiced with Indian flavours.

Dinner by Heston Blumenthal Get your meat fruit here. It's as good as the version at the London branch.

Hakkasan Designer dim sum and reimagined Cantonese classics.

Hoseki Arguably, the UAE's best sushi restaurant.

Moonrise Solemann Haddad merges Middle East and Asian cuisine at this 12-seat restaurant.

Ossiano Leading French chef Grégoire Berger helms this 'underwater' haven.

Tasca by José Avillez The best of Portuguese cuisine, from rich stews to red prawns.

Torno Subito Massimo Bottura's homage to Italian dishes from his childhood.

Abu Dhabi One-star

Hakkasan Dubai's sister branch, serving the same dishes with even more vibe.

99 Sushi Haute Japanese cuisine at the elegant Four Seasons on Al Maryah Island.

Talea by Antonio Guida Slurp posh pastas inside the landmark Emirates Palace Mandarin Oriental.

3 FILS

A casual and contemporary Asian eatery perched alongside an old fishing port in Jumeirah.

KINOYA

Dubai-born supper club-turned-restaurant is now open in Harrods, London – a testament to how good the ramen is.

REIF KUSHIYAKI

Reif Othman's Dar Wasl Mall eatery now has a licensed sibling at Dubai Hills and a chef's table experience.

GAIA, DUBAI

Named after the Greek goddess, this upscale DIFC taverna has a fish counter, roast goat and other Aegean staples.

DUBAI

THE GUIDE

Chapters in this section are organised by hubs and their surrounding areas. We see the hub as your base in the destination, where you'll find unique experiences, local insights, insider tips and expert recommendations. It's also your gateway to the surrounding area, where you'll see what and how much you can do from there.

Deira
p49

Bur Dubai
p61

Downtown Dubai & Business Bay
p75

Jumeirah
p89

Dubai Marina & Palm Jumeirah
p103

South Dubai
p117

Bur Dubai Souq (p70)

NEIGHBOURHOODS AT A GLANCE: DUBAI

Find the neighbourhoods that tick all your boxes.

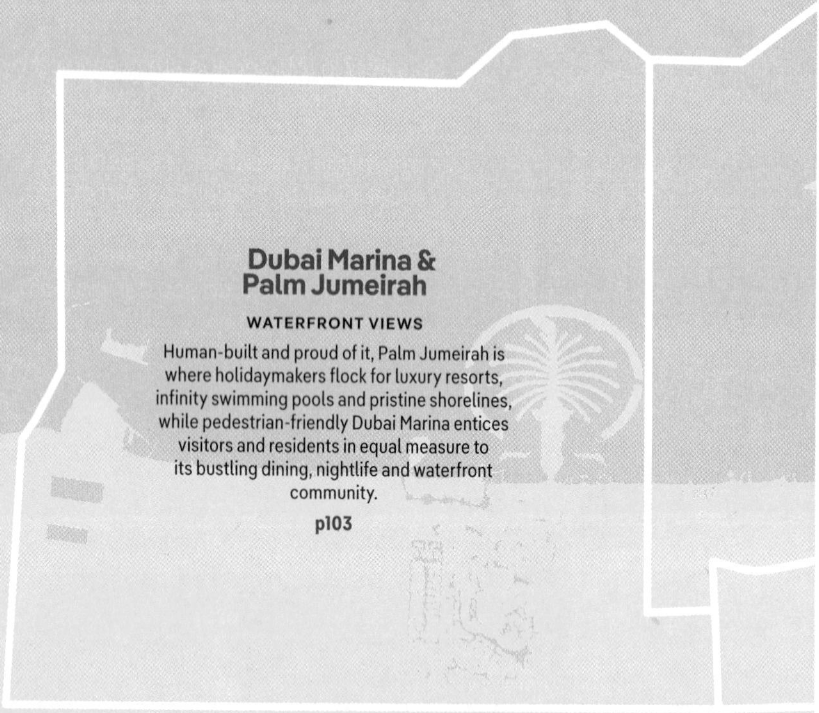

Dubai Marina & Palm Jumeirah

WATERFRONT VIEWS

Human-built and proud of it, Palm Jumeirah is where holidaymakers flock for luxury resorts, infinity swimming pools and pristine shorelines, while pedestrian-friendly Dubai Marina entices visitors and residents in equal measure to its bustling dining, nightlife and waterfront community.

p103

Bur Dubai

THE CITY'S OLDEST NEIGHBOURHOOD

The emirate's oldest district, waterfront Bur Dubai enchants travellers with labyrinthine-like lanes filled with traditional wind towers and historic buildings, all melded together via never-ending atmospheric Creek views and a multicultural community. Blossoming Al Jaddaf adds a touch of modern culture.

p61

Jumeirah

COASTAL VIBES

Whitewashed villas and seaside views await in this shoreline neighbourhood that runs parallel to Sheikh Zayed Rd. In a few decades, Jumeirah has gone from a sleepy residential hub to a holidaymaker's haven filled with dining, drinking and shopping, plus plenty of under-the-radar boutiques, all just a stone's throw from the beach.

p89

Deira

CREEKSIDE NEIGHBOURHOOD

Colourful, charismatic and crowded, this Creekside neighbourhood is one of Dubai's early settlements and very much the old part of a city that's known around the world for its futuristic attractions. Famed for its bustling port, its twisting roads are loaded with atmospheric souqs, colourful dhows and must-visit heritage sites.

p49

Downtown Dubai & Business Bay

THE HEART OF DUBAI

Dubai's beating centre is lorded over by the Burj Khalifa, the tallest building in the world. With its tower-filled skyline, entertainment options galore and one of the biggest shopping malls on the planet, not to mention a healthy smattering of culture at Dubai Opera, this neighbourhood packs a punch.

p75

South Dubai

EXTENDING THE CITY'S REACH

This new kid on the block packs a hefty punch via Expo City Dubai with its pavilions, attractions and urban parks. It's also a family favourite thanks to its collection of theme parks, laid-back resort hotels and the chance to reconnect with nature in the desert.

p117

TOP TIP

Deira's Dubai Islands is a waterfront neighbourhood that's still under construction, but it's already home to two hotels, both of which are great for families and offer lots of kid-friendly facilities, at a fraction of the price you'd pay for an equivalent hotel in any of Dubai's other waterfront resorts.

Above: Dubai Gold Souq (p50); Right: Spice Souq (p51)

I LIVE HERE: DEIRA MUST-DOS

Sarah Ameen was born and raised in Dubai and is an influencer marketing consultant. Here's her pick of things to do and see in Deira.

Dubai Creek Resort & Golf Club

Home to several restaurants and bars, including my favourite, QDs – a lounge overlooking the Creek with beautiful views of the Dubai skyline, and a fantastic Ramadan tent each year.

Dampa Seafood Grill

The place to go for an authentic Filipino seafood experience, where staff pour your food directly onto the table. This casual hangout space guarantees a great meal.

Take an abra to Al Fahidi Historical Neighbourhood

Hop on an abra and head across the Creek to this old neighbourhood for plenty of instaworthy pictures and TikTok content.

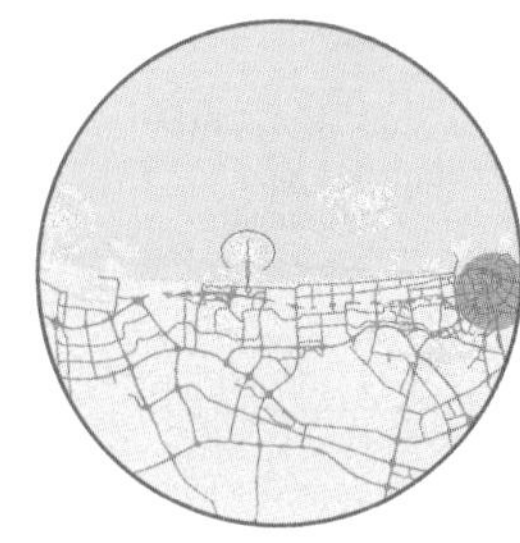

Deira

DUBAI'S CHARISMATIC AND CROWDED CREEKSIDE NEIGHBOURHOOD

One of the settlements that made up early Dubai, Deira is very much the old part of the city.

Lying across the Creek from Bur Dubai, Deira is famed for its bustling port where colourful wharves are piled high with goods. The region's early dwellings were made of palm fronds, but these were soon replaced by sturdier structures made of coral stone and gypsum, many of which remain today, making Deira a good place to get a sense of what life was like in the city in days gone by. From Al Ahmadiya School, the city's first formal educational establishment, to Dubai's first police station, a wander around Deira can shed light on a city that's undergone massive and rapid development in just a few short decades.

Deira's most famed landmark is the Dubai Gold Souq – a sprawling network of shops in the Al Ras neighbourhood near the mouth of the Creek. Piled high with earrings, necklaces, bracelets, tiaras and rings made from the precious metal, it's one of the biggest gold markets in the world as well as one of the best regulated. Sharpen your haggling skills and you could be going home with some bargain bling. Just beyond the Gold Souq, Deira's Spice Souq and Perfume Souq were the forerunners to Dubai's luxury shopping malls.

Home to a huge multi-ethnic population, Deira is also a place to go for eats from around the world. Whether you're craving Indian dishes, Middle Eastern fare or food from around Asia, you'll find it in this multicultural neighbourhood.

DON'T MISS...

DUBAI GOLD SOUQ

Almost all that shimmers is gold in this warren of shops piled high with the precious metal.

p50

DEIRA CREEKSIDE

People-watch as goods are loaded and unloaded on the dock, or hop aboard an abra for one of Dubai's cheapest must-do activities.

p57

DUBAI CREEK RESORT & GOLF CLUB

Not just for golfers, this palm-lined resort has excellent culinary options and a first-rate spa.

p54

GOLD TIPS

No matter what you're in the market for, here's a few pointers that will help you get the best deal. First up, know the going market rate for what you're buying, an easy one as prices are displayed on billboards at the entrance of the souq. Shop around and when you've found a piece you like, deploy the art of bargaining. While the gold rate is fixed, with a bit of persuasion you can often haggle down additional charges. Paying in cash can also boost your bargaining power.

Dubai Gold Souq

MAP P50

Shopping in the City of Gold

Known as the **City of Gold**, this den of side-by-side shops, piled high with gleaming rings, dazzling necklaces and shimmering pendants, is Deira's most famous attraction. Wander underneath the wooden-latticed central arcade to wonder at what is a simply staggering array of the precious metal for sale in some 300 shops. Dubai began trading in gold after the demise of the pearl industry, well before it discovered oil, so it's been an important market for the emirate for a long time. Today, all of the city's gold is government-regulated, so there's no need to worry about buying anything fake. Prices are fair, and haggling is expected. It's not just gold you'll find here: shopfronts also gleam with silver, platinum, pearls, diamonds and precious gemstones. Enter through Gate 3 and you'll come face-to-face with the world's heaviest gold ring. This monster piece might not be the world's prettiest, but its 21-carat frame weighs in at a whopping 64kg and is studded with 5kg of diamonds and 615 Swarovski crystals.

DEIRA CORNICHE & DEIRA MARKETS

HIGHLIGHTS
1 Deira Creek
2 Dubai Gold Souq

SIGHTS
3 Al Ahmadiya School
4 Deira Corniche
5 Heritage House
6 Museum of the Poet Al Oqaili
7 Naif Market
8 Naif Museum
9 Perfume Souq
10 Spice Souq
11 Women's Museum at Bait Al Banat

SLEEPING
12 Hyatt Regency Dubai

EATING
13 Al Bait Al Qadeem Restaurant and Café

Al Ahmadiya School

MAP P50

The origins of the city's education

Near the Gold Souq, this well-preserved example of one of Dubai's first **schools** has been lovingly restored using authentic materials like coral stone, sandalwood and gypsum. It was founded in 1912 and famed alumni include Sheikh Mohammed Bin Rashid Al Maktoum, Dubai's current ruler, and his late father. It's now a small museum with classrooms, corridors and an external courtyard. Next door is **Heritage House**, the restored home of the wealthy pearl merchant who founded Al Ahmadiya School.

TOP RIGHT: MARCOBRIVIOPHOTOGRAPHY/SHUTTERSTOCK ©; BOTTOM LEFT: GALLO IMAGES/GETTY IMAGES ©

Al Ahmadiya School

Perfume Souq

MAP P50

A place to awaken your senses

Looking like an old apothecary, shops in this **souq** are fronted by bulbous glass bottles filled with hundreds of oil-based fragrances. The scents are a traditional part of Middle Eastern life and range from heavy wood-based smells to mild floral traces. Decide which is right for you, and the storekeepers will siphon some off into a smaller glass bottle. If you have a favourite scent bring it with you – some shopkeepers can custom-make scents to suit. This is also the place to learn about *oud*, a scented oil made from agarwood and loved by Emiratis, and *bakhoor* – fragranced wood-burning chips.

Perfume Souq

Spice Souq

MAP P50

Heady scents in a vibrant bazaar

Disembark at Deira Old Souq abra station and you'll find yourself in front of the **Spice Souq**. Smaller than it once was, this pungent market is made up of narrow alleyways lined with stalls selling saffron, frankincense, cardamom, cinnamon, rose petals and other herbs and spices typically used in the Middle East, stored in colourful rows of burlap sacks. Shopping here makes for a great photo opportunity and friendly traders will invite you to taste, try and smell. Further into the warren-like souq, the market becomes **Deira Old Souq**, with a variety of groceries and kitchen utensils on sale – if you go this far, turn back – there's nothing more interesting to be found.

Deira Clocktower

Deira Clocktower

MAP P56

Keeping track of time

Perfect for a drive-by visit, Deira Clocktower is located on the roundabout between Umm Hurair Rd and Al Maktoum St, the first paved road in the neighbourhood. It is significant as it was erected to mark the UAE's first oil exports, a turning point for the city. Dating back to 1963, the landmark is often used as a reference point for directions and was revamped in 2023 with multicoloured lights and new greenery at its base.

Al Ghurair Centre

MAP P56

Dubai's first shopping mall

Before it was known as a shopping metropolis, Dubai's first mall was Deira's **Al Ghurair Centre**, which opened in 1980. Some four decades later, the mall is dwarfed by the city's more famous, upmarket shopping centres, but remains a decent place for retail therapy, with around 400 shops including the likes of Mango, Marks and Spencer, Aldo and Bath & Body Works. There's also a large Carrefour supermarket and a good selection of restaurants and food court options. Attached to the mall is the Swissotel Al Ghurair hotel, where room rates tend to be more affordable than five-star hotels in other parts of the city.

Al Ghurair Centre

Children's City

MAP P56

Imagination-building fun

On the outskirts of Deira inside Creek Park, **Children's City** is an often-overlooked attraction that's worth a visit if you have little ones with you. Designed to be fun and educational, the entertainment centre has interactive, hands-on activities themed around various subjects including the human body, Arab culture and nature. There's also a planetarium with regular shows exploring the night skies, stars and galaxies, and an aeronautics section where children can learn about gravity, create a tornado and see what it's like to fly a plane. A soft play area keeps younger children entertained and there's an outdoor park, a library and a cafe. The Dhs50 entry fees are a lot lower than many of Dubai's other kid-friendly draws.

Naif Museum

MAP P50

Dubai's first police station

Originally the Naif Fort, this **museum** gives visitors a glimpse into the UAE's judicial and criminal system. Built in 1939, the fortified building with its round watch towers was Dubai's first police station and was also previously used as a prison. It's filled with artefacts including a display of police uniforms over the years, weaponry and wrought-iron cannons, which shed light on how policing in the emirate has changed from a modest security detail to the supercar-driving force that Dubai has today.

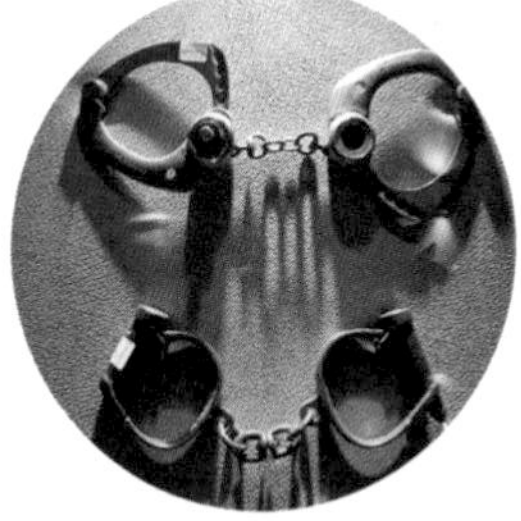

Naif Museum

Museum of the Poet Al Oqaili

Museum of the Poet Al Oqaili

MAP P50

A well-preserved heritage house

Behind heavy teak doors and under a house of beamed ceilings, this ornate building on the edge of the Spice Souq was built in 1923 and was formerly the home of Mubarak Bin Al Oqaili, a Saudi-born poet that moved to Dubai and is considered one of the most prominent poets of classical Arabic. The building was constructed by a team of workers that Al Oqaili brought with him from Saudi's Al Ahsa region and is filled with artistic writings and ornamental details. Now a **museum**, the space is split into nine wings where visitors can see examples of his writings and poems, as well as original manuscripts and some of the late poet's belongings, including his much-used writing desk and pen.

Women's Museum at Bait Al Banat

MAP P50

Behind every great man is an even greater woman

While men play the lead role in the story of Dubai's development, they have always been supported by a vast network of women who were hugely instrumental in shaping the origins of the country. Trace some of the stories of these pioneers at the **Women's Museum at Bait Al Banat**, the UAE's only museum documenting the history of Emirati women. Tucked away in the Gold Souq, this is the place to see the work of Ousha Bint Khalifa Al Suwaidi, one of the country's most famous female poets, or that of Muneera al Mazrou, the first female photographer from Sharjah. It also has pop-up exhibitions documenting various achievements of local women in sports, literature, politics and science.

Deira Waterfront Market

Bait Al Mandi Restaurant MAP P56

Huge portions with not so huge prices

Part of a chain, this casual **restaurant** specialises in *mandi* – a traditional Middle Eastern dish that originated in Yemen and consists of meat and rice cooked in a special blend of spices. It's a bit like a Middle Eastern version of a biryani. There's a few other Emirati dishes on the menu, as well as some choice Indian options. Portions are huge, unlike your bill, which will happily be the opposite.

Deira Waterfront Market MAP P50

The Middle East's largest fish and seafood market

Open all day but busiest first thing in the morning, this purpose-built **market** is located on the Deira corniche on the site of what was previously the city's old fish market. It's now the Middle East's largest fish and seafood market, with more than 400 stalls selling everything from tuna and snapper to hammour, sardines and more. Porters push loaded trolleys filled with the day's catch around the covered market halls as stallholders yell loudly about their wares. Hungry visitors can choose their catch and let chefs grill it up at one of the market's live cooking stations.

Dubai Creek Resort & Golf Club

Dubai Creek Resort & Golf Club MAP P56

Waterside luxury in old Dubai

Set on the banks of the Creek, this **sports club** was previously listed in *Golf World* magazine as one of the world's top 100 must-play courses, so it's a hit with golfers, but it's the resort side of things that make it worth a visit for most. Tucked away from the hubbub of Deira via a winding palm-lined driveway, it's home to a temperature-controlled swimming pool, an outdoor mini-golf course, and padel and tennis courts. Popular waterside lounge **QDs** is the best place to enjoy sundowners with Creek views, and **Casa De Tapas** has some of the city's best Spanish bites. It's also where you'll find the **Park Hyatt Dubai**, a gorgeous five-star resort that looks like it's been transplanted to Dubai directly from an Aegean coastline.

Dubai Islands

MAP P50

A floating archipelago and work in progress

Formerly called Deira Islands, this constructed **archipelago** is still something of a work in progress. Spread across five isles off the Deira coastline, it's where you'll find **Souq Al Marfa**, an indoor traditional-style bazaar selling handicrafts, cosmetics, spices and clothing; it's also home to the **Thai Market**, which sells Asian crafts and authentic street food. Two family-friendly hotels make Dubai Islands a popular base for those travelling with children – the all-inclusive **Hotel Riu Dubai**, and kid-centric **Centara Mirage Beach Resort**, which has its own waterpark and candy-themed spa.

Deira City Centre

Al Mamzar Beach Park

Al Mamzar Beach Park

MAP P56

One of the city's best beaches

Almost as far north as you can get in Dubai, this huge space in **Dubai Public Parks** is spread over 106 hectares with more than 1600 palm trees and 300 coconut trees. Inside, there's five sandy beaches, green parks, playgrounds, BBQ facilities, bike paths and an amphitheatre. There's also three swimming pools, and the daily entry fee is one of the lowest you'll find if you're on the hunt for a budget pool day in Dubai. Changing rooms, showers and restrooms are available, or choose to make a day of it by hiring a chalet. This is also one of the city's first smart parks, with solar-powered benches offering free wi-fi and wireless charging, plus smart oasis pods that convert seawater into cooling spray systems.

Deira City Centre

Shopping, wellness and a live herb wall

One of Deira's largest **malls**, this space has a broad selection of high-street, high-end and bargain brands on sale. Near Port Saeed and with a metro stop right outside it, this sprawling mall attracts shoppers seeking fashion, jewellery, technology, homewares and toys. There's a 20-screen **Vox Cinema** and lots of dining options. The **Food Central Hall** has cuisine from around the world, a herb wall and a wellness corner with free yoga classes taking place on weekends. Licensed dining options are on offer at the cluster of hotels that is attached to the mall.

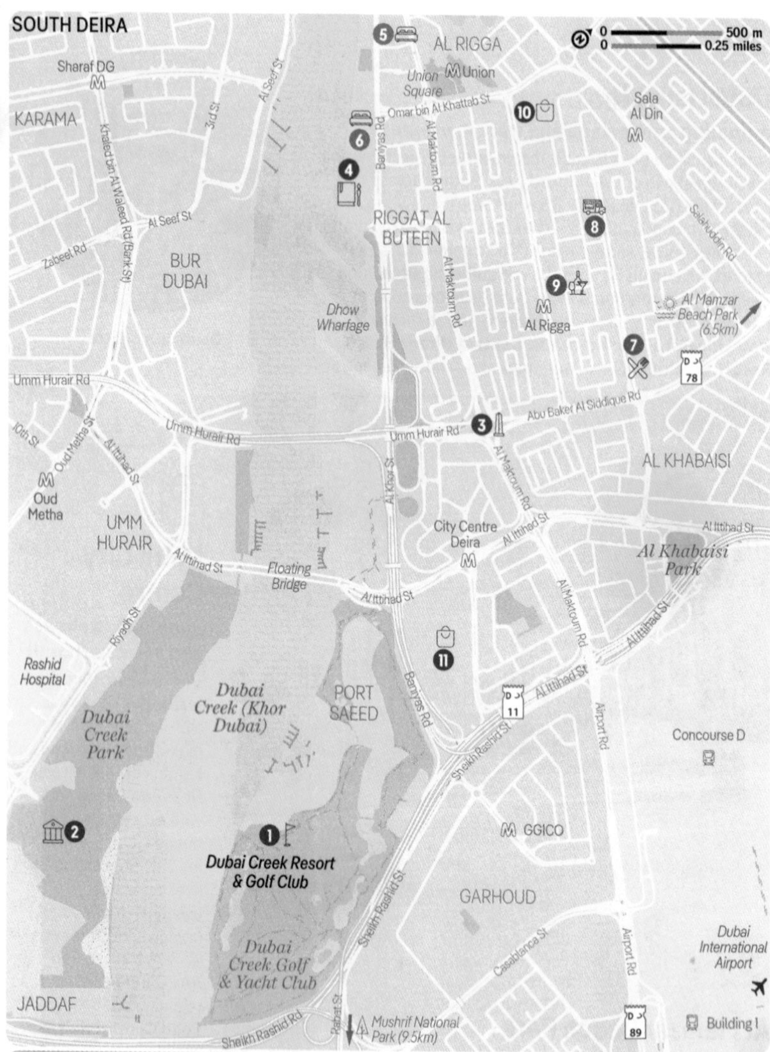

HIGHLIGHTS
1 Dubai Creek Resort & Golf Club

SIGHTS
2 Children's City
3 Deira Clocktower
4 National Bank of Dubai

SLEEPING
5 Radisson Blu Dubai Deira Creek
6 Sheraton Dubai Creek Hotel and Towers

EATING
7 Bait Al Mandi Restaurant
8 Sultan Dubai Falafels

DRINKING
9 Juice World

SHOPPING
10 Al Ghurair Centre
11 Deira City Centre

Exploring Deira Creekside

MAP P56

The story of Dubai's beginnings

Known as Al Khor in Arabic, the **Creek** has long been the trading point in Dubai. This watery channel meandering between Deira and Bur Dubai was the hub of the local fishing and pearling industries in the early 20th century, and was also the city's first airport – long before Dubai International Airport opened its doors. From 1935 until 1947, the creek was used as a landing area for Imperial Airways' mammoth 'flying boats' and a permanent jetty was built on the Deira side that received up to eight flights per week.

The waterfront on the Deira side is a lot busier than on the Bur Dubai coastline, thanks to the dhow wharves that line it. Here, wooden boats that have long been used for transporting cargo to and from Dubai are still widely used today. Stroll by and you'll spot hardworking sailors and ship hands stacking goods high on the quayside or balancing dizzying heights of wares on the vessels.

Today, the Creek's banks are connected via four bridges, a tunnel and the Dubai metro, but the best way to go between the two is via an abra ride. These little wooden boats chug along the water day and night and the five-minute ride costs a mere Dhs1. Make it a longer experience by hiring an abra at one of the docking stations; it should only cost around Dh120 for a one-hour charter. The best time is at sunset: step aboard and drink in the atmospheric views of the skyline where you can see the clear contrast between the centuries-old buildings and souqs of the old city, and the distant modern peaks of its skyscrapers in the new.

Crossing Dubai Creek

MAP P56

See Old Dubai from the water

Traditional **abras** – wooden water taxis with a name that means 'to cross' in Arabic – line either side of the Dubai Creek and the vehicles are still used by many people today as a way to cross from Deira to Bur Dubai. Boarding one of these vessels is a good way to step back in time and experience the Dubai of days gone past.

Several abras dock at Deira Old Souk Abra station and run to Bur Dubai Abra Station, just beyond the Textile Souq. Operational times are from around 6am until midnight each day, and boats can fit about 20 passengers, though you may spot

DUBAI INTERNATIONAL AIRPORT

Dubai Creek may have been Dubai's first airport of sorts, but the city's main air hub today lies just north of the neighbourhood. Dubai International Airport is one of the busiest in the world, receiving more than 80 million passengers annually. A high-speed train whizzes visitors between terminals and there's spas, shopping, drinking and dining galore. The airport also has its own gaming lounge and in-terminal hotel with a swimming pool. It's the hub for Emirates Airline – Dubai's homegrown airline with flights arriving and departing exclusively in Terminal 3.

SOUQ-SIDE SPOTS TO REFUEL

Juice World
Sprawling Saudi Arabian juice bar that serves over 200 different fruity concoctions. $

Sultan Dubai Falafels
Palestinian street food serving some of the city's best falafel with all the accompaniments. $

Al Bait Al Qadeem Restaurant and Café
Traditional hearty Middle Eastern food, just a short walk from the Gold Souq. $

DEIRA CORNICHE

Not to be confused with Deira Creekside, the **Deira Corniche** on the northeastern side of the neighbourhood remains under development as work progresses to transform it into a broad waterfront esplanade. The first part of the corniche is primarily a dhow wharf, one that's able to accommodate much bigger vessels than the wharves in the Creek, as well as being home to some decent waterfront hotels where room rates tend to be a lot more reasonable than the city's other coastlines. Further north, great city views can be had from the bridge leading over to Dubai Islands, and this is also where you'll find the waterfront market and emerging new residential areas.

Abras, Dubai Creek

some vessels that have packed in a few more if you happen to be here during the morning or early evening rush hours.

Head to the pier and step aboard. Onboard, passengers sit on a central wooden bench and the abra driver or his hand will pass down the boat collecting the Dhs1 fare from each rider – make sure you have this in cash.

You'll pass scenes of old Dubai including traditional houses, towering minarets and impressive wind towers, nestled beside modern signs of the city like glass-fronted buildings and multi-level hotels. Spot merchants dropping anchor at the banks and look out for wooden dhows – large colourful boats that hark back to Dubai's pearling and fishing heritage. After a journey of just over five minutes, travellers can disembark at the Bur Dubai Abra Station, which is within easy walking distance of the historic Al Fahidi neighbourhood, as well as several of the city's markets.

Tracing Dubai's History in Deira

MAP P56

A time-lapse of transformation

Amid renovated souqs and modern developments lie centuries-old buildings in this **historical neighbourhood**, a place that pays testament to an ever-evolving city. On the banks of the Creek, watch traders loading wooden ships with everything from televisions and car tyres to spices and instant coffee. These traditional Arab sailing vessels have been the backbone of the region's port trade for centuries, facilitating

DEIRA'S BEST DHOW CRUISES

Deira Dhow Cruise
Has a small fleet of boats with budget prices starting from Dh30 to more luxurious dinner cruises.

Al Mansour Dhow Cruise
A full-service bar and live music are part of the lunch and dinner cruises on this wooden dhow.

Tour Dubai
Luxury dinner cruises on a traditional wooden dhow with an open-air upper deck and air-conditioned lower deck.

easy trade with countries like Oman, Pakistan, India and Iran. Long before Dubai discovered black gold, it was trading in the yellow stuff, and the Gold Souq (p50), one of the largest gold markets in the world, is a worthy stop for some perspective on how important the precious metal is to the city, not to mention Aladdin-esque photo moments. Along the banks of the Creek, look out for the headquarters of the **National Bank of Dubai**. Set in a shimmering gold-coated glass-and-granite building that looks like the billowing sails of a boat, this '90s-built tower was one of the first modern buildings to be erected in deliberately luxury-focused new Dubai. The city's ever-evolving narrative can also be pieced together via visits to Al Ahmadiya School (p51), the first formal educational establishment in the city; **Burj Nahar**, a water tower constructed as one of the emirate's original security fortresses, and Deira Clocktower (p52) - erected to mark the first ever oil export from the UAE, a turning point in the UAE's history.

A Day in Nature at Mushrif National Park

MAP P56

Horse riding, hiking and heritage houses

Lying to the east of Deira, **Mushrif National Park** is Dubai's grandfather of outdoor spaces, and is the place to go to find nature. First opened in 1974, this national park is rich with indigenous wildlife and greenery, including a 35,000-sq-metre protected forest of Ghaf trees. Bird-spotters should bring their binoculars and keep a look out for Arabian babblers, yellow-throated sparrows and the rare pallid scops owl.

Bigger than all of the city's other parks, this sprawling green space has picnic and BBQ facilities, two swimming pools, basketball, volleyball and tennis courts, and a jogging track. It's also home to a newly opened hiking trail where active travellers can enjoy 10km of marked trails, all of which are free to use, open year-round and suitable for everyone from beginners to seasoned hikers. Lace up your walking boots and hit the ground to trek over the park's sandy, sloped, grassy terrains. The new trail is dotted with public restrooms, sculptures and bridges.

An afternoon in the saddle is also on offer here at **Winners Equestrian Club**, best visited during the winter months for desert and forest hacks or even riding lessons. One of the more quirky attractions at Mushrif National Park is **World Village**, a collection of miniature models of traditional houses from around the globe. And adrenaline-seekers heading to Mushrif can get their fix at **Aventura Nature Adventure Park**, a high-ropes course in the treetops with ziplines, net falls and rope challenges, although it's only open seasonally.

DEIRA'S MULTICULTURAL DINING SCENE

Having a bite to eat in one of Dubai's most multi-ethnic neighbourhoods comes with an array of choices, from stalwart Indian restaurants to authentic Asian eateries, not to mention an endless range of Middle Eastern spots. Dine around the world with a shawarma at **Ashwaq** and Syrian dishes at **Aroos Damascus**. Head to **Pravin Bhai Naashata Wala** in the Gold Souq for Indian food - it's one of the city's oldest - or settle down on the carpet for Yemeni meals at **Al Tawasol**. Feast on steaming delights at **Xia Wei Yang Hotpot** or enjoy authentic local cuisine with a meal at **Aseelah** at the Raddison Blu Hotel, where Emirati dishes are best served with terrace views.

WATERFRONT HOTELS IN DEIRA

Hyatt Regency Dubai
Five-star services and Gulf views from the corniche, plus Dubai's first and currently only revolving rooftop restaurant. **$**

Radisson Blu Dubai Deira Creek
The first five-star hotel in the city, this place has 15 dining and drinking options. **$**

Sheraton Dubai Creek Hotel and Towers
Spacious rooms overlook Dubai's historic waterway, with beautiful views by night. **$**

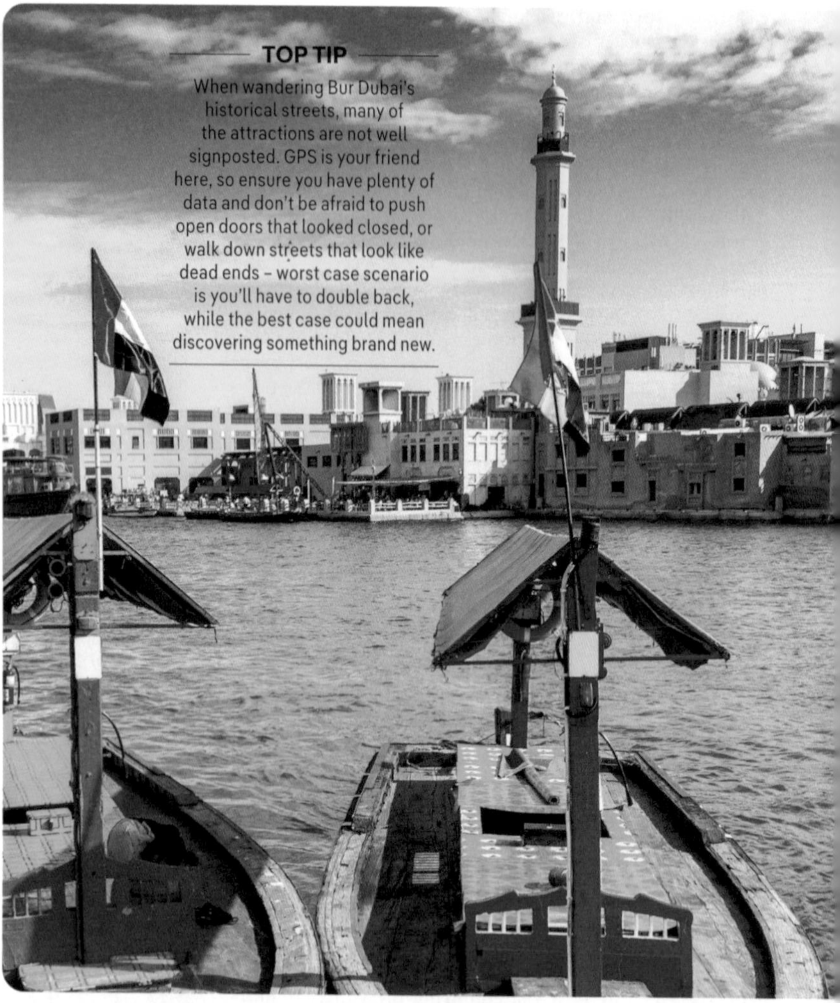
TOP TIP
When wandering Bur Dubai's historical streets, many of the attractions are not well signposted. GPS is your friend here, so ensure you have plenty of data and don't be afraid to push open doors that looked closed, or walk down streets that look like dead ends – worst case scenario is you'll have to double back, while the best case could mean discovering something brand new.

SERGII FIGURNYI/SHUTTERSTOCK ©

Above: Abra, Dubai Creek; Right: Al Fahidi Historical Neighbourhood (p66)

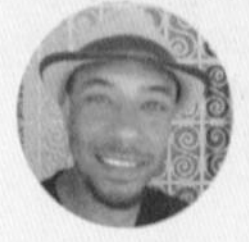

I LIVE HERE: FAVOURITE BUR DUBAI SPOTS

Saeed Saeed (@Saeed_squared) is a music journalist in Dubai. Here he shares his favourite Bur Dubai spots.

Al Fahidi Historical Neighbourhood
It might be a little bit of a tourist spot, but it's really lovely and like walking in an open-air museum. Afterwards, take an abra cruise, it's cheap and very cool to do.

The Coffee Museum
Recommended for caffeine aficionados. Designed by a coffee-lover, for coffee-lovers, it tells the history of the grain and how it came to the Arab world.

Q's Bar & Lounge at Palazzo Versace
One of the best live-music venues in the UAE. Named after Quincy Jones, it has music five days a week and an authentic speakeasy vibe - it's simply dynamite.

Bur Dubai

THE CITY'S OLDEST NEIGBOURHOOD

Waterfront Bur Dubai is the city's oldest area, encompassing atmospheric narrow lanes, traditional wind towers and a bustling Creek.

Bur Dubai is a sensory experience and a wonderful place to just go and take in the sights, the sounds and the smells.

Trace the city's past in Al Shindahga, formerly an independent neighbourhood that is thought to be the site of Dubai's fishing and pearling origins and which has now been swallowed by Bur Dubai.

The Al Fahidi District is the place to lose yourself for an afternoon, exploring labyrinthine streets filled with galleries, cafes, museums and other hidden gems. Stop by the Sheikh Mohammed Centre for Cultural Understanding to learn more about the local culture, customs and traditions, and break bread with locals over an authentic Emirati meal.

Away from the water, Bur Dubai's neighbourhoods are far removed from the luxury that many people imagine when they think of Dubai, but that doesn't mean they are without charm. Head to Meena Bazaar, akin to Dubai's little India, to shop for shiny trinkets, beautiful fabrics and sparkling jewellery, or go bargain-hunting in Karama for cheap souvenirs and budget-friendly dining. Wafi was one of the city's first themed districts and is where ancient Egypt has been given a Dubai-style makeover with hieroglyphics, tombs and towering pyramids. Finally, wander to Port Rashid where you'll see evidence that Dubai's growth is not over yet. The deep-water port is growing in popularity alongside the city's cruising industry, which is on track to welcome nearly 100,000 annual tourists.

DON'T MISS...

AL FAHIDI HISTORICAL NEIGHBOURHOOD
Restored 19th-century neighbourhood that captures Dubai's old-world charm.
p66

ARABIAN TEA HOUSE
Pretty tablecloths, friendly servers and authentic local cuisine.
p70

DUBAI FRAME
Picture-perfect views of old and new Dubai from a golden vantage point 150m above the city.
p65

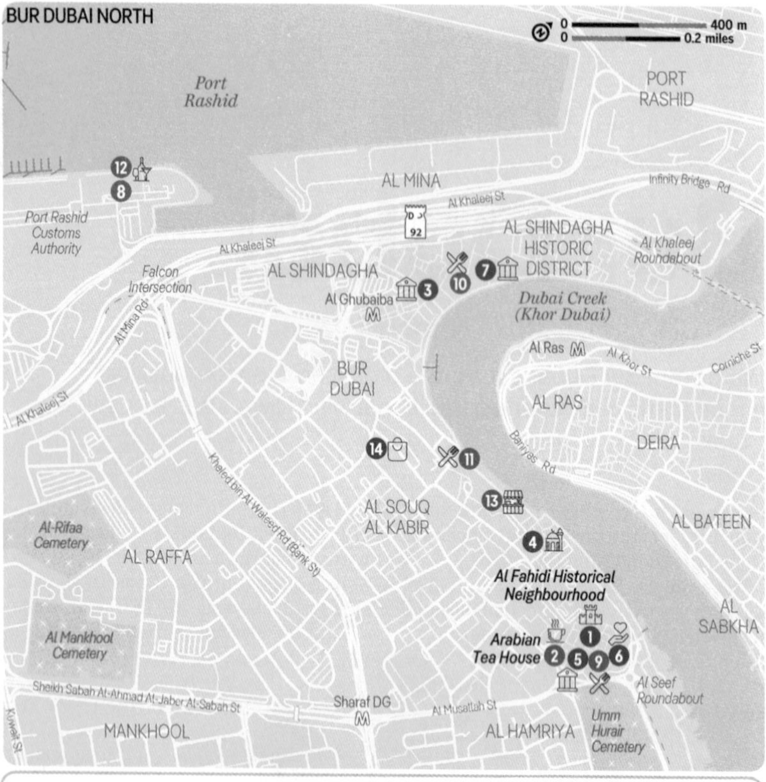

BUR DUBAI NORTH

HIGHLIGHTS
1 Al Fahidi Historical Neighbourhood
2 Arabian Tea House

SIGHTS
3 Al Shindagha Museum
4 Bur Dubai Grand Mosque
5 Coffee Museum
6 Sheikh Mohammed Centre for Cultural Understanding
7 Sheikh Saeed Al Maktoum House

SLEEPING
8 QE2

EATING
9 Al Khayma Heritage Restaurant
10 Bait Al Jeyran
11 Bayt Al Wakeel

DRINKING & NIGHTLIFE
12 Golden Lion

SHOPPING
13 Bur Dubai Souq
14 Meena Bazaar

Bur Dubai Grand Mosque

MAP P62

Experience Islamic culture

Also referred to as **Grand Bur Dubai Masjid**, this house of worship in the Al Fahidi Historical Neighbourhood is the largest in the city, with capacity for some 1200 worshippers. Reaching into the air like a lighthouse is its 70m minaret, Dubai's tallest. In its past life, the mosque was a school dedicated to the study of the Quran. It's also one of the only mosques in old Dubai open to non-Muslim visitors. Visit on Sunday, Tuesday or Thursday morning for a free tour and a unique insight into Islamic culture with ablution and prayer demonstrations. Questions are welcome and refreshments provided post-tour.

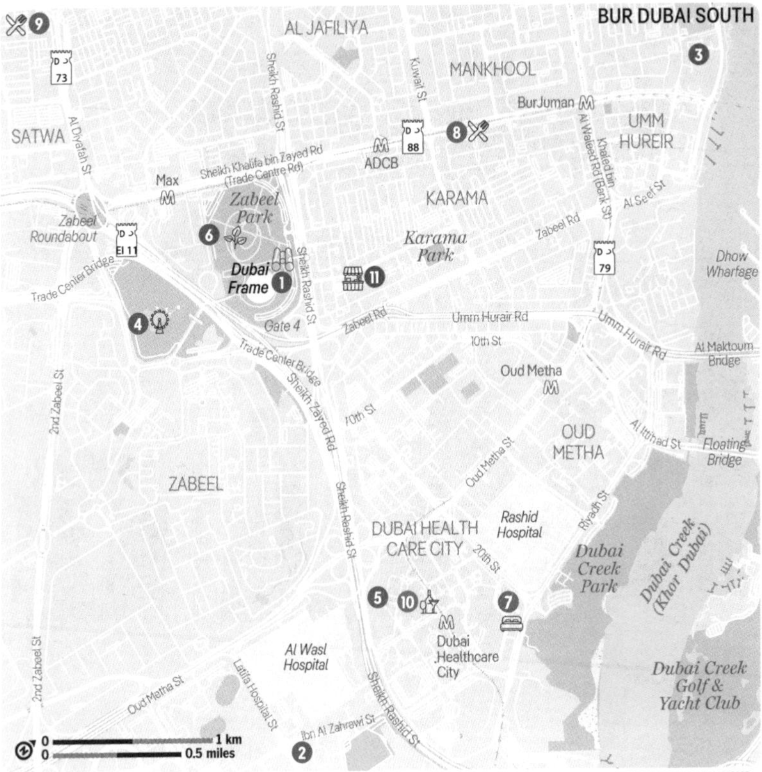

BUR DUBAI SOUTH

HIGHLIGHTS
1 Dubai Frame

SIGHTS
2 Al Jaddaf
3 Al Seef Dubai
4 Dubai Garden Glow
5 Wafi City
6 Zabeel Park

SLEEPING
7 Hyatt Regency Dubai Creek Heights

EATING
8 Chappan Bhog
9 Ravi's

DRINKING & NIGHTLIFE
see 7 Eve Penthouse and Lounge
10 McCafferty's Bar and Restaurant

SHOPPING
11 Karama Market

Al Shindagha Museum

MAP P62

What life was like before

At the mouth of Dubai Creek, this **museum** is one of the focal points of the restored historic district where the ruling sheikhs used to live. Beautifully laid out with interactive exhibits, multimedia elements, recovered artefacts and restored historic houses, it ushers visitors around on a self-guided tour that's a great reminder of the fact there was life in the city before its commercialisation. Afterwards, check out the old watch tower that was once used in the city's defence plans then follow your nose to the nearby **Perfume House** to find out more about Emirati scents, from the traditional incense of *oud* to the sought-after exotic perfumes that once influenced sea trade in this port city.

Sheikh Saeed Al Maktoum House

Sheikh Saeed Al Maktoum House

MAP P62

Step inside the former home of Dubai's ruling family

Located on a quiet stretch of the Creekside promenade, this two-storey courtyard residence was once the home of Sheikh Saeed, the grandfather of Shiekh Mohammed and where the current ruler of Dubai was born. Built from coral stone with high-vaulted ceilings, it's a fine example of Emirati architecture. Now a museum depicting early life in Dubai, it's home to one of the city's most extensive collections depicting what life was like in the emirate in days gone by, including previously unseen photographs of the royal family. Upstairs, peek inside the majlis where balconies open out to views over the Dubai Creek.

Bait Al Jeyran

MAP P62

Charming, old-school eatery

Located right on the Creek, this unassuming **restaurant** is a great stop when sightseeing in Al Shindagha. Serving traditional Middle Eastern food such as mixed grills, hummus and tabbouleh, it also has a huge selection of smoothies, juices and mocktails. Step inside where stonework walls offer respite from the sun, or settle down on *majlis*-style benches under bamboo canopies with views over the water when the weather allows.

Dubai Frame

MAP P63

A view from above

Visible for miles around and towering over Bur Dubai is this gigantic golden landmark, one of the newer additions to the skyline in this part of town. Located in **Zabeel Park**, Dubai Frame stands at 150m tall and more than 93m wide, and is designed to look like a giant photo frame offering unique views of old Dubai and new Dubai when looked through from either side. Visitors can go inside where a lift whisks you to the top floor and a glass panel offers 360-degree views of the city. A gallery on the ground floor sheds more light on the city's past, from fishing and port village to one of the world's most popular tourist destinations.

Dubai Frame

QE2

QE2

MAP P62

The city's only floating hotel

One of a kind, the *Queen Elizabeth 2* – or **QE2** as it was more commonly known – is enjoying retirement in the Dubai sunshine. Permanently moored on the docks of Port Rashid Marina, the historic ocean liner is now a floating hotel. Journey back in time on the ship's heritage tour and enjoy a drink in the **Golden Lion**, Dubai's oldest pub. Then settle in for the night in a lovingly restored cabin; room rates are entirely reasonable.

Al Fahidi Historical Neighbourhood

MAP P62

Heritage, culture, art and architecture

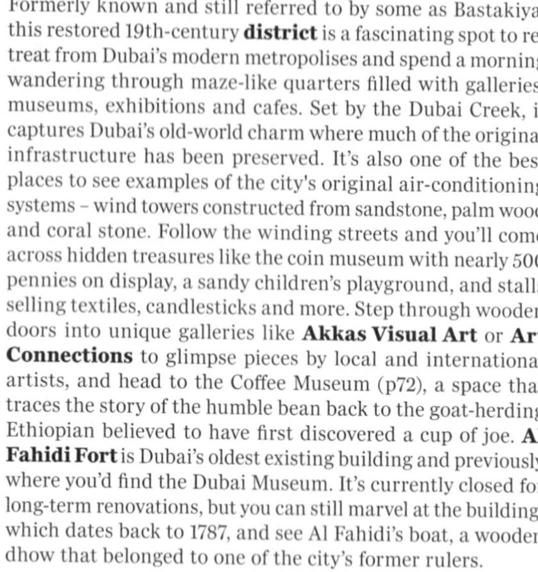

Formerly known and still referred to by some as Bastakiya, this restored 19th-century **district** is a fascinating spot to retreat from Dubai's modern metropolises and spend a morning wandering through maze-like quarters filled with galleries, museums, exhibitions and cafes. Set by the Dubai Creek, it captures Dubai's old-world charm where much of the original infrastructure has been preserved. It's also one of the best places to see examples of the city's original air-conditioning systems – wind towers constructed from sandstone, palm wood and coral stone. Follow the winding streets and you'll come across hidden treasures like the coin museum with nearly 500 pennies on display, a sandy children's playground, and stalls selling textiles, candlesticks and more. Step through wooden doors into unique galleries like **Akkas Visual Art** or **Art Connections** to glimpse pieces by local and international artists, and head to the Coffee Museum (p72), a space that traces the story of the humble bean back to the goat-herding Ethiopian believed to have first discovered a cup of joe. **Al Fahidi Fort** is Dubai's oldest existing building and previously where you'd find the Dubai Museum. It's currently closed for long-term renovations, but you can still marvel at the building, which dates back to 1787, and see Al Fahidi's boat, a wooden dhow that belonged to one of the city's former rulers.

XVA HOTEL DUBAI

A former residential home in Al Fahidi Historical Neighbourhood, the **XVA Hotel Dubai** is now a boutique hideaway welcoming guests to spend the night in Dubai's oldest community. Within its 15 individually decorated rooms, you can expect hanging lanterns, wooden beams and cosy alcoves. The **XVA Cafe** is a quaint spot serving vegetarian and vegan food in a leafy shaded courtyard, far removed from the hustle of the big city, and on-site **XVA Gallery** specialises in contemporary art, with changing exhibitions throughout the year.

PHOTOPANKPL/SHUTTERSTOCK ©

Al Fahidi Historical Neighbourhood

Al Seef Dubai

Al Seef Dubai

MAP P63

Vibrant waterfront neighbourhood

A mix of old and new awaits at this bustling **district** on the banks of the Dubai Creek. Developed in 2017 and inspired by old Middle Eastern villages, the waterfront area combines markets, restaurants, cafes, hotels and walkways. The architecture pays homage to the city's heritage with traditional wind towers, winding alleyways and stone-coloured buildings. There is a floating market, nodding to the importance of the Creek and how its trading days were instrumental in shaping Dubai as we know it today. The district hosts pop-up events throughout the year, from fashion-themed markets to craft fairs and a Christmas-themed festival.

Stay at **Al Seef Heritage Hotel** for a real sense of stepping back in time. Rooms have wooden shutters and private *majlis* areas. When it comes to dining there's plenty of choice, from traditional Emirati eats at **Al Fanar** and fine-dining Egyptian at **Khofo** to Palestinian dishes from **Nablus**. It's also where you'll find the UAE's prettiest **Starbucks** – a Middle Eastern-themed cafe with thatched roofing, timber-framed windows and lantern lighting.

Sheikh Mohammed Centre for Cultural Understanding

MAP P62

Learn about Dubai's past and present

Learn more about Emirati culture with a visit to this **centre** in Al Fahidi Historical Neighbourhood. Founded by Dubai's ruler some 25 years ago, the centre's primary purpose is to teach visitors more about traditions, religion and practices in the UAE. Set inside restored wind towers, visitors can take part in basic Arabic lessons and calligraphy workshops, join a guided heritage tour or tuck into authentic Emirati meals, sitting Bedouin-style on carpets and pillows. The Heritage Express tour sees a local guide accompany visitors as they're whisked around Dubai's oldest neighbourhood in a trolley-style tram.

TOP LEFT: LIUDMILA LEGKAIA/SHUTTERSTOCK ©; BOTTOM RIGHT: BSIP SA/ALAMY STOCK PHOTO ©

Dubai Garden Glow

Dubai Garden Glow

MAP P63

A magical garden

One of Bur Dubai's more surreal attractions is this illuminated **theme park** in Zabeel Park. Spanning several different fantasy lands, it's part art, part technology and a surefire winner for those visiting with children. Consisting of more than 10 million energy-saving light bulbs, it's open daily after dark. This is also where you'll find **Dino Park**, filled with moving, life-like prehistoric reptiles, and **Magic Park**, which defies logic with its hypnotic, optical illusions.

Karama

MAP P63

Bargain-hunting galore

Pocket-friendly dining and great bargains are to be found in this low-rise residential district. **Karama Market** has about 300 shops and stalls spread across several buildings, selling everything from camel keyring souvenirs to luxury handbags – don't forget to barter. Also spot large-scale graffiti murals bringing a burst of colour to some of the district's walls, and take your pick from plenty of casual eateries where you can easily score a south Asian dinner for two for under Dhs100 – **Patiala House Restaurant** with its unlimited *pani-puri* is recommended.

Camel keyrings

Al Jaddaf

MAP P63

A growing waterfront suburb

Set along the western side of Dubai Creek, this is one of the city's rapidly evolving **neighbourhoods**. It's largely a residential spot, but has a growing number of places to shop and dine along the Jaddaf waterfront. The **Jameel Arts Centre** is well worth a visit for culture, exhbitions and art, and this is also where you'll find the **Mohammed Bin Rashid Library**, a literary hub that towers over the water in the shape of a traditional Islamic lectern. Free to enter, it has fiction and nonfiction books, a collection just for children, and a Treasures of the Library section with hundreds of rare encased works, some dating back to the 13th century. A 4km tree-lined boulevard wraps around Al Jaddaf's coastline. It's typically not very busy and a great place for a stroll with views of the Dubai skyline.

Bayt Al Wakeel

MAP P62

A historic place to dine

Next to the Textile Souq and set along Dubai Creek, this historic **eatery** is built of mud, coral and wood and dates back to 1935. Having borne witness to the city's ever-evolving sea trade, it houses a small maritime museum, as well as being a popular restaurant serving up dishes that are a cross between the Middle and the Far East. Dine inside the original or sit on the outdoor deck to eat alfresco, and watch abras and dhows glide over the water.

Wafi City

Wafi City

MAP P63

Walk like an Egyptian

Step back to a time of hieroglyphics, pharaohs and tombs at this pyramid-shaped **complex** in the heart of Bur Dubai. One of the city's first themed districts, it centres on **Wafi Mall** – a huge shopping complex guarded by mammoth stone sphinx statues. Inside, the grand Egyptian theme continues alongside luxury and high-street fashion shops and the five-star pyramid-shaped **Raffles Dubai** hotel. There's several places to dine, including licensed venues like **McCafferty's Irish Pub**, vintage cheese specialists, and **Biella**, a popular pizzeria. The underground **Khan Murjan** market is a souq-style shopping space centred on a marble courtyard and divided into four regions from across the Arab World – Egypt, Syria, Turkey and Morocco. Immersive light-and-sound park **Aya Universe** is the place to go for striking visuals and thought-provoking experiences.

Meena Bazaar

MAP P62

Dubai's little India

Not a bazaar in the traditional sense of the word but more a tightly packed **neighbourhood** filled with multi-ethnic shops selling everything from crafts and jewellery to souvenirs – this is Dubai's Little India. It's also the place to go for made-to-measure suits, jackets and dresses, with many textile stores offering quick turnaround and low prices. Fabrics on reel in every colour, shade and textile imaginable can also be purchased here. Bring patience with you, as the bustling alleys get busy and vendors, although harmless, can be rather persistent. When you've had enough, buy some cheap street eats and enjoy alongside the area's views over Dubai Creek.

TOP LEFT: ALEKSANDRA TOKARZ/SHUTTERSTOCK ©; BOTTOM RIGHT: GLEN BERLIN/SHUTTERSTOCK ©

Arabian Tea House

Ravi's

MAP P63

Legendary Pakistani eats with the T-shirt to match

This authentic Pakistani **eatery** has been serving up chicken *handi,* fresh nan and tasty curries since 1978. Located in Satwa, the family-run eatery started as a place to serve traditional Pakistani food to workers in Dubai who were homesick, and has evolved into something of a Dubai institution. Expect fuss-free interiors and daily menu specials as well as pocket-friendly prices. You can also pick up funky Ravi's streetwear, and the restaurant recently created a retro green-and-white trainer with global sportswear giant Adidas.

Arabian Tea House

MAP P62

Best breakfasts in Bur Dubai

One of the prettiest places in Old Dubai to dine, this **tea house** will draw you in with the heady scent of freshly baked bread. Located in Al Fahidi, it's open for all-day dining – breakfast here is eternally popular. Sit on turquoise wooden benches at whitewashed tables, surrounded by pretty lace curtains and draping foliage. Old black-and-white photographs adorn the walls giving diners a glimpse of Dubai's yesteryear. The Emirati breakfast tray is served sharing-style on a big silver platter with pretty flower-adorned crockery.

Bur Dubai Souq

Bur Dubai Souq

MAP P62

Traditional market shopping in old Dubai

Also known as **Bur Dubai Grand Souq**, this traditional shopping area on the southern side of the Creek is famed for its array of textiles and also sells homewares, spices, perfumes and toys inside a network of narrow shopping streets and sand-coloured buildings. A trip here is an experience – expect a heady assault on the senses, from the colours of myriad textiles and the scents of Arabian *oud* to the sounds of the traders calling to shoppers as they pass by. Pick up kaftans, cashmere shawls, intricately patterned abayas and crisp *kandouras* (long robes worn by men). It's also a good place to find cheap souvenirs like stuffed camels and Dubai keyrings, with prices lower than those you'd pay in the malls.

Al Fahidi Historial Neighbourhood

MORE IN BUR DUBAI

Embark on a Guided Walking Tour of Old Dubai

Get under the city's skin

Cast your imagination back hundreds of years and envision what the city of Dubai was like long before it was filled with luxury shopping malls and beachside resorts. Accompanied by a local guide, get set to navigate Old Dubai's bylanes on a curated, off-beat walking tour. Organised by **Dubai by Foot**, the two-hour heritage, culture, art and architecture tour starts in the historic Al Fahidi neighbourhood, weaving in and out of traditional homes and heritage buildings with stops at art galleries and cafes, and a chance to interact with some of the people who live and work in the district. Let your guide enthral you with stories and narratives about Dubai and its personalities – from artists to architects. From here, cross the Dubai Creek on a wooden abra to Deira and, as you bob along the water, learn more about how the city has always had such an appeal for immigrants, and how it is home to nationalities from over 120 countries. On the other side of the water, be prepared for a heady assault on the senses with

WHERE TO EAT IN AL JADDAF

As a neighbourhood that's still developing, Al Jaddaf has some great places to eat that showcase the district's dynamism. Try **Mandi Man**, an easy-going, rustic spot serving Yemeni style *mandi* – rice dishes with cooked meat and spices. Sit down on the floor and dig in with your hands. On the other end of the scale is **Enigma** in the Palazzo Versace hotel. This Iranian fine-dining restaurant keeps its home-cooking ethos – you'll feel like you're eating your Iranian grandmother's food, but in fancier surrounds. Finally, **Teible** inside the Jameel Arts Centre is an artisanal bakery and restaurant with a focus on farm-to-table eating and a menu that celebrates local produce.

BUR DUBAI'S BEST CASUAL RESTAURANTS

Chappan Bhog
Budget restaurant panning North and South Indian cuisine with a focus on vegetarian thalis. $

Ravi's
Pakistani dishes in a low-key setting at this popular, long-running restaurant. $

Al Khayma Heritage Restaurant
Middle Eastern restaurant in Al Fahidi serving all-regional fare, done really well. $$

COFFEE MUSEUM

Satisfy your inner caffeine addict with a stop at Dubai's **Coffee Museum**, a small, privately owned space in Al Fahidi Historical Neighbourhood. Housed in a former residential villa, this beautifully laid-out exhibit traces the origins of the humble bean, from Ethiopian goat herders to Yemen's cultivated coffee plants, and shares more details on the caffeinated drink and its standing in Middle Eastern social occasions. Follow your nose to the scent of freshly brewed beans and you'll find staff in traditional garb waiting to serve you *gahwa* and dates. Free entry.

RITU MANOJ JETHANI/SHUTTERSTOCK ©

Sheikh Mohammed Centre for Cultural Understanding (p67)

stops at the Gold Souq (p50) and pungent Spice Souq (p51). You'll leave with both an appreciation of how a small fishing village transformed itself into a global brand in one generation, as well as having some common myths about life in the Middle East debunked. Tours run from October to May and cost from Dhs155.

The Wonders of Arabic Coffee

MAP P62

A symbol of generosity

Fragrant, piping hot and yellow coloured, **Arabic coffee** *(gahwa)* is an important part of Emirati hospitality that was traditionally served to guests as a symbol of generosity. In the past, the coffee was made fresh whenever guests arrived in a home. The traditional method sees the beans lightly roasted in a shallow pan then pounded inside a mortar and pestle.

SOUVENIRS WORTH TAKING HOME

Sand art
Bring home a piece of the desert with you, but do so in style with a colourful creation from a local sand artist.

Dates
Intrinsic to Emirati culture and the fruit used to break fast during Ramadan.

Camel chocolate
Created from the milk of camels instead of cows, this sweet dairy treat is creamy and surprisingly moreish.

Once ground, the beans and water are added to a large coffee pot that's placed on a fire. When its brewed, the liquid is decanted into a smaller coffee pot and poured into tiny cups, not much larger than a shot glass. Travellers keen to find out more about *gahwa* can do so at the Sheikh Mohammed Centre for Cultural Understanding (p67), where cultural speaker Khawla Al Marzooqi explains that Arabic coffee is traditionally served as soon as guests arrive and continuously served throughout a gathering. The oldest person in the room would typically be served first, then the order extends from their right to circle around the *majlis*. As coffee is continuously served, it's good to be able to politely let your server know you've had your fill and you can do this without using words, just gently tip your cup from one side to the other when the coffee pot comes your way. In the past, it was polite to drink at least three cups, but in modern times, it's more acceptable to stop earlier, or even refuse altogether if you do not like it.

Exploring Bur Dubai's Tailoring Scene

MAP P62

Go home with some custom-made clothing

Ditch Dubai's malls in favour of Bur Dubai's well-trodden streets where scores of talented **tailors** create custom-made outfits, personalised to your liking. All good creations start with the basics, so take your time selecting a fabric. Bur Dubai Grand Souq (p70) on the southern side of the Creek, or shops in Meena Bazaar (p69), stock every kind and colour of material imaginable. Ask questions about how it drapes, wears, washes and tears – having a picture of what you're hoping to use it for can be helpful. Hold the fabric up in different light, even if this means taking it outside of the shop to see it better in natural daylight. And when it comes to how much to purchase, opt for a metre or two more than what you need. Bur Dubai's tailoring shops are mostly located in Meena Bazaar and range from cupboard-sized shops hidden down back alleyways to multiple-level shops filled with reels of fabric and noisy sewing machines. Some of the city's long-running favourites include **Parmar**, which has been piecing together creations since 1956, Sartor near the Royal Ascot Hotel, and **Tichi's Tailoring Boutique**. Share your idea with the tailor and make sure they understand your vision before you commit. You'll need to visit at least twice – once to drop off fabrics and have measurements taken, and another time to pick up the finished piece. Turnaround times range from a few days to a few weeks, depending on complexity and availability.

WHAT DO THE LOCALS WEAR?

When donning traditional garb, Emirati men dress in a long robe known as a *kandoura* that is typically white in colour. This is paired with a *gutra* (headscarf), kept in place by a thick rope *(agal)*. The rope used to be a multifunctional accessory – used not only to keep headgear from blowing off in the wind, but also to bind camels' hooves together to stop the precious animals wandering off when Bedouins made camp for the evening. Women traditionally wear long black robes known as *abayas*, although today these come in every colour and material imaginable. Some women also choose to cover their heads with hijabs or *shaylas*.

WATERING HOLES IN BUR DUBAI

Eve Penthouse and Lounge
Sleek rooftop spot with skyline views, cocktails, shisha and live music at the Hyatt Regency Dubai Creek Heights.

Golden Lion
This QE2 watering hole is a quintessential British pub that's easily Dubai's oldest.

McCafferty's Bar and Restaurant
Traditional Irish pub inside Wafi City with great food, live music and happy hours.

TOP TIP

One of Dubai's most popular places to ring in the New Year is the Burj Khalifa, and while tickets to the spectacle are free, the logistics of getting here can be a minefield. Dubai Police begin closing roads and streets in the area early in the day on 31 December, so get there early. You can spend time shopping at Dubai Mall, then walk to your chosen viewing spot closer to the countdown.

Above: Burj Khalifa (p78); Right: Museum of the Future (p80)

I LIVE HERE: EXPERIENCE DOWNTOWN DUBAI

Emma Laurence (emmalaurence.net), freelance writer, editor and mum-of-one, shares her favourite ways to experience all that Downtown Dubai has to offer.

In Dubai's buzzing heart you can scale the world's tallest building or wander the world's biggest mall – but the best seats (and the best live music) in town lie just across the water at Time Out Market, where you can catch the Dubai Fountain show while dining on a curated selection of the city's freshest food concepts. From there, follow the urban sculpture trail along the twinkling Boulevard and duck into an eclectic mix of art galleries (don't miss Foundry), restaurants (Masti's fusion dishes and cocktails are hard to beat) and even a luxury licensed movie theatre, Cinemacity.

Downtown Dubai & Business Bay

THE HEART OF DUBAI

Wind the clock back just a few decades and what we now know as Downtown Dubai and Business Bay was mostly untouched desert sand.

Today, it's the city's most-frequented neighbourhood, packing more than its fair share of iconic tourist attractions into its 200+ hectares.

Topping the billing is the Burj Khalifa, the world's tallest building and Dubai's most recognised landmark. Piercing the skyline at 828m high, the glistening tower offers one of the best vantage points from where to see the sprawling emirate in all its glory, from its low-lying coastal villas and Gulf waters to its tower-filled skyline and vast desert lands. Seemingly rising from a lake at its base, the Burj Khalifa is also where you'll find the Dubai Fountain – a waterjet show that rivals the Bellagio Fountain in Las Vegas. Dinner and a show is a great way to spend an evening in Downtown Dubai, and there's an impressive year-round calendar of events to check out at Dubai Opera with its Swarovski-lined interiors.

As the centre of forward-thinking Dubai, the neighbourhood has plenty of distinctive architectural destinations dotted along its core, from the stunning Museum of the Future, inlaid with windows cut to the shape of Arabic calligraphy, to the block-like bricks of Dubai Design District, where you'll find a host of the city's creatives.

Art-lovers will be in their element in this neighbourhood, which brims with galleries, sculptures and exhibits. And of course it's a shopaholic's dream at Dubai Mall, the city's largest shopping centre, with more than 1200 shops, an ice rink and an urban aquarium.

DON'T MISS...

BURJ KHALIFA
An 828m architectural wonder that's become synonymous with the city.
p78

DUBAI FOUNTAIN
Twinkling lights, dancing jets and crescendo-building musical scores.
p79

MUSEUM OF THE FUTURE
A new landmark that catapults visitors 50 years into the future.
p80

SOUK AL BAHAR
Middle Eastern-inspired complex with great dining and drinking options.
p77

DOWNTOWN DUBAI & BUSINESS BAY

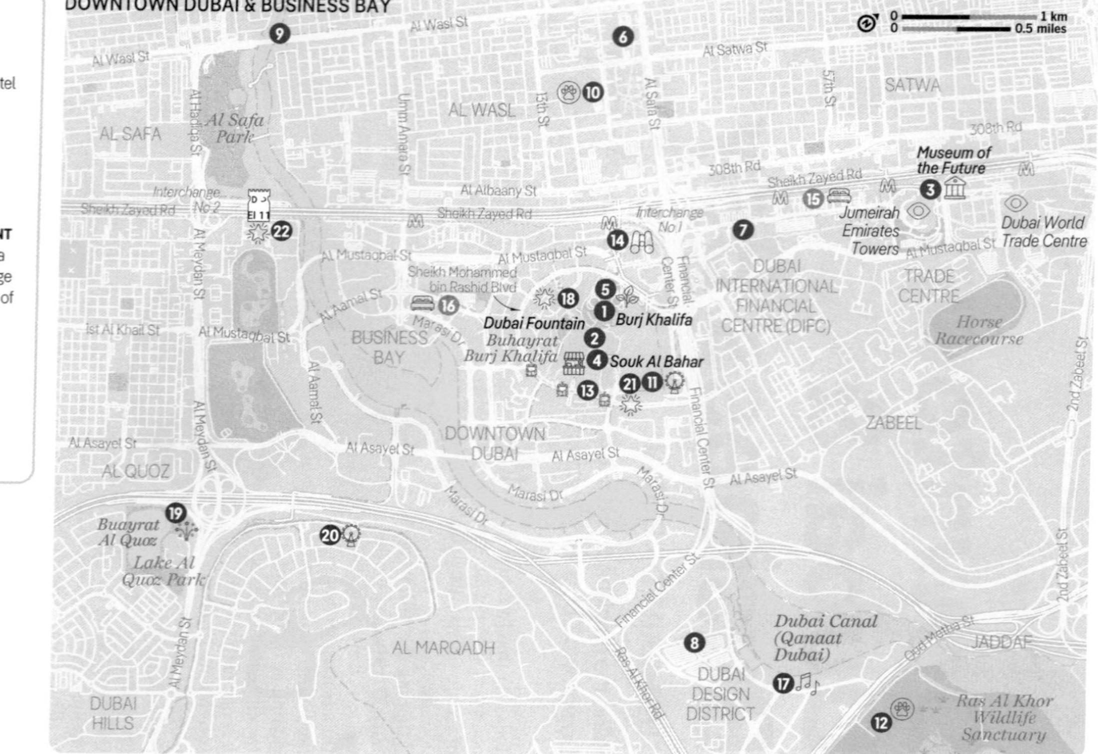

HIGHLIGHTS
1 Burj Khalifa
2 Dubai Fountain
3 Museum of the Future
4 Souk Al Bahar

SIGHTS
5 Burj Park
6 City Walk
7 DIFC
8 Dubai Design District
9 Dubai Water Canal
10 Green Planet
11 Play DXB
12 Ras Al Khor
13 Sheikh Mohammed bin Rashid Boulevard
14 Sky Views

SLEEPING
15 Gevora Hotel
16 ME Dubai

DRINKING & NIGHTLIFE
17 Sky 2.0

ENTERTAINMENT
18 Dubai Opera
19 Global Village
20 IMG Worlds of Adventure
21 KidZania
22 La Perle by Dragone

Pedestrian bridge over Dubai Water Canal

Souk Al Bahar

Arabesque hub for dining and drinking

Right next to Dubai Mall over a small pedestrian bridge is **Souk Al Bahar**. Designed as a traditional Middle Eastern market, it has 20 restaurants, cafes and bars, many of which come with fountain views. The **Time Out Market Dubai** is popular – a giant sprawling food hall featuring food concepts from the local restaurants and some of Dubai's best chefs, plus a bustling bar and outdoor terrace. The dining destination also has a handful of shops mostly selling souvenirs.

Dubai Water Canal

A new waterfront neighbourhood

Extending 3.2km from Old Dubai's Creek through Business Bay and into the Gulf, this constructed **channel** slices through Downtown Dubai, transforming it into a waterfront destination. Wide pavements flank the canal – popular with runners, cyclists and meandering tourists. As night falls, the canal and the neighbourhoods that surround it come alive as buildings and bridges are illuminated and waterfalls glow in brightly coloured lights, creating a shimmering cityscape. The pedestrian bridges lining the canal are also good picks for photographers seeking alternative vantage points of the city.

Souk Al Bahar

Jumeirah Emirates Towers

Triangular shaped grandeur

This visually striking twin tower gateway to Dubai's financial district was once Dubai's tallest building. Today, **Jumeirah Emirates Towers** is dwarfed by many of its skyscraper neighbours, but the hotel remains a favourite with visitors, locals and members of the country's ruling family, not to mention its flock of resident peacocks that wander the grounds. There's a ladies-only floor with nine Chopard-themed rooms and suites, and high-end shopping at the **Emirates Towers Boulevard**. Stop by the **Office of the Future**, the world's first 3D-printed office, then take your pick from drinking and dining options aplenty including chic, Parisian-inspired **La Cantine De Fauborg**, and **Ninive** with its urban *majlis* setting and contemporary Middle Eastern fare.

KIRK FISHER/SHUTTERSTOCK ©

TOP SIGHT

Burj Khalifa

PRACTICALITIES

Scan this QR code for opening hours and tickets:

The tallest building in the world and Dubai's most-visited attraction, the 828m peak of Burj Khalifa sits well above the city, visible for miles. This ground-breaking feat of architecture marked a landmark moment in the UAE's growth story when it opened in 2010. Housing residences, restaurants, a hotel and sky-high observation tower, it's also directly connected to Dubai Mall, the emirate's largest shopping metropolis.

DON'T MISS

- At the Top
- Dubai Fountain
- Dubai Aquarium & Underwater Zoo
- Dubai Dino
- Diving Waterfall Fountain

The Tallest Building in the World

Dubai has some of the world's best architectural wonders, but the glimmering jewel in its crown is the Burj Khalifa. The tallest building on the planet, this pencil-like skyscraper sits at the heart of Downtown Dubai and has become a defining symbol of the city.

The megastructure is also a pandora's box of engineering triumphs and cutting-edge technology. While you might not think it from looking at the ultra-modern exterior, the building's design was inspired by the geometry of the spider lily, a desert flower found across the region, and by intricate patterns common in Islamic architecture. Inside, the lifts have the world's longest travel distance from lowest to highest stop, soaring at speeds of up to 10m per second, guaranteed to make your ears pop.

Spiralling upwards, the building also has the highest outdoor observation deck in the world at 555m on the 148th floor. Taking in the views from here is a bucket-list experience and a trip to **At the Top** observation tower is the only way to do so.

SERGII FIGURNYI/SHUTTERSTOCK ©

Above: Dubai Mall; Left: Burj Khalifa

The experience doesn't come cheap, but is set up like a VIP visit with complimentary refreshments and a guided tour. Stand on the edge of the ledge and drink in the unforgettable views. If you feel a little unsteady while you're up here, don't worry. The building is designed to be able to sway and on its highest floor can experience up to 2m back-and-forth movement.

A slightly less expensive way to get a very similar experience is to opt for an At the Top ticket. This includes access to the observation deck on the 124th level, where the views are just as spectacular, but you may need to contend with a few more people for the perfect selfie.

Dubai Mall

A super-sized shopping experience is a key part of any visit to Burj Khalifa as the skyscraper is attached to Dubai Mall (p38). With over 1200 shops, this mammoth mall sells everything from homewares, toys and high-street fashion brands like Gap and H&M to upmarket luxury shops like Fendi, Valentino and Faberge at Fashion Avenue. The souq on the ground floor is the place to go for Middle Eastern wares, and the Dubai Mall Gold Souq houses endless jewellery shops, but prices are unlikely to be better than those found in Deira. Hungry? There's a dizzying array of places to eat, from the uber-popular Din Thai Fung to contemporary Emirati dishes at Loga, plus food courts for cheaper eats. Recent extensions to the already monster-sized mall include the Dubai Mall Zabeel with family-friendly shops and supermarkets, and the city's very first Chinatown.

Dubai Fountain

In the lake flanked by the Burj Khalifa, dancing fountains come alive nightly, putting on a free show that's guaranteed to impress. The jets shoot water up to 140m high and are perfectly choreographed to match the accompanying soundtracks, which range from traditional Khaleeji music to well-loved pop ballads.

MORE THAN JUST SHOPPING

Dubai Mall (p38) has lots to explore. Go ice-skating at the Olympic-sized rink, visit **KidZania**, where children can play make believe as a doctor, firefighter or pilot, get spooked at **Hysteria**, the city's first haunted house, and visit **Dubai Dino**, a 24m long and 150-million-year-old dinosaur skeleton. **Dubai Aquarium & Underwater Zoo** is home to sharks, rays and thousands more marine life.

TOP TIPS

- Book a room in the Armani Hotel and you'll have unrivalled views of the Dubai Fountain. The music from the show is piped into each suite inside the Burj Khalifa, and there's also secret access directly into Dubai Mall for guests staying at the designer hotel.
- A unique way to experience Burj Khalifa is by booking a table at At.mosphere on the 122nd floor. This modern French restaurant serves an upscale dinner menu and is also open for breakfast, afternoon tea and sunset experiences, all served with serious views.

Dubai Opera

Perfect for dinner and a show

Dubai's premier address for the performing arts opened in 2016 and has welcomed some of the biggest performers from around the world. Glass-fronted with twinkling Swarovski chandeliers, **Dubai Opera** is a place to dress up for a night of musical, theatrical or comedic entertainment. The dhow sail-shaped structure is much more than just an opera house thanks to its ingenious design that allows it to be transformed into a multi-purpose venue for concerts, gigs, exhibitions, theatre, comedy and more.

CREATIVEHYMMS/SHUTTERSTOCK ©

Dubai Opera

Museum of the Future

A peek ahead to 2070

Looking like a spaceship that landed on a grassy mound on the side of Sheikh Zayed Rd, this eye-opening **museum** fast forwards visitors 50 years into the future to a land of robot-served coffee, virtual tour guides and impossible twisting skyscrapers. With a gleaming silver exterior, it's inlaid with Arabic calligraphy-shaped windows, taken from poems penned by Dubai's ruler Sheikh Mohammed. Inside, interactive exhibits are spread over seven floors and include a sci-fi-like virtual DNA library, a moon mission where visitors soar into orbit, and a futurist children's fantasy land where kids can apply gaming skills to real-life challenges. There's also a calming sanctuary that priorities mediation and mental health. It's always popular; tickets must be booked in advance.

ME Dubai

The only hotel in the world designed by Zaha Hadid

Designed by the late British Iraqi starchitect, this gleaming **hotel** in the Business Bay district is part of the the Opus building, a cube-like structure formed from two separate towers. Featuring Hadid's mastery of curves, the building's central void is the focal point on the exterior, while the interior ME Dubai hotel is one of the city's best five-star boutique places to stay. With space-age-like rooms and futuristic good looks, the hotel has a strong focus on art with regular exhibitions and pop-up galleries, and is also where you'll find the first international branch of popular London restaurant **Roka**.

Sheikh Mohammed bin Rashid Boulevard

Downtown Dubai's restaurant-lined strip

Encircling the Burj Khalifa, this palm-lined **boulevard** runs for 3.5km and is peppered with hotels, restaurants and cafes. With wide, well-lit pavements, it's one of the few places in Dubai where you can easily walk from one place to another. Dining options are plentiful, with something for all tastes and budgets. Try **Ting Irie**, the UAE's first Jamaican restaurant and lounge, or head to **Fouquet's** for upscale French eats. **Bohox** is a homegrown cafe serving vegan and veggie options, and newcomer **Jun's** ranks for its American-Asian flavours. Rent a bike from one of the stations along the foothpaths and cycle the near-perfect circular boulevard, or take a ride on the fire-engine-coloured **Dubai Trolley**. This retro hop-on, hop-off tram trolley is the world's first hydrogen-powered, zero-emission street trolley. Stop by *The Wings of Mexico*, a golden sculpture of angel wings created by Mexican artist Jorge Marin, then skip the steps down towards Burj Park and instead take the **Downtown Slide**, a 19m insulated steel slide.

Dubai Trolley, Sheikh Mohammed bin Rashid Boulevard

Sky Views

Taking city sightseeing to new highs

On the top floor of the Address Sky View hotel, this elevated experience is probably not one to try if you have a fear of heights. But at more than 200m above ground, **Sky Views** is a good spot for anyone seeking the best vistas over Downtown Dubai. The **Observatory experience** sees guests take a panoramic lift ride to level 52 for a 46m walk along a clear glass bridge that links the hotel's two towers. One level up, hop inside the **Sky Slide**, a transparent tunnel that lets visitors whizz down the outside of the tower. Thrill-seekers can harness up and take things up a notch at the **Edge Walk**, a nail-biting outdoor amble along the towering ledge that encircles the hotel.

Address Sky View

Play DXB

A land of imagination

Play DXB is the newest iteration of VR Park, the world's biggest indoor virtual reality zone inside Dubai Mall. Geared towards children and teenagers, the indoor attraction has more than 30 immersive games and rides to entertain youngsters. Don an Oculus headset to battle demons and dragons, ride into the eye of a storm on a roller-coaster or go head to head in a bumper car challenge. There's also a classic carousel ride, arcade games and trampolines.

Sheikh Hamdan sculpture, Dubai Design District

Burj Park

Dubai Design District

Where creatives converge

One of the city's newer neighbourhoods, the colourful **Dubai Design District**, also referred to as D3, located just off Al Khail Rd about 4km from Dubai Mall, is a fashionable shopping, art and creative region that's evolving. With edgy architecture, wall murals and unique brands, it's home to concept boutiques, art studios, co-working spaces and showrooms. Eating inspiration is plentiful with everything from hipster favourite **Joe and the Juice** and home-grown **Akiba Dori**, to **Yui**, the UAE's first handmade ramen house. It's also where to come for some of Dubai's annual pop-up events including **Sole DXB** and **Dubai Design Week**.

Burj Park

Perfectly manicured grass and views of the Burj Khalifa

A sprawling **public park** that's open round-the-clock and free for everyone to access, this green space is in the heart of Dubai's busiest urban area. Reachable via bridges from the mainland, Burj Park is set on a little island next to the Dubai Fountain Lake. It's a spot where Dubai locals walk their dogs, go for a jog, cycle or enjoy a picnic, and often gets busy in the evenings. What makes this park extra special is its unparalleled views of the world's tallest building and the nightly shows of Dubai Fountain. It also has a sculpture park and a busy calendar of pop-up events including Christmas fairs, fashion shows and alfresco markets. Bike hire and parking are available at the entrance.

City Walk

From fine dining to family-friendly activities

This funky, pedestrian-friendly, open-air district on Al Safa St is one of Dubai's most popular communities. Inspired by European boulevards, the streets here stretch over several blocks and are lined with boutiques, outdoor terraces and chic cafes. As you wander, keep your eyes peeled and you'll likely spot art from a team of global artists that transformed some of the district's walls into canvases via large-scale murals, graffiti-inspired artwork and hidden paintings. A central fountain area gets busy in the evenings as children ride pedal boats and diners sit at terraces surrounding the water. It's also where you'll find the **Coca-Cola Arena**, one of the Middle East's largest indoor arenas. At night, many of the buildings are illuminated and the neighbourhood takes on a whole new persona.

Green Planet

Sky 2.0

Year-round rooftop parties

Taking clubbing to the next level, this standalone **open-air venue** in Dubai Design District is fast becoming the city's hottest place to party. Expect high-energy rooftop parties under the stars at this sphere-shaped venue where weekend nights are hosted by some of the city's most popular DJ's. Dazzling projections, curved screens and light shows add to the atmosphere, and the fun doesn't stop for summer as the venue has a special cooling system designed to keep partygoers cool no matter what the outside temperature is.

Green Planet

A rainforest in the desert

You might be in the desert, but that doesn't mean you can't enjoy rainforest views. **Green Planet** is Dubai's very own tropical microclimate that's home to more than 3000 plants and animals. Set in a cube-shaped biodome that's spread over four levels, visitors to the City Walk attraction can learn more about the importance of every part of the rainforest, from the forest floor to the canopy. Sloths, anteaters, toucans and armadillos can all be found here and there are some unusual experiences like snorkelling with African cichlid fish, zookeeping sessions and overnight camping.

A WALKING TOUR IN & AROUND DUBAI MALL

Downtown Dubai's wide boulevards and Dubai Mall are the ideal spot for a self-guided walking tour ticking off some of the city's big sights. Take the metro downtown, disembarking at the **1 Dubai Mall/Burj Khalifa metro station**, and from here, walk across the glass **2 Metro Link Bridge**, enjoying neighbourhood views from this elevated air-conditioned bridge. Enter the mall at **3 Pylones**, a funky French brand selling quirky homewares, and turn left in the direction of Bloomingdales towards Galleries Lafayette. Take the lift to the ground floor, turn right and you'll be in the atrium of the souq. Continue in the same direction, window shopping at ultra-high end shops like Patek Philippe and Cartier, turning left at Rolex. Head down this walkway, past a statue of a golden camel, and you'll soon reach the almost wholly complete structure of **4 Dubai Dino** (p79). Turn right here toward the huge blue tank that houses the **5 Dubai Aquarium & Underwater Zoo** (p79). Descend the nearest lifts to the lower lobby level and head for the Star Atrium, walking out of the mall and crossing the bridge to **6 Souk Al Bahar** (p77). Stop in the centre for good snaps of the Burj Khalifa. Returning to the main side of the bridge, turn left towards **7 Burj Lake**, where you can see the Dubai Fountain in action. This pedestrian-only boulevard leads to a bridge that will take you over the water to **8 Burj Park** (p82) with its sculpture *Win Victory Love* – a model of a hand giving Sheikh Mohammed's famous three-finger gesture. Continue across the park, and over the bridge, making a stop for a picture at the **9 Wings of Mexico Statue** (p86). From here, you'll soon find yourself on **10 Sheikh Mohammed bin Rashid Boulevard** (p81) with its myriad cafes and restaurants.

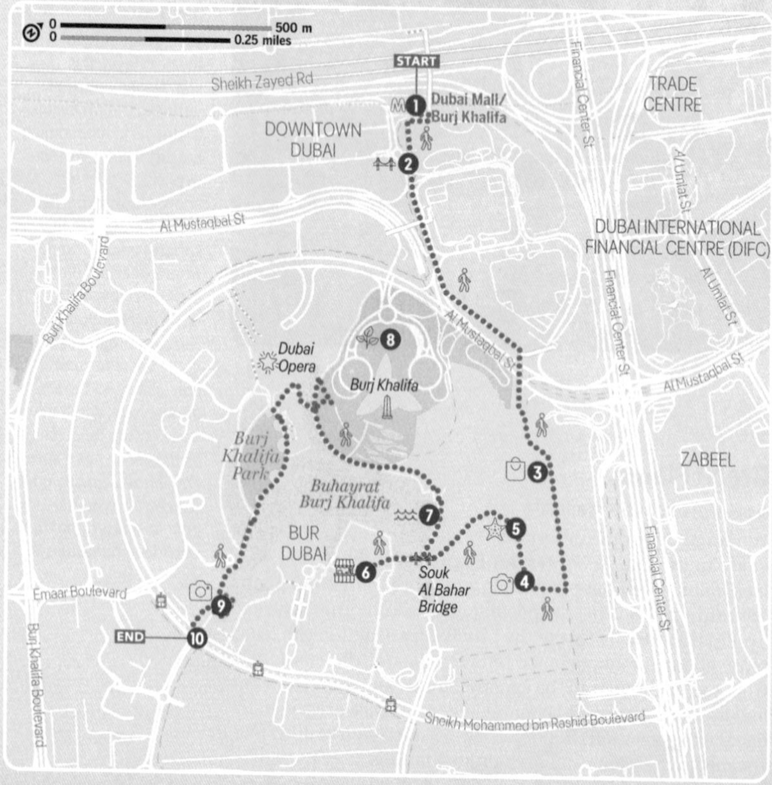

Dubai Fountain Lake

MAKING THE MOST OF DUBAI WATER CANAL

Visitors can find plenty of ways to make the most of the Dubai Water Canal (p77) and its 6.4km promenade. Book a luxury dinner cruise along the water to take in panoramic views of the city skyline accompanied by great food and live entertainment. Or put on your walking shoes and hit the pavement: wide paths wind along either side of the canal. Runners, walkers and cyclists can also traverse three of the canal's five bridges, including the purple-hued **Bridge of Tolerance** and the **Twisting Bridge**, previously hailed one of the most beautiful bridges in the world.

MORE IN DOWNTOWN DUBAI & BUSINESS BAY

Tables with a View

Front-row seats for Dubai Fountain

As water jets soar overhead and the music builds, spectators vie for space around the edge of the **Dubai Fountain**, with everyone keen on catching the spectacle. But there's no need to jostle for position, as there are plenty of ways you can get a front-row seat to the water-tastic spectacle. Take an abra ride on the **Dubai Fountain Lake** to set sail just as the show kicks off – but be prepared to get wet. Or keep your feet on dry land at the **Dubai Fountain Boardwalk**, a floating platform that gets visitors closer to the action. The 272m boardwalk is only open to ticketed spectators and at its closest point is just 9m away from the dancing jets. Restaurants surround Burj Lake, many with terraces overlooking the fountains. Reserve ahead of time to guarantee lake-side seating. Push the boat out with a reservation at **Novikov Café** in Fashion Avenue where the elevated location comes with awesome waterside views. At Palace Downtown hotel, elegant **Thiptara** offers authentic Thai cuisine and lives up to its name, which

UNUSUAL FINDS IN DUBAI MALL

Pinocchio World by Bartolucci
Beautifully crafted, handmade Italian wooden creations, toys and gifts that are perfect for souvenirs.

Candylicious
One of the world's largest confectionary stores. Sweets from around the world, plus a huge jellybean-filled wall.

Sauce
Homegrown Dubai concept store known for its curated fashion and lifestyle finds.

FINDING ART IN DOWNTOWN DUBAI

From well-established galleries to pop-up exhibits, it's easy to get your art fix in Downtown Dubai. The **MB&F M.A.D Gallery** in Dubai Mall is part horology shop, part kinetic gallery where you can see curated mechanical art devices. In DIFC, **Opera Gallery** showcases an enviable collection of works from established and up-and-coming artists; or head to boutique Hotel **Indigo Dubai Downtown** where you can appreciate over 200 curated artworks from local and Dubai-based artists, all of which combine to tell the story of Dubai and its evolvement. Immersive urban art can also be found at *The Wings of Mexico* sculpture on Shiekh Mohammed bin Rashid Boulevard, an iconic piece by Mexican artist Jorge Marin that's uber popular with Instagrammers.

Flamingo, Ras Al Khor Wildlife Sanctuary

means 'magic at the water', via front-row fountain seats. Lakeside **Wafi Gourmet** is popular thanks to a menu that serves dishes from around the region and terrace tables overlooking the water. Across the bridge in Souk Al Bahar (p77), enjoy Turkish dining on the waterfront promenade at **Gunaydin Dubai** with Anatolian-inspired dishes as impressive as the accompanying views. For a budget option, head to **Five Guys** and enjoy your burger at a table on the terrace with a side of fries and dancing fountain views.

An Evening of Entertainment at La Perle

Art and aquatics combine in this watery extravaganza

A metal spherical cage begins to rise above the ground, with five full-size motorbikes and their riders inside. The accompanying music builds dramatically as a girl with a pearl watches on from a bench below, just metres away from a 5m-deep pool. Reaching its pinnacle, the globe hovers and the riders start their engines. The audience gaps as the stunt riders whiz at top speeds around the globe, almost defying reality as they zoom narrowly past each other in the extremely tight quarters. This is just one scene from **La Perle by Dragone**, Dubai's first ever permanent show. Telling the tale of a prince and a young woman, the show explores themes of Dubai's pearl-div-

TOP THINGS TO DO WITH KIDS

Global Village
Outdoor festival running from October to April that's one of the city's most affordable family-friendly attractions.

IMG Worlds of Adventure
Dubai's largest indoor theme park with Cartoon Network and Marvel themed rides.

KidZania
Fun-filled edutainment centre where kids can play dress up and take a starring role in an incredible make-believe town.

ing history, ancestry and globalisation in a 90-minute extravaganza filled with death-defying stunts, special effects and unbelievable water theatrics. Running five days a week at Al Habtoor City, the spectacle is a Cirque du Soleil–style extravaganza and the work of creative director Franco Dragone. Taking place in a purpose-built aqua theatre, it's a has-to-be-seen-to-be-believed show. No matter where you sit, you'll have a good view thanks to the 270-degree seating layout. Expect to be transfixed as the cast of 65 artists, athletes and stunt performers depict a fantasy story supported by amazing sets, colourful costumes and dramatic scores. Be prepared for some nail-biting moments as the show's aerial feats, aquatic plunges and circus-like stunts unfold.

City Centre Bird-Watching at Ras Al Khor

The Cape of the Creek

A hushed silence falls over the wooden hut as a bright pink bird swoops in to land on the water, just metres from where you sit. Gathering its cerise plumage neatly behind its body, the long-beaked bird looks around – scoping out its surrounds. Seemingly satisfied with what it observes, it raises a leg – balancing on one long, slender matchstick-like limb. Quick as a dart, it plunges its head below the water's surface, emerging a few moments later with salty liquid dripping from its black and pink beak. This isn't a scene straight out of Africa or the retelling of a tale from the Caribbean, but instead a scene from the urban metropolis of Dubai. That's because in Ras Al Khor, just 14km from the world's tallest building, is a protected nature reserve that's home to hundreds of flamingos. Entirely free to enter, several bird-watching hides have been setup around the periphery of **Ras Al Khor Wildlife Sanctuary**. Park on the street and make your way through the palm-frond-lined walkway to sign in at one of the wooden huts, then pull up a stool, whip out some binoculars and sit quietly. In the marshy water in front of you, flocks of flamingos bathe, feed, soar and dance at their winter home. No reservations are needed to visit, but guests must agree to respect the environmental rules in place such as not littering or making loud noises.

MEYDAN CITY

Not far from Ras Al Khor are the sprawling grandstands of Meydan Racecourse. Home to the world's richest horse race, the spectacular structure is evidence of how seriously Dubai takes it horses. Identifiable via the **Meydan Bridge**, which glows brilliant blue every evening, it's also where you'll find the **Meydan Hotel**, a five-star resort with a fantastic rooftop infinity pool. Each year, the Dubai World Cup is hosted at Meydan, offering some of the sport's highest prizes, and well-dressed fans flock to the city for the event, and the super-star-fronted concerts that accompany it. A calendar of lower-key race meets take place in the run up to the World Cup, frequented both by racing fans and local families who come to enjoy the on-track entertainment.

ANIMAL EXPERIENCES

Camel Farm
Open seasonally, this farm in the Dubai desert is the place to get hands-on with camels, goats, donkeys and more.

Butterfly Garden
Next to Dubai Miracle Garden, this place is home to more than 15,000 butterflies housed in custom-built domes.

Al Maha Desert Resort
Luxury five-star tented retreat in Dubai's protected conservation area; spot oryx, gazelle, foxes, hares and more.

TOP TIP

There are no metro stops serving Jumeirah, which means getting around by public transport can be tricky. Take the Red Line to whichever stop is closest to where you want to go, and then taxi or uber from there. Local buses run regularly, operating the length of Jumeirah Beach Rd.

Above: Burj Al Arab (p92); Right: Kite Beach (p91)

I LIVE HERE: JUMEIRAH'S HIDDEN GEMS

Carla Baz (@carlabazstudio) is a Lebanese product designer based in Dubai. She shares some hidden gems of Jumeirah.

Orfali Bros
This is at the top of my list for places to eat, it's a fresh, creative and delicious take on Levantine cuisine. It's earned several accolades and is not to be missed.

Villa Margot
Housed in a typical Jumeirah villa, this quaint space has a coffee shop, a flower shop – with the nicest bouquets in Dubai – and a great concept store where you can shop a curated selection of clothes, jewellery and homeware.

The Grey
My favourite coffee shop with a gorgeous interior in sleek shades of grey and beautiful designer pieces, as well as the best coffee and pastries in the neighbourhoodand TikTok content.

Jumeirah

LOW-SLUNG WHITEWASHED VILLAS AND COASTAL VIBES

Running parallel to Sheikh Zayed Rd, Jumeirah is the city's beach-fringed coastline that begins just beyond Palm Jumeirah and stretches almost to Old Dubai.

Originally a residential area, the neighbourhood is full of low-rise villas and in the 1960s, '70s and '80s became increasingly popular as a place for expats to live. This gave rise to the term 'Jumeirah Janes' – a tongue-in-cheek name for the wives of the wealthy expat businessmen who reportedly spent their days in Dubai lounging on the beach, indulging in beauty treatments and having long lunches.

Running the length of the neighbourhood is Jumeirah Rd, behind which is Al Wasl Rd. Many of Jumeirah's original villas here have been redeveloped and house independent businesses with quirky cafes, art galleries, coffee houses and more.

With countless beaches dotted along Jumeirah's length, many of which run into one another, it's a popular spot with sunseekers and families with beach babies. Finding a quiet undeveloped spot of shoreline is now much harder in Jumeirah than it used to be, which sadly takes away a little of the neighbourhood's charm. On the other hand, Dubai's tourism authority has been busy developing the coastline and many formerly untouched beaches now boast changing rooms, toilets, lifeguards and places to eat and drink. Three have also recently been designated as night swimming spots where floodlights and round-the-clock lifeguards allow beachgoers to dip in the Gulf after dark, a welcome treat during the hot summer months.

Jumeirah's most important landmark is its towering flagpole that marks the site of Union House where the UAE was first formed in 1971. Etihad Museum, at the same site, is a worthy destination for travellers looking to understand more about the nation's five-decade history.

DON'T MISS...

BURJ AL ARAB
The world's only seven-star hotel and one of Dubai's iconic landmarks.
p92

MADINAT JUMEIRAH
Authentic Middle Eastern charm at a megacomplex of souqs, shopping, drinking and dining.
p90

KITE BEACH
Some of Dubai's most popular strips of shoreline, home to golden sand, waterside activities and more.
p91

JUMEIRAH GRAND MOSQUE
Discover more about Islamic culture and Emirati traditions at this house of worship.
p95

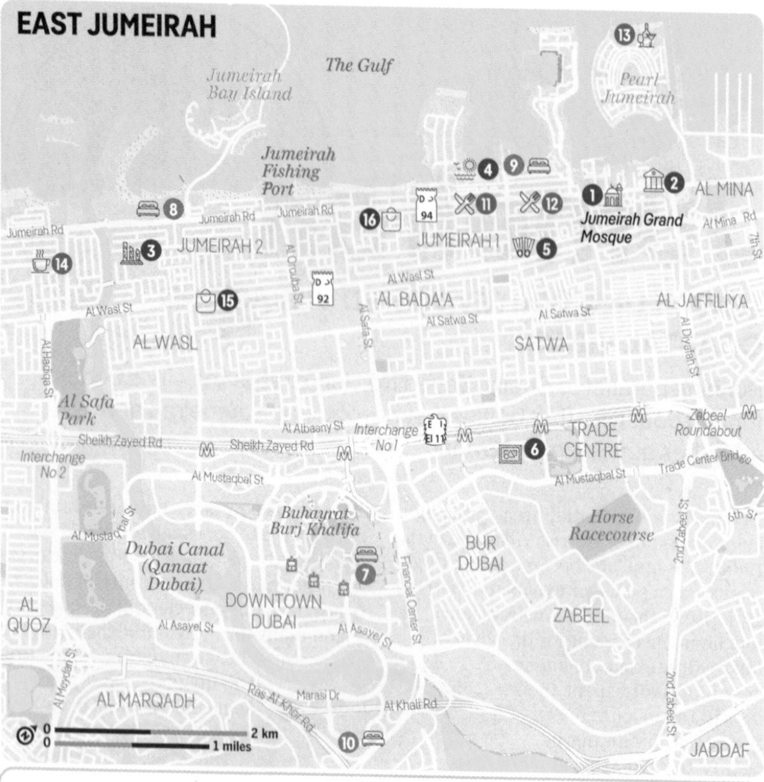

EAST JUMEIRAH

HIGHLIGHTS
1 Jumeirah Grand Mosque

SIGHTS
2 Etihad Museum
3 Jumeirah Archeological Ruins
4 Jumeirah Public Beach

ACTIVITIES, COURSES & TOURS
5 Al Boom Diving
see 10 Ciel Spa
6 DIFC Sculpture Park
see 7 The Spa

SLEEPING
7 Address Downtown
8 Four Seasons Resort Dubai at Jumeirah Beach
9 Rove La Mer Beach
10 SLS Dubai

EATING
11 Comptoir 102
12 Seva

DRINKING & NIGHTLIFE
13 Bungalo34
14 Rx Coffee Apothecary & Kitchen

SHOPPING
15 BoxPark
16 Mercato Mall

Madinat Jumeirah

MAP P93

Middle Eastern charm meets modern eating and dining

Madinat Jumeirah is a modern reinterpretation of a traditional Arabian village that mixes the wind towers of Al Fahidi District with the bustle of the city's old souqs and elements of its early humble palaces. Part resort and part entertainment arena, at its heart is **Souq Madinat Jumeirah** – a warren of lantern-lined alleyways filled with stalls selling everything from bottled sand art and glass-blown ornaments to babouche-style shoes and colourful kaftans. It's also a great spot for dining and drinking, with many of the restaurants offering palm-fringed waterway vistas. Head to **Trattoria** for Italian dining by the water or **Pai Thai** for upmarket Thai food that's only reachable via an abra ride, and try **Folly** for rooftop sundowners.

Jumeirah Public Beach

MAP P90

Day to night on the shore

There's no shortage of beaches in this coastal neighbourhood, and **Jumeirah Public Beach** is a popular choice. Located behind Sunset Mall, it's often referred to as NessNass Beach by Dubai's old-timers, and offers a laid-back stretch of golden sand for lazy beach days. Free to access, it isn't as well developed as nearby Kite Beach, but this means it's often a less crowded choice. It's also open for after-dark dips, thanks to floodlights and round-the-clock lifeguards. Changing rooms, toilets and showers are available.

Ski Dubai

Mall of the Emirates

MAP P93

Skiing, shopping and serious retail therapy

While it's no longer the city's largest mall – it was eclipsed when Dubai Mall opened back in 2008 – **Mall of the Emirates** remains one of the city's most popular shopping destinations. Home to an indoor ski slope, huge cinema complex and **Magic Planet** – an arcade and mini amusement park rolled in to one – the mall has more than 500 shops, restaurants and cafes. Harry Potter fans will want to visit the Wizarding World Shop to stock up on themed goodies, and the city's only **Harvey Nichols** offers an upmarket department shopping experience. The **Fashion Dome** – with its glass and wrought-iron ceiling – is the place for luxury finds or window shopping, with brands like Christian Louboutin, Jimmy Choo and Tiffany's holding fort beneath the skylight.

Ski Dubai

MAP P93

Off-piste adventure

It might be sunshine and rising temperatures outside, but travellers can always cool off at **Ski Dubai**, the Middle East's first indoor ski slope where temperatures hover around an icy 0°C (32°F). Located inside Mall of the Emirates, this artificial alpine ski resort has five ski runs of up to 400m, including the world's first indoor black run. There's also a snow park where you can hop on a bobsled, or tackle the climbing wall or career down snow-covered slopes in an inflatable zorb ball. If you're new to winter sports, ski and snowboard lessons are available.

Kite Beach

MAP P93

Sunshine-filled days and panoramic views

Kite Beach is one of Dubai's most popular strips of shoreline, home to pristine golden sand and plenty of activities including beach tennis, kitesurfing, volleyball, bike paths and an inflatable on-the-water obstacle course. It has showers, toilets and changing rooms, plus a host of food trucks and quirky cafes. The public beach is free to access and, at 5km from the Burj Al Arab, is a great spot for sunset selfies with the seven-star hotel in the background.

BEST BARS IN JUMEIRAH

Bahri Bar
Upmarket waterside bar at Jumeirah Mina A'Salam with sea views, live music and eclectic cocktail list. **$$$**

Bungalo34
Retro Riviera bar serving ice-cold cocktails beachside at Nikki Beach Resort & Spa. **$$**

Loca UAE
Fiesta vibes await at this popular laid-back Mexican bar that gets livelier after dark. **$$**

Burj Al Arab

MAP P93

The world's only seven-star hotel

The jewel of Dubai's Jumeirah coastline is the **Burj Al Arab** – branded the world's only seven-star hotel since it first opened in 1999. An icon of the emirate, Burj Al Arab is to Dubai what the Eiffel Tower is to Paris or Big Ben is to London. The sail-shaped tower rises 320m above sea level and dominates the Jumeirah skyline, reflecting the bright sunshine by day and being illuminated via colour-changing lights after dark. Built on a constructed island, the hotel, which in reality is a five-star property, has luxurious suites, all of which come with Gulf views, private butlers and a choice of 17 pillow options. Interiors are gilded in gold and you can see more than 30 different types of marble. The resort is also home to some of the city's best restaurants, including Michelin-starred **Al Muntaha**, and **Ristorante L'Olivo at Al Mahara**, which has a floor-to-ceiling aquarium. Travellers that want to learn more about the landmark can book a spot on the Inside Burj Al Arab tour, which highlights secrets of the hotel's design and gives guests a glimpse inside the opulent Royal Suite. If you're not going inside, the best photo opportunities are to found on the public beach to the north of the hotel, from vantage points inside the Madinat Jumeirah, or from the water.

Wild Wadi

MAP P93

A watery adventure inspired by Arabia

In the shadow of the Burj Al Arab, next door to Jumeirah Beach Hotel, **Wild Wadi Waterpark** is Dubai's original waterpark, dating back to 1999. The park remains a favourite with holidaymakers seeking a place to cool off. Themed around a traditional Middle Eastern village, it's home to the Jumeirah Sceirah – the tallest free-fall slide outside North America; Tantrum Alley, with its plunging waterslide and twisting tornado-style tube rides; and Juha's Journey, a meandering 360m-long lazy river. Travellers staying at select Jumeirah hotels get free access, as does anyone presenting a disability card.

MARIEKE KRAMER/SHUTTERSTOCK ©

Wild Wadi

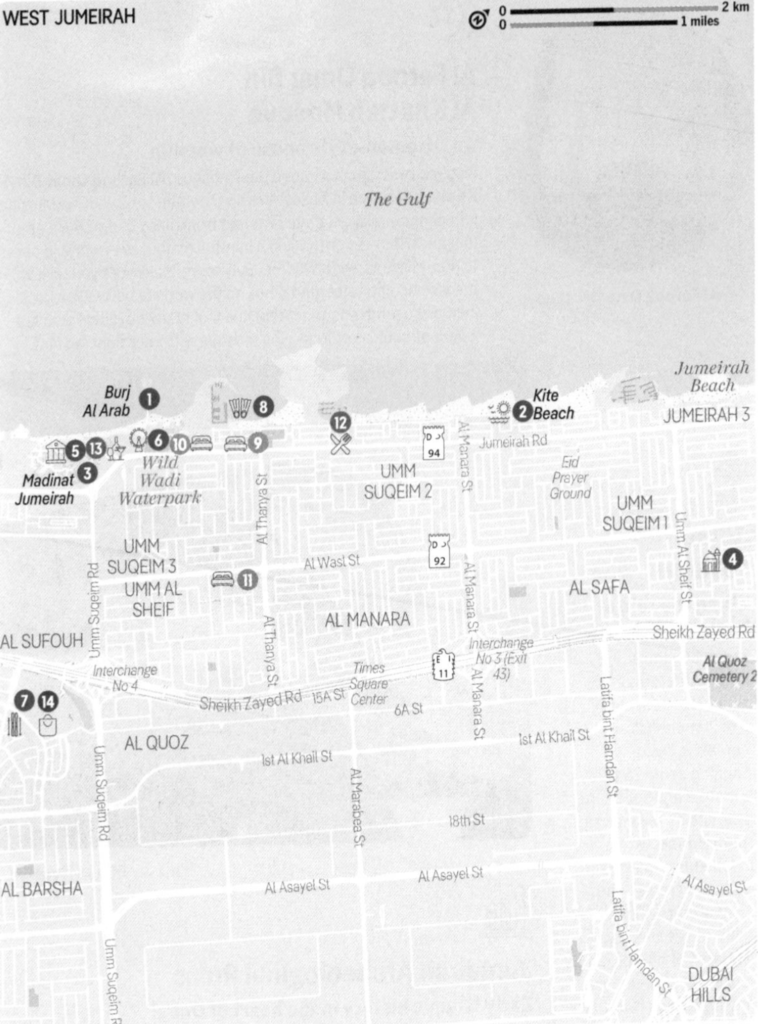

HIGHLIGHTS
1 Burj Al Arab
2 Kite Beach
3 Madinat Jumeirah

SIGHTS
4 Al Farooq Omar Bin Al Khattab Mosque
5 Theatre of Digital Art
6 Wild Wadi Waterpark

ACTIVITIES, COURSES & TOURS
7 Ski Dubai
8 Sunset Beach

SLEEPING
9 Beach Walk Boutique Hotel
10 Jumeirah Beach Hotel
11 Lemon Tree Hotel Jumeirah

EATING
12 Jumeirah Fishing Harbour 3

DRINKING & NIGHTLIFE
13 Bahri Bar

SHOPPING
14 Mall of the Emirates

Al Farooq Omar Mosque

Al Farooq Omar Bin Al Khattab Mosque

MAP P93

An Ottoman-style house of worship

Inspired by Istanbul's famed blue mosque, **Al Farooq Omar Bin Al Khattab Mosque** in Al Safa has an Ottoman style with Andalusian influences, making it quite different from many of the UAE's other mosques. It's also one of just a handful of houses of worship open to non-Muslims, with two free daily tours. Make sure you review the visiting etiquette guidelines on the website before you go; it includes useful recommended tips that many travellers won't be aware of, such as entering the mosque with your right leg first.

Etihad Museum

Etihad Museum

MAP P90

Telling the tale of the UAE

Chronicling the story of the UAE's formation, **Etihad Museum** at the tip of Jumeirah is an impressive building spanning some 25,000 sq metres and set on the same site as the historic **Union House**, where documents signed 52 years ago created the country that we know today. Inside there are hundreds of photos, films, books and other archival media showing how the emirates has developed, plus interactive pavilions, a library, exhibition hall and a cafe. It's also where you'll find the 123m-tall flag pole sporting the massive UAE flag fluttering in the wind above Jumeirah.

Jumeirah Archeological Ruins

MAP P90

Early Islamic history in the heart of Dubai

The UAE might only be five decades old, but its history runs much deeper, something you can see at **Jumeirah Archaeological Ruins**. Located between Jumeirah Rd and Al Wasl Rd, this history-laden spot is one of the largest and most important early Islamic sites in the Gulf Region. Archaeologists here have discovered the ruins of a port town dating back some 1000 years. The original settlement was on the ancient trade route and excavated ruins include the foundations of houses, market buildings, a mosque, and a roadside inn where travellers would rest and meet to conduct business. Ruins are in a fragmentary state so not much is recognisable to the untrained eye, but it's a great place to witness Middle Eastern history juxtaposed against Dubai's skyscraper-filled skyline.

Comptoir 102

MAP P90

Health-conscious eats and great coffee

In a low-rise former residential building in old Jumeirah, **Comptoir 102** on Beach Rd is a cosy cafe and boutique that's been serving up organic breakfast, lunch and dinner to health-conscious diners for over a decade. The menu changes according to the season and there's a host of raw, vegan, gluten-dree, dairy-free and sugar-free options available. It's also the place to find souvenirs as it's stocked with designer homewares, one-off jewellery pieces, and quirky clothes, candles and gifts.

TOP RIGHT: AMINA7/SHUTTERSTOCK ©; BOTTOM LEFT: CHECCO2/SHUTTERSTOCK ©

Jumeirah Fishing Harbour 3

Jumeirah Fishing Harbour 3

MAP P93

The freshest catch of the day

Swathed in ocean breezes, **Jumeirah Fishing Harbour 3** is a working boatyard and yesteryear wharf peppered with wind towers and lantern-lit walkways. It's home to **Jumeirah Fish Market** and a handful of seafood restaurants including **Bu Qutair**, a much-loved former beach shack that serves up no-frills fresh seafood in an unpretentious indoor and outdoor setting. Close to the Burj Al Arab, don't confuse this spot with Jumeirah Fishing Harbours 2 and 1 further east, although the latter is also worth a visit for any foodies keen to dine at **3Fils**, Dubai's most unassuming Michelin-recommended eatery.

Jumeirah Grand Mosque

Jumeirah Grand Mosque

MAP P90

Shining a light on Dubai's Islamic culture

Travellers keen to learn more about Dubai and the UAE as a Muslim country can head to **Jumeirah Grand Mosque**. Dating back to 1979, the sandstone and marble structure is one of just a handful of mosques open to non-Muslim visitors. Twice-daily guided tours run every day except Friday, and an Emirati guide leads guests around the venue and explains more about religions practices, celebrations and cultural traditions, with guests able to ask any burning questions they may have. Tours end with traditional Emirati refreshments. Modest dress is required and women should bring a scarf to cover their hair. The mosque is also home to a small museum showcasing pieces documenting life in the city in the '70s and '80s.

Seva

MAP P90

Holistic, plant-based goodness

Part cafe, part wellness shop and part secret garden that plays host to wellness events, **Seva** is one of Dubai's longest-standing health spots. Formerly known as Life n One, it's located in a traditional villa in Jumeirah 1, just behind the popular Magrudy's bookshop. The food here is plant-based and free from gluten, sugar, dairy and artificial ingredients, but there's no compromise on taste. Eating aside, you can join regular group yoga, meditation and sound healing classes, with drop-ins welcome. There's also a boho-style shop where you can find a host of earth-inspired products including candles, sage, botanical oils and more.

Four Seasons Resort Dubai at Jumeirah Beach

MAP P90

Beachside elegance and a restaurant village

This elegant **beach resort** on the northern tip of Jumeirah has rooms overlooking the waters of the Gulf on one side and Dubai's skyline on the other. With two temperature-controlled swimming pools and a sprawling stretch of private beach, it's a favourite with families. It's also popular with foodies thanks to 11 drinking and dining options, including retro-style **Hendricks Bar**, which has one of the city's most extensive gin selections, and a restaurant village that's home to upmarket Italian **Scalini**, Peruvian favourite **Coya**, and **Nammos**, a Mediterranean eatery with beachside views.

STANISLAV71/SHUTTERSTOCK ©

Four Seasons Resort Dubai at Jumeirah Beach

Mercato Mall

MAP P90

Dubai's first themed shopping district

While it's not one of Dubai's biggest malls, **Mercato Shopping Mall** near Jumeirah Mosque is home to a good selection of international fashion brands, homewares and local jewellery shops. There's also a Spinney's supermarket, a cinema and **Fun City** – an indoor family entertainment hub with arcade games, rides and soft play zones. First opened in 2002, it was the Middle East's first themed mall and is designed to replicate an Italian Renaissance town with its colourful architecture, cafe-lined piazza, pretty fountains and huge vaulted skylight roof. If you're visiting at Christmas, pass by to see some of the best decorations in the city – with a sparkling tree, Santa's grotto, and a huge red ribbon designed to wrap up the mall's exterior like a present.

BoxPark

MAP P90

An upcycled shipping container district

Inspired by the original high-street pop-up mall in London, **BoxPark** Dubai is an outdoor mall on Al Wasl Rd that's been constructed from upcycled shipping containers. Here you'll find trendy boutiques, concept stores, beauty shops, hip restaurants and quirky cafes including the monochromatic 2D-style **Forever Rose** cafe. It's also a good place to catch a movie at the arty **Roxy** cinema, and there's **Escape the Room** for sleuth-loving visitors. BoxPark is best visited in the winter months when the weather is a little cooler.

Forever Rose, BoxPark

Alserkal Avenue, Al Quoz

Rx Coffee Apothecary & Kitchen

MAP P90

Scandi-style coffee spot

Caffeine-addicts can make a beeline to **Rx Coffee Apothecary & Kitchen** in Jumeirah 3 for one of the city's best cups of joe. One of four branches in Dubai, this soothing cafe is all sleek lines and soft lighting with natural-shaped fittings, apothecary-style drawers and Scandinavian-style finishings. Downstairs is the brew bar where light-roasted Fuglen coffee beans from Norway are served in handcrafted ceramics, while upstairs is a communal dining area filled with local artwork. There's also a moreish menu of baked goods, light bites, salads, breakfast dishes and more.

Al Quoz

Dubai's industrial-turned-creative zone

Technically **Al Quoz** isn't part of Jumeirah, but the sprawling district lies directly opposite the neighbourhood on the other side of the Sheikh Zayed highway. One of Dubai's oldest manufacturing hubs, housing autoshops and factories, the busy industrial area is still the place to take cars to be repaired, but it has also blossomed into one of the city's most creative districts. Boasting several art galleries, studios and performance spaces, it's also home to the uber-popular **Alserkal Ave**, a sprawling cluster of cutting-edge art galleries. The neighbourhood is dusty and traffic-filled, but has a blossoming active scene including trampoline parks, padel courts, boxing rings and marital arts studios, plus a growing number of concept stores, organic coffee roasters and inventive cafes.

Theatre of Digital Art

MAP P93

A 360-degree cultural immersion

Inside Madinat Jumeirah, this immersive **art space** is a relative newcomer to the city's art scene, having only opened in 2020. Spread over 1800 sq metres, it showcases famous artwork giving it a modern twist via technology and imaginative storytelling. Multimedia, multi-sensory exhibitions change seasonally; previous shows have featured Banksy and Van Gogh. There's also hands-on edutainment-style exhibits for children, a virtual reality area, wellness workshops, and musical performances and concerts, including weekly Friday jazz nights.

Jumeirah Beach Hotel

Jumeirah Beach Hotel

MAP P93

Dubai's original family resort

Rising into the sky with its glass-encased 26-storey wave-shaped design, Jumeirah's original beach hotel is something of a Dubai landmark. Having opened back in 1997, the recently renovated hotel is geared towards families, with five swimming pools, a private beach, indoor and outdoor kids club, and no fewer than seven restaurants. Soon to be part of the oceanic trilogy from the homegrown Dubai hotel group, this five-star resort also gives all guests complimentary unlimited access to nearby Wild Wadi Waterpark (p92).

World Islands

Dubai's most ambitious project

Leave it to Dubai to build a floating replica of the entire world. Jutting off the coast of Jumeirah, this **constructed archipelago** has been several years in the making and is still not complete, but the first few attractions are now open. Made up of 260 islands, grouped into seven sets to represent different continents, it's designed to look like the world map when seen from above. Accessible from the mainland via a 15-minute boat ride, current attractions include the **Royal Island** beach club on Lebanon, which is open for day guests, the French Riviera-inspired **Côte d'Azur** resort on the Heart of Europe island, and **Anantara World Islands Dubai Resort**, a luxury Thai-inspired hotel on the South American continent of the development.

Exploring Offshore

MAP P93

Going into the big blue

Dubai may have risen from the desert, but the city is surrounded by the warm waters of the Gulf and offers a variety of experiences for those keen to go diving in the big blue. Novice divers can try an easy shore dive from **Sunset Beach** where there's plenty of corals and several fish species to be seen. Those with a bit more experience can venture out to *Zainab,* a shipwreck some 40 minutes off the coast of Dubai. This 1969-built vessel sank in 2001 and has settled at a depth of 30m on a sandy shore. It's home to several marine creatures including oysters, large rays, yellowtail barracuda, snappers and batfish. There are several dive schools in the city, mostly located in Jumeirah and catering to all levels of divers. Of course, this being Dubai, there's also a host of artificial dive sites to explore including **Deep Dive Dubai**, the world's deepest diving centre where you can go down to a depth of 60m or enjoy a game of chess under the water; the **Ambassador Lagoon** at Atlantis, The Palm, where you'll find over 60,000 marine creatures; and Dubai Aquarium & Underwater Zoo (p39) in the heart of Dubai Mall, which is a good place for divers keen to swim with sharks as it's home to over 400 sharks and rays, including the world's biggest collection of sand tiger sharks. Non-divers can get in on the action with a Shark Walk, which lets adventurers immerse themselves in the tank wearing an oxygenated helmet that makes breathing underwater easy.

Dubai's Blossoming Arts Scene

MAP P90

From urban street art to priceless pieces

Having expanded on its reputation as a place to visit for unrivalled luxury, Dubai has evolved and its arts scene is now one of the most sophisticated in the Middle East. Long a capital for artistic expression, the city's contemporary cultural heritage sees cutting-edge galleries rub shoulders with inspirational installations, dynamic exhibits and urban street art. Surrounded by the glistening skyscrapers of Dubai's Financial District, **DIFC sculpture park** is open seasonally as a way to make art accessible to all. See surreal visions from Salvador Dalí, immersive yourself in pop artwork from Jeff Koons, and wander the gardens filled with works of local and regional artists.

SCUBA DIVING IN DUBAI

Dani Beentjes (@ scubahubdivingclub) is a diving instructor in Dubai who spills the tea on the best place to explore the big blue.

Scuba Hub's dive site is located on Dubai Islands. It's one of the very best dive sites in Dubai where you can see amazing marine life. More often than not we spot seahorses, eagle rays, stingrays, nudibranches, groupers, angel fish, batfish and even turtles on our dives. The depth here reaches up to 13m ,and visibility is about 4m or 5m, which is better than other common spots in Dubai. It's an easy-access shore dive without any current; perfect for spotting marine life and taking photographs.

WHERE TO STAY ON A BUDGET IN JUMEIRAH

Rove La Mer Beach
Funky, beachfront hotel with a pool from Rove Hotels, a Dubai brand known for its fuss-free rooms and easy-going vibe. $

Beach Walk Boutique Hotel
A stone's throw from Jumeirah's beaches, this tiny boutique hotel has a boho-Middle Eastern vibe. $

Lemon Tree Hotel Jumeirah
In the heart of Jumeirah, a few streets back from the shoreline; comfortable, clean rooms and a rooftop pool. $

WHERE TO SEE ART IN DUBAI

Slava Noor (@slava noor @arte8lusso), founder and editor of online art magazine *Arte & Lusso* and a PR girl, shares details on her favourite art galleries in Dubai.

Galleria Continua This international gallery is a great addition to Dubai's art scene. Located in the Burj al Arab, it has a picturesque space coupled with stunning views of the sea.

Firetti Contemporary, Alserkal Avenue My absolute favourite gallery in Dubai and a space dedicated to showcasing established contemporary artists, as well as focusing on emerging talent. It's located in the vibrant Alserkal area.

XVA Art Hotel and XVA Cafe A beautiful gem in the heart of Al Fahidi Historical Neighbourhood that's a unique space with a boutique art hotel, art gallery, shop and cafe.

Arabian oryx, Dubai Desert Conservation Reserve

Nearby Dubai Design District (p82) is still a work in progress, but is fast shaping up to be one of the city's hippest art-filled haunts with edgy architecture, concept stores, pop-ups and showrooms; it's also a place to attend cultural events.

Alserkal Ave in Al Quoz (p97) is popular for galleries prioritising emerging underground and experimental art, including an outpost of New York's **Leila Heller Gallery**, while more high-end Middle Eastern art galleries including **Ayyam** can be found in Gate Village, Downtown Dubai. And you don't even have to go looking for art – instead just keep your eyes peeled as you wander Satwa, City Walk and Jumeirah to spot artistic graffiti and wall murals decorating many of the city's buildings.

Unwind at Some of the World's Best Spas

MAP P90

Unwind, pamper and restore

There's spa days and then there's Dubai spa days. In a city famed for all things luxury, there's a plethora of retreats where you can escape the hustle and bustle of the big city and allow skilled therapists to calm your mind, body and spirit. As a melting pot of cultures, Dubai's spa scene also spans continents and the array of treatments on offer across the city is second to none.

DIVING SCHOOLS IN DUBAI

Divers Down
Friendly instructors teach a range of Padi courses and organise water clean-up days. Branches in Dubai and Fujaira.

Al Boom Diving
One of the city's best-known dive schools, with courses, day trips and guided excursions in Dubai and Fujairah.

Scuba Shade
Full-service diving centre inside the Habtoor Grand Resort. Retail and rental equipment, plus a range of Padi courses.

Talise Spa is an award-winning outpost from homegrown hotel brand Jumeirah that's located in most of the group's hotels, and is open to day visitors as well as in-house guests. The 8200-sq-metre **Talise Ottoman Spa** at Jumeirah Zabeel Saray is one of the largest in Dubai and a haven of relaxation with thalassotherapy pools, ice rooms, Turkish hammams and Ottoman-inspired treatments.

If you prefer old-school Dubai bling try the Gold Dust treatment at **Ciel Spa** on the 69th floor of SLS Dubai, where therapists exfoliate skin with 14-carat gold. Or take it one step further at the **Palazzo Versace**, where the diamond and gold royal hammam journey includes a gold rhassoul body treatment followed by a massage using oil infused with real diamonds. At the other end of the spectrum, **The Spa** at Address Downtown offers a Vibra Healing massage that's based on ancient eastern practices and uses Tibetan singing bowls to align chakras and stimulate brain waves. Children aren't neglected either, with the **Candy Spa** at Centara Mirage Beach Resort Dubai specialising in sweet-themed treatments for little ones.

Escaping to Dubai's Desert Dunes

Embrace the call of the wild

The Arabian Desert surrounds Dubai and is a place where many tourists go for dune-bashing adventures and safari tours that show another side of the city, one filled with henna painting, belly dancing and slow-cooked lamb ouzi, roasted under the midday sun.

It's also where much of the city's conservation efforts take place, with **Dubai Desert Conservation Reserve** designated as the UAE's first protected national park. Wildlife thrives in this desert terrain, with 225 sq km of land where gazelle, oryx and Arabian tahr roam freely. And camels, long a symbol of Emirati heritage, are easily spotted meandering along its ever-changing mounds and ridges.

If you want to immerse yourself in the desert, consider booking a night at one of Dubai's desert retreats. **Al Maha**, a Luxury Collection Desert Resort & Spa, is located inside the national park and guests are likely to see gazelles meander by as they lounge in private plunge pools. Or head to Bab Al Shams (p122), a stalwart in the city that's recently been renovated and is surrounded by the glistening dunes of the desert. Of course, you don't need to spend a whole night in the desert to be touched by its magic. A dusk visit is more than enough to see families and friends swapping tourist-trodden hot spots for an evening barbecue, a lengthy dog-walk or a spot of stargazing.

RESPECTING DUBAI'S WILDERNESS

Rob Nicholas (@sandshepra) is the founder of eco-tourism company Sand Sherpa. Working in the Dubai Desert Conservation Reserve, he's keen to make sure the city's wilderness is preserved.

A spike in the number of visitors venturing into the city's wilderness areas has led to some disrespectful behaviour, with fires being set on the ground, gathering of indigenous plants and collecting of brush wood. Driving on the *sabhka* (gravel plains) is also harmful and car tracks through these areas can take the environment years to recover from. Travellers should be aware of new measures designed to protect the desert, including restrictions accessing some natural beauty spots, designated tracks in and out of the dunes, and regular patrols of the area.

BEST DESERT SAFARI COMPANIES

Sand Sherpa
Offers eco-adventures in Dubai's desert conservation area including desert and falcon safaris.

Arabian Adventures
A long-running stalwart offering door-to-door pickups, decent entertainment and highly skilled drivers.

Platinum Heritage
This upmarket company has knowledgeable guides, night safaris and the option to explore in a vintage LandRover.

TOP TIP

Get your thrill on at Dubai Marina's XLine Dubai, the world's longest urban zipline where riders descend from a platform 170m above the city before soaring for 1km over the blue waters of the marina. Reaching speeds of up to 80km/h in a Superman-style harness, it's worth a whirl (even if you've ziplined before) for its panoramic skyscraper-surrounded urban views.

RASTO SK/SHUTTERSTOCK ©

Above: Pier 7 (p110), Dubai Marina; Right: Atlantis,The Palm Dubai (p108)

I LIVE HERE: EATING & DRINKING IN DUBAI MARINA & PALM JUMEIRAH

Jakob Vermehren, head of retail at Jysk UAE, hails from Denmark and lives in Dubai Marina. He shares the best places to eat, drink and lounge in the waterfront neighbourhood.

Azure Beach
An upscale beach club in Rixos Premium Dubai JBR that has good vibes, great music and in my opinion is the best beach bar in JBR.

Clay
On Bluewaters Island, this Japanese-Peruvian restaurant is a favourite, it serves up some of the best sushi in the city.

Massimo's Italian Restaurant
This laid-back restaurant has waterfront views, great food and, even better, authentic Italian ice cream.

Dubai Marina & Palm Jumeirah

CONSTRUCTED ISLANDS AND WATERFRONT VIEWS

On the city's southern side, Dubai Marina is one of the most popular places to live and visit.

Having grown from an untouched patch of sand along the Gulf, the district is now centered on its 3km-long marina and fabricated waterfront where boats bob up and down in the greeny-blue waters. Around this, towering buildings have risen up to form one of the city's buzziest residential areas. One such skyrise is the Palm Tower, where travellers can find Aura, the world's highest 360-degree infinity pool.

In front of the marina, JBR was once a quiet residential area on the shoreline, but it has evolved into one of the busiest entertainment and holiday districts in Dubai, which hasn't been great news for residents that originally bought sea-view property here – ocean views have vanished as the neighbourhood's coastline has edged ever further into the Gulf. Jutting into the water 400m off the JBR coastline is Bluewaters Island, one of Dubai's newer districts that's home to a host of bars and restaurants, plus the world's largest observation wheel.

Further north along the coast, Palm Jumeirah is perhaps Dubai's most impressive constructed landscaping project to date. Having added a whopping 56km to the city's coastline when it opened back in 2007, this palm-tree-shaped island is Dubai's favoured destination for holidaymakers, and tourists flock to its golden beaches, cafe-lined boulevards and luxury resorts. Affluent residents and several celebrities own private villas on the palm fronds, most of which come with beach and direct sea access. This is also where you'll find the pink and turquoise turrets of Atlantis, The Palm, the underwater themed megahotel that commands pride of place on the tip of the Palm Jumeirah trunk, and its recently added bigger, more glamourous sibling Atlantis, The Royal.

SERGII FIGURNYI/SHUTTERSTOCK ©

DON'T MISS...

ATLANTIS, THE PALM DUBAI
Family-friendly resort with a giant aquarium and waterpark.
p108

ATLANTIS, THE ROYAL
Swanky new luxury hotel with celebrity-backed restaurants and 90 swimming pools.
p108

SKYDIVE DUBAI
Tandem jumps with views over Palm Jumeirah and the Gulf.
p107

THE VIEW AT THE PALM
Elevated views from a glass-framed observation deck in Nakheel Mall.
p106

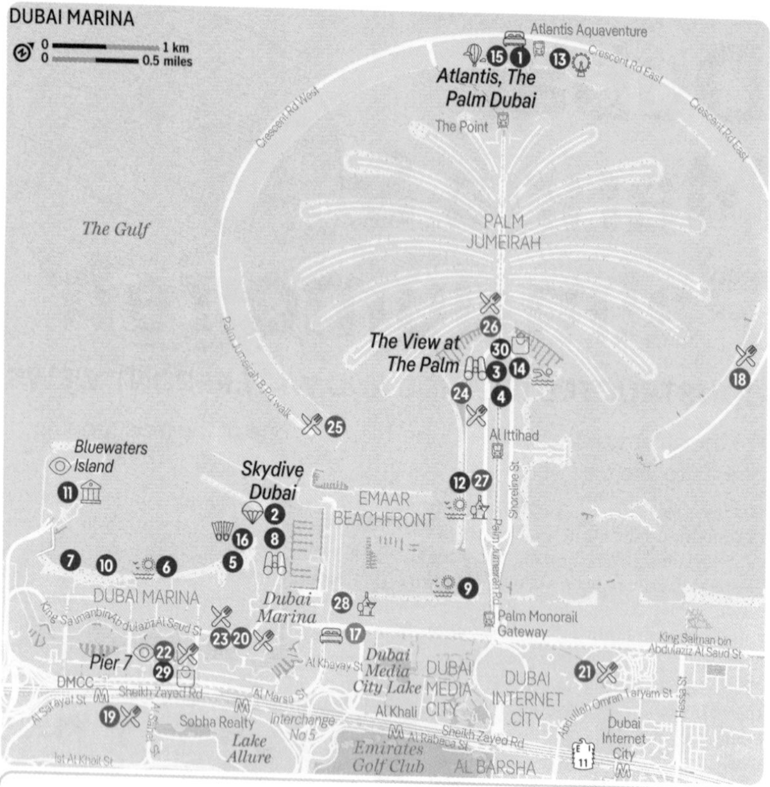

DUBAI MARINA

HIGHLIGHTS
1 Atlantis, The Palm Dubai
2 Skydive Dubai
3 The View at The Palm

SIGHTS
4 Al Ittihad Park
5 Andreea's
6 Azure Beach
7 Bla Bla
8 Dinner in the Sky
9 Drift Beach
10 JBR
11 Madame Tussauds
12 Palm West Beach

ACTIVITIES, COURSES & TOURS
13 Atlantis Aquaventure Waterpark
14 Aura Skypool
15 Dubai Balloon
16 Scuba Shade

SLEEPING
17 Mina Seyahi

EATING
18 Anantara The Palm Dubai Resort
19 Bait Maryam
20 Ceylonka Restaurant
21 Holiday Inn Express
22 Le Pain Quoitiden
23 Massimo's Italian Restaurant
24 SAN Beach
25 STAY by Yannick Alleno
26 Strand Kraft Kitchen

DRINKING & NIGHTLIFE
27 Above Eleven
28 Attiko Dubai

SHOPPING
29 Dubai Marina Mall
30 Nakhell Mall

Nakheel Mall

MAP P104

Shopping, dining and drinking

Standing on the tip of Palm Jumeirah's trunk, **Nakheel Mall** is one of the city's newer shopping destinations and is easily reachable via the Palm Monorail. Filled with high-street brands, boutiques, homeware shops and a few designer outlets, it also has a Waitrose supermarket and **Depachika**, a luxury food hall that's home to several of Dubai's favourite dining venues including Lime Tree Café, city-famous for its carrot cake. There's also entertainment options including a Vox Cinemas and Trampo extreme, an indoor trampoline park, as well as **Soho Garden** on the rooftop for dining and drinking with views over Palm Jumeirah.

Anantara The Palm Dubai Resort

Anantara The Palm Dubai Resort

MAP P104

A taste of Thailand

For a visit to Thailand without leaving the UAE, head to **Anantara The Palm Dubai Resort**. On the east crescent of Palm Jumeirah, this secluded tropical resort has swaying palm trees, colourful tuk-tuks, overwater villas and red-roofed temple-inspired architecture. Unwind on the 400m stretch of private shoreline or explore the coast on the resort's traditional Thai longtail boat then dine at a rickshaw-style table in **Mekong**, an upmarket Asian eatery serving Thai, Vietnamese and Chinese favourites.

Palm West Beach

MAP P104

Waterfront strip with sunset views

Part public beach and part promenade, **Palm West Beach** on Palm Jumeirah's trunk has something for everyone. Stretching 1.6km along the Dubai coast, the beachfront has some of the city's best sunset views. Get your steps up on the promenade's walking and running trails, or enjoy meandering along the boulevard until you come across a waterfront restaurant that takes your fancy – try **Senor Pico's**, **Koko Bay** or **Lucky Fish**. It's also pet-friendly, making it popular with dog-loving residents. Several hotels are now open on the strip, including the family-friendly **Hilton Dubai Palm Jumeirah** and **Marriott Resort Palm Jumeirah**, which look like carbon copies of one another, the party-centric **Raddison Beach Resort Palm Jumeirah**, and a local favourite, **Voco Dubai The Palm**.

Koko Bay

Viewing deck, Palm Tower

The View at the Palm

MAP P104

Elevated 360-degree vistas

For a chance to drink in Palm Jumeirah's impressive outline while keeping your feet firmly on ground, this outdoor **viewing deck** on the 52nd floor of the Palm Tower is a good choice. Perched at a lofty 240m atop an architectural tower designed in the shape of a palm tree, the glass-surrounded platform is a lookout point to the Gulf and the sprawling city skyline. Tickets also include access to The View Exhibition, an interactive digital display that sheds more light on Dubai's constructed island. For the best bragging rights, purchase a ticket to The Next Level, which lets you skip the queue and gives you access to highest viewpoint on Level 54.

Dubai Marina Mall

MAP P104

High-street shopping by the water

Underneath a sparkling dome atrium, this **neighbourhood mall** has over 100 shops, including high-street favourites, sports shops and a few upmarket fashion brands. It's spread over four levels, and is a much more manageable size than some of the city's megamalls. The ground floor opens out onto a promenade where you can enjoy a bite to eat with views of the yachts bobbing in the adjacent marina. Up on level four, there's a multi-screen cinema complex, a food court and an indoor soft play area for little ones to burn off some energy when its too hot to do so outside.

Dubai Marina Mall

Dubai Balloon

MAP P104

Rise up over Atlantis

Newly opened in 2023, the **Dubai Balloon** is an aerial experience that takes travellers 300m up in the air where mind-boggling 360-degree views of the city await. Located at Atlantis, The Palm, the helium-operated balloon fits up to 20 people in its gondola and rides last approximately 10 minutes, which gives you just enough time to drink in the vistas and snap a few selfies. On a clear day, you'll be able to see all the way to the Burj Khalifa.

Bluewaters Island

MAP P104

A record-breaking destination

In a city of constructed islands, **Bluewaters** is one of the newest. Located across from Dubai Marina, its most famous resident is the record-breaking **Ain Dubai observation wheel**, which towers 210m above the coastline, although it was closed at the time of writing. This popular residential area has several drinking and dining options; try **Puerto99** for fun-fuelled Mexican fiestas, or enjoy the lush garden at the **London Project**. **Banyan Tree Dubai** hotel is also here – visit for great Asian, Italian and International restaurants as well as epic ocean views.

TOP RIGHT: CREATIVE FAMILY/SHUTTERSTOCK ©; BOTTOM LEFT: RITU MANOJ JETHANI/SHUTTERSTOCK ©

Ain Dubai observation wheel, Bluewaters Island

Madame Tussauds

MAP P104

Frozen in time

Madame Tussauds made its waxwork debut in the Middle East in Dubai in 2021 and visitors to the museum on Bluewaters Island will find plenty of lifelike models from the worlds of music, film, politics, royalty and fiction. Some of the most popular include Taylor Swift, Justin Bieber and the Beckhams, and visitors can also see famous faces from the Arab world including singer Nancy Arjam and make-up artist Huda Kattan. A Bollywood zone hosts Salman Khan and Katrina Kaif, and guests can sit down to tea with Audrey Hepburn.

Madame Tussauds

Skydive Dubai

MAP P104

Adrenaline-pumping action

Thrill-seekers can get their adrenaline rush by jumping out of a plane then floating back to earth with views of Palm Jumeirah and the waters of the Gulf. **Skydive Dubai** offers tandem parachute flights year-round. The day starts in the venue's training facility where participants get geared up, meet their instructor and undergo basic safety training. After that, you're whisked into the air via a tiny plane and once you reach 13,000ft, its go-time. Don't forget to breathe in before you jump – it can be hard to catch a breath in those few moments of freefall. Smile for the camera – instructors will film the entire experience for you to share with friends and family once your feet are back on the ground.

Atlantis, The Palm Dubai

MAP P104

Dubai's ultimate destination resort

With its pink-toned towers and turquoise-topped turrets, this themed five-star **hotel** sits on Dubai's Palm Jumeirah island, dominating the skyline as you drive towards it. Keep it in view as you take the Palm Jumeirah tunnel, then wait for the surprise on the other side as the mammoth structure seems to disappear – a trick of the eye thanks to the underwater tunnel. With 1500 rooms, including an underwater suite with floor-to-ceiling windows gazing out to sharks, rays and fish, plus 23 restaurants and bars, this opulent hotel based on the legend of the lost city of Atlantis is a firm favourite with families.

The main attraction is Aquaventure (p112), the Middle East's largest waterpark, with over 30 slides, rides and rivers including Blackout, a near-vertical drop that's not for the fainthearted. It's free to enter for hotel guests, while day visitors access it via **The Avenues**, a marble-lined retail walkway. The **Lost Chambers** aquarium has 21 exhibits sharing mysteries of the deep, and 65,000 marine animals call the **Ambassador Lagoon** home.

World-famous Japanese chef Nobu Matsuhisa has a restaurant here and is in good company alongside Gordon Ramsey's **Bread Street Kitchen**. More casual dining is on offer at **Wavehouse**, where there's a bowling alley, games arcade and views over the resort's wave-rider machine. **White Beach Club** is one for the winter season: the day-to-night venue has two pools, in-water loungers, a breezy outdoor terrace and endless Insta-worthy vistas.

ATLANTIS THE ROYAL

A big sister to Dubai's original Atlantis hotel, this glass-encased **resort** opened in a star-studded ceremony headed up by Beyoncé at the start of 2023. The hulking 795-room hotel dwarfs its neighbour in size and splendour. Sleek, upmarket design incorporates statement sculptures and water and fire features and there's 17 restaurants, six of which are helmed by celebrity chefs. There are also no fewer than 90 swimming pools dotted across the resort, including a rooftop infinity pool suspended some 100m above Palm Jumeirah.

KIEVVICTOR/SHUTTERSTOCK ©

Lost Chambers, Atlantis, The Palm Dubai

Dinner in the Sky

MAP P104

Seriously elevated dining

Floating in the air above Skydive Dubai, this unique **restaurant** takes elevated dining to an entirely new level. Diners are strapped into bucket seats placed around a table on a platform that is then hoisted 50m above ground by a crane for one of the most unusual dining experiences in the city. Once up there, tuck into a three-course feast as bar staff keep diners supplied with cocktails and drinks, all of which are served alongside epic views over Dubai Marina, Palm Jumeirah and the Gulf.

Dinner in the Sky

Westin Mina Seyahi

Aura Skypool

MAP P104

Poolside lounging in the sky

Take a dip 200m in the air at the world's highest 360-degree infinity swimming pool. Curving around the 50th floor of Nakheel's Palm Tower, **Aura Skypool** measures 9m higher than Singapore's famous Marina Bay Sands infinity pool. Bookings are essential and you can choose from sunrise, morning, afternoon or evening slots – the latter allowing bathers to swim under a star-filled sky. Take in views of Palm Jumeirah and the ocean, all the way to Downtown Dubai, from the temperature-controlled pool. Lounge on a sunbed, enjoy a bite to eat then go for a dip; just don't forget the obligatory selfies. Sunsets here are highly recommended.

Mina Seyahi

MAP P104

Three beachfront hotels

Beyond Jumeirah but before your reach Palm Jumeirah and Dubai Marina is a little slice of Dubai known as **Mina Seyahi**. Set along 500m of golden shoreline here are three hotels, a marina and a waterpark. The **Westin Mina Seyahi** has landscaped gardens and **El Sur**, one of the city's best Spanish restaurants, while **Le Meridien Mina Seyahi** offers family-friendly stays and the uber-popular, pink-toned health cafe **Bounty Beets**. **Jungle Bay Waterpark**, possibly Dubai's prettiest with cool Aegean vibes, is also here alongside adults-only **W Mina Seyahi**, a skyscraper hotel located next to **Barasti**, one of Dubai's oldest and most raucous beach bars that transforms into a giant air-conditioned dome in the summertime.

Al Ittihad Park

Al Ittihad Park

MAP P104

A secret slice of greenery

Tucked away under the shadow of the Palm Monorail, this little **park** is popular with Palm Jumeirah residents, families and pet-lovers, but is open to anyone. There's a shaded walking and jogging track, cascading water features and over 100 species of plants and herbs, many of which are handily labelled. There are also a few playgrounds with slides and swings for children and new enclosed dog parks, as well as plenty of coffee shops and cafes in the adjacent **Golden Mile** mall to grab a refreshment.

Pier 7

MAP P104

Fine-dining, drinking and harbourside views

Attached to Dubai Marina Mall via a glass-encased walkway, this circular **tower** is spread over seven levels and is a nice choice when you fancy a night out with the option of several venues in one building. **Asia and Asia** and **Atelier M** offer elegant dining and nightlife, **Cargo** and **Bedrock** are the places to go for casual bites, while **Abd el Wahab** is one of the most popular Lebanese brands in Dubai. All restaurants come with harbourside views and are licensed for drinks.

Pier 7

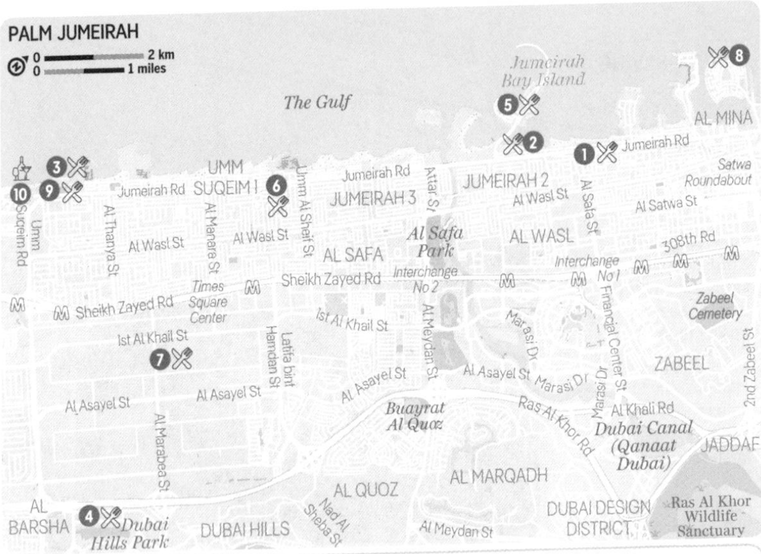

PALM JUMEIRAH

EATING
1 Il Woodfire
2 3Fils
3 Al Muntaha
4 Avatara
5 Il Ristorante – Niko Romito
6 Just Vegan
7 La Nena
8 Nikki Beach
9 Summersalt Beach Club

DRINKING & NIGHTLIFE
10 Folly

JBR

MAP P104

One of Dubai's buzziest, busiest neighbourhoods

Having started life as a quiet beachside residential area, **Jumeirah Beach Residence**, to give it its full name, is now one of Dubai's busiest and liveliest neighbourhoods. Home to beachside hotels, buzzy bars and upmarket restaurants, it's also known for its ever-busy traffic, so give yourself plenty of time if you're meeting someone here. The popular public **beach** is free for all and has showers and toilets, but can get very busy on weekends and holidays. Cool down with a run around on **AquaFun**, the world's largest inflatable park floating just off the shoreline. Stroll along **The Walk**, a beachside boulevard lined with cafes and restaurants, then shop at the handful of shops at outdoor shopping mall **The Beach, JBR**.

Jumeirah Beach Residence

DIRHAM-SAVING TIPS

Susan Syrek and Selma Selma Abdelhamid (@ dirham_stretcher_ by_sum) are the founders of Sum, a UAE platform for saving dirhams in Dubai. They share top tips for tourists.

One of the best places to shop for dates and regional sweets to take home as souvenirs is at Carrefour hypermarket in Mall of the Emirates (p91), which often has offers on chocolate covered dates. The bakery counter sells freshly made pastries and local sweets by the kilogram, and if you ask they'll package these up for you so that they will survive the flight. If you're only staying for a week or so, it's worth purchasing the **Entertainer Tourist**. This discount app has a selection of buy one, get one free offers on dining, theme parks, entertainment and more across the city.

BY KIEVVICTOR/SHUTTERSTOCK ©

Palm Jumeirah Monorail

MORE IN DUBAI MARINA & PALM JUMEIRAH

A Day on Palm Jumeirah on a Budget

MAP P104

Experience the city without breaking the bank

With more than its fair share of five-star hotels, swanky restaurants and reservation-only bars, you'd be forgiven for thinking that a visit to Palm Jumeirah is an expensive affair, but it doesn't have to be. Start your day with a scenic ride on the **Palm Jumeirah Monorail**, where an unlimited day pass costs Dh35 and children under 110cm ride free. Disembark at Al Ittihad Park (p110) and take a leisurely stroll around this shaded green space filled with playparks, picnic benches, shrubs and trees. Pop into the Golden Mile and pay a visit to **Thrift for Good**, Dubai's secondhand shop selling preloved fashion, books, homewares and more, where prices start at Dh1. After rummaging the racks, hop back on the monorail to the next stop, Nakheel Mall (p104). Window-shop to your heart's content then visit the **J Café**, a Scandi-inspired coffee shop that serves a tasty breakfast combo for Dh25, or a lunch meal deal for Dh40. Board the train again and soar over to the station at **Atlantis Aquaventure Waterpark**.

WHERE TO FIND PET-FRIENDLY DINING IN DUBAI

La Nena
Boho contemporary coffee house in Al Quoz welcomes dogs of all sizes indoors. **$$**

Just Vegan
Converted villa in Jumeirah serves a plant-based menu and allows pets indoors and out. **$**

Strand Kraft Kitchen
Mediterranean-inspired kitchen and cocktails on Palm West Beach, where dogs can also dine-in. **$$**

No tickets are needed to wander inside the sprawling hotel so go gawp at the giant aquarium and see the glass-blown marble sculpture in the lobby. Afterwards, head towards the ocean – you can walk or cycle around the rock-lined boardwalk without paying a dirham. And as the sun begins to set, hotfoot it back to the Shoreline Apartments where **Peaches & Cream** serve up pitchers of wine for just Dh80 every Sunday to Thursday from 6pm and 8pm, one of the best happy-hour options in this part of town.

Let's Do Brunch

MAP P104

Silly Saturday afternoon revelry

Ice-sculpture adorned seafood bars, hand-rolled sushi stations and candyfloss machines can only mean one thing – **Dubai brunch**. Something of an institution in the city, all-inclusive Saturday brunches are a big part of the social scene here and almost every hotel in town offers them. Setups range from elaborate all-you-can-eat feasts where unlimited cuisine from around the world is laid out buffet style, often paired with limitless drinks and cocktails, to slightly more sensible set-menu affairs.

Leave it to Atlantis, The Palm (p108) to serve up one of Dubai's most elaborate brunches. The **Saffron 2.0** brunch takes place in the hotel's Asian restaurant, which transforms into a huge party venue inviting dolled-up revellers to feast on nonstop food and drinks where chefs head up live cooking stations, DJs spin hits and magicians keep everyone entertained. While the focus begins on the food, with hundreds of dishes spanning Asian, Indian, Mediterranean, Japanese, American and European cuisines, it inevitably ends on the party vibes supplemented by unlimited vodka-filled pineapples, jelly shots and tropical cocktails. At nearby Westin Mina Seyahi (p109), long-running **Bubbalicious Brunch** is another decadent affair, with everything from prime steak and lobster to oysters and a flowing chocolate fountain on the menu. A family-friendly option, there's also entertainment for children including face painting, a petting zoo and a play area. Not every brunch experience needs to be a splurge though – **Muchachas Mexican Cantina** at the **Holiday Inn Express** offers a wallet-friendly fiesta-style brunch with a set menu of guacamole, quesadillas, tacos and more, plus free-flowing sangria, loud music and raucous party games.

ON THE MOVE IN THE MARINA

As a city set by the sea, Dubai has long relied on boats to move people around, so it makes sense to consider using the **Water Bus** to skirt around Dubai Marina. One of the most scenic ways to travel, the floating public transport vehicle is fully air-conditioned and shuttles passengers between the Marina Walk, the Marina Terrace, Marina Mall and the Promenade every day, running on a 15-minute schedule. Hop on and hop off for a scenic way to explore this part of town.

WHERE TO EAT ON THE WATERFRONT IN DUBAI MARINA

Le Pain Quoitiden
This cosy cafe is part of Dubai Marina Mall, but has a terrace with waterside views to go with its European-style menu. **$**

Massimo's Italian Restaurant
Casual Italian eatery with tables on the terrace over the water, large portions and delicious gelato. **$$**

Ceylonka Restaurant
Sri Lankan restaurant right on the marina, serving traditional flavours and seafood from the teardrop nation. **$**

POOL-DAY DEALS

Dubai can be an expensive city but there are ways to cut down costs when it comes to finding things to do, and that includes spending a day lounging at a **beach club**. Start by checking the social media accounts or websites of the places you want to go – often different beach clubs will run special offers on set days of the week or between certain visiting times, and they tend to shout about them on socials. Travellers visiting Dubai during summer, or low season, can also find cheaper day rates on pool passes as part of the emirate's annual **Dubai Summer Surprises** festival. Finally, check discount voucher sites such as Groupon and Cobone for deals, but be aware most of these need to be pre-booked.

KIEV.VICTOR/SHUTTERSTOCK ©

Habtoor Grand Resort

A Day at the Beach, Dubai Style

MAP P104

Cabanas, DJs and perfectly chilled pools

The city's coastline is peppered with sandy beaches that are ideal for a day on the beach, but in true Dubai style, the city also has a buzzy **beach club** scene that's geared towards those who want more than just a pristine shoreline. Rolling sand, sun and luxury into one, these chic venues can be found across the city, but the highest concentration are in Dubai Marina and Palm Jumeirah. Whether you're seeking fine dining by the pool, top-rate DJs to spin hits while you tan, or simply a nonstop party atmosphere under the sun, there's plenty of options to choose from. Head to **Azure Beach** at Rixos Pre-

DUBAI'S HIPPEST BEACH CLUBS

Summersalt Beach Club
Upmarket menu with by Burj Al Arab views, this Jumeirah Al Naseem beach club is one of the city's most relaxed. **$$$**

SAN Beach
Beautifully boho, this toes-in-the-sand beach club takes sun-soaked days to a whole new level of chill. **$$**

Nikki Beach
Its crisp white aesthetic attracts beautiful bathers to its coastal Jumeriah location. **$$**

mium JBR where you'll find good vibes, good music and perfect sunset views of Ain Dubai from the club's infinity swimming pool. **Andreea's** at the **Habtoor Grand Resort** near Skydive Dubai is another popular choice and offers sun beds, cabanas and a swim-up bar, all with picture-perfect views of the shoreline, which you can also head down to via complimentary golf cart. Upmarket **Drift Beach** at the One&Only Royal Mirage not only has a 1km-stretch of private beach and a panoramic infinity pool, but it also has a poolside restaurant serving delicious Mediterranean dishes – perfect when the post-swim hunger kicks in. And **Bla Bla** at JBR, a venue that is perhaps better known for its snobby bars and restaurants, also has a buzzy beach club that's popular with a younger crowd and features plush daybeds shaded by bright orange umbrellas and a nonstop summertime soundtrack.

AIN DUBAI

Standing at an eye-watering 250m tall, **Ain Dubai** is officially the world's largest observation wheel. The giant sphere dominates the skyline around Palm Jumeirah and the Dubai Marina and opened to much applause in 2001. Until recently, riders in one of the wheel's 48 high-tech pods were treated to half-hour spins with unrivalled views over the city, and had the option to book private cabins and in-pod skybars. Since March 2022, however, the wheel has been closed, with no official reason given for the interruption. Rumour has it that parts needed to fix the high-tech pods are proving difficult to source, hence the lengthy delay, but that's not been confirmed by operator or owner.

Michelin-Starred Dining in Dubai

MAP P111

Table excellence

In a city with more than 10,000 restaurants it's perhaps surprising that it was only last year that the Michelin Guide, a hallmark of culinary excellence, decided to include Dubai as one of its featured destinations. In the 2023 edition, 14 top restaurants across the city received stars. Culinary connoisseurs looking to enjoy a two-starred meal should head to **Il Ristorante – Niko Romito** at the luxury fashion-focused Bulgari Resort Dubai, or to **STAY by Yannick Alléno** at One&Only The Palm for innovative French dining. And in Nakheel Mall, **Trèsind Studio** has an ever-evolving menu of modern Indian cuisine complemented by two stars. There's also several one-star restaurants to try including **11 Woodfire**, a contemporary restaurant specialising in open-fire cooking, and **Al Muntaha** at the seven-star Burj Al Arab, which serves Mediterranean-influenced fare served with epic views. Plant-eaters can head to **Avatara** at Voco Dubai where the focus is on pure, clean, plant-based produce creatively served as soulful Indian cuisine. For Michelin-starred dining on a budget, the guide's inspectors handpicked venues that serve quality meals with pocket-friendly prices. Try **3Fils** for contemporary Japanese food overlooking the Jumeirah Fishing Harbour, or tuck into homey Middle Eastern fare at **Bait Maryam** in Jumeirah Lakes Towers.

BRILLIANT ROOFTOP BARS

Folly
Ice popsicle prosecco cocktails make perfect sundowners at this Madinat Jumeirah favourite. **$$**

Above Eleven
Exported from Bangkok, this funky rooftop venue comes with twinkling views of the Dubai Marina skyline. **$$$**

Attiko Dubai
Panoramic ocean views and a creative cocktail menu await on the rooftop of W Dubai Mina Seyahi. **$$**

TOP TIP

It's easy to get around in this neighbourhood, thanks to the recent extension of the Dubai Metro red line from Jebel Ali to seven new stations, including popular residential areas Discovery Gardens and Jumeirah Golf Estates, business hub Dubai Investment Park, and a new end destination, Expo City Dubai.

Above: Al Wasl Dome (p120); Right: Motiongate Dubai (p119)

I LIVE HERE: SOUTH DUBAI'S MUST-DOS

Nila Pendarovski hails from Germany and is based in Dubai, where she's hotel manager at Rove Expo 2020. Here are her must-do's in the neighbourhood.

Terra Pavilion, Expo City

One of my favourite pavilions at Expo City – it takes visitors on a journey to understand their impact on the environment and showcases mind-blowing technologies that will make our future greener.

Al Qudra Love Lake

You can stroll around this heart-shaped lake, surrounded by golden sands. It's great for picnics, barbecues, camping, and catching desert sunsets.

Dubai Parks and Resorts

Kids and adults alike will have a blast at this theme park destination, which is home to Legoland theme park and waterpark, and the movie-tastic Motiongate.

South Dubai

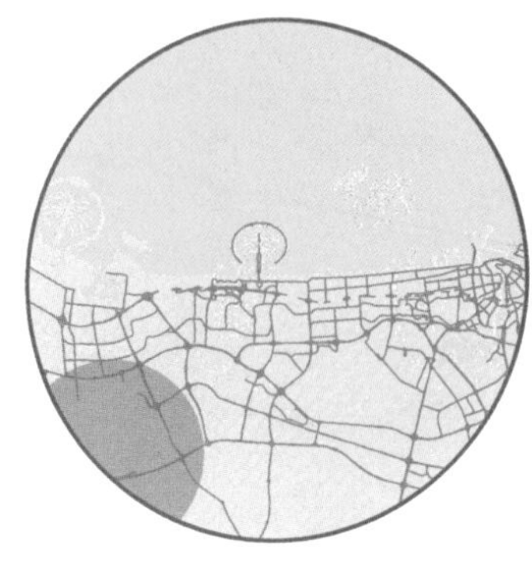

EXTENDING THE CITY'S REACH

South Dubai is an expanding neighbourhood via which the emirate is creeping ever closer to its neighbour Abu Dhabi.

This multi-faceted region comprises Jebel Ali, Dubai's hard-working industrial area, Dubai Parks and Resorts, with its theme parks and entertainment zones, Dubai Investment Parks, several residential areas, and the city's second international airport, currently used primarily for cargo. It's also a great spot for nature-seekers, as it's home to Al Marmoom Conservation Area, the largest unfenced nature reserve in the entire country.

RZULEV/SHUTTERSTOCK ©

One of the biggest new additions in South Dubai is Expo City Dubai. Located on the site where the Dubai Expo2020 international fair took place after a year's delay due to the global COVID-19 pandemic, the city spans an area twice the size of Monaco. It's being hailed as the emirate's city of the future to be powered by smart and sustainable technology, with residents expected to move in by 2026. Today, the community already has several attractions, most of which were left over from the expo. These include Al Wasl Dome, a spaceship-shaped elevated disc over a tiered green park, a 55m-high tower called Garden in the Sky, food trucks, coffee shops, exhibitions and several green spaces and cycling tracks.

And there's more expansion coming in the city's southern region, with Sheikh Mohamed, ruler of Dubai, recently announcing the revival of Palm Jebel Ali, a constructed island jutting into the Gulf that's twice the size of the existing Palm Jumeirah, and where new luxury hotels, resorts, beaches, restaurants and villas are on the cards.

DON'T MISS...

EXPO CITY DUBAI
A sprawling purpose-built neighbourhood that's being transformed into Dubai's first smart city.
p120

DUBAI PARKS AND RESORTS
Theme parks galore on the edge of the city – explore rides and slides at Legoland and Motiongate Dubai.
p119

AL MARMOOM DESERT CONSERVATION RESERVE
Golden sand dunes, ghaf trees and Arabian oryx thrive in this protected desert space.
p122

SOUTH DUBAI

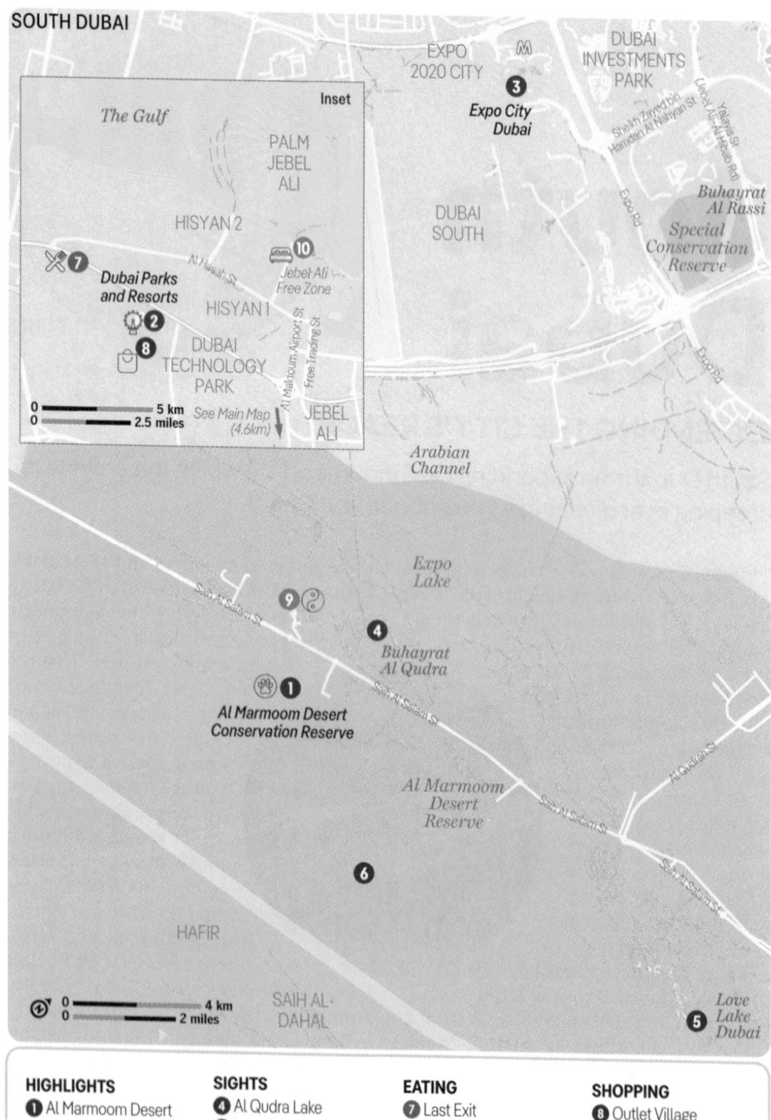

HIGHLIGHTS
1 Al Marmoom Desert Conservation Reserve
2 Dubai Parks and Resorts
3 Expo City Dubai

SIGHTS
4 Al Qudra Lake
5 Love Lake Dubai
6 Moon Lake

EATING
7 Last Exit

ENTERTAINMENT
see 2 Legoland Dubai Resort

SHOPPING
8 Outlet Village

SLEEPING
9 Bab Al Shams
10 JA The Resort

Legoland Dubai

Legoland Dubai Resort

Brick-tastic fun

The Middle East's first **Lego-themed hotel** is located in Dubai Parks and Resorts. The 250-room hotel is plastered head-to-toe in brick-related design, which touches everything from the lifts to the carpets. Step past the Lego-dragon guarding the entrance into the hotel lobby where a huge Lego pit is open for all to play with. Standard rooms sleep up to five with a separate bunk-bed space and built-in treasure hunts for children. There's also a castle-themed play area and masterclasses where kids can learn from Lego experts, as well as an outdoor swimming pool filled with Lego brick floating toys.

Dubai Parks and Resorts

Theme-park heaven

Take Sheikh Zayed Rd in the direction of Abu Dhabi and you'll eventually arrive at an exit adorned with a colourful character-lined archway and the road towards the entertainment haven that is **Dubai Parks and Resorts**. Movie-lovers can explore **Motiongate Dubai**, a park themed around three of Hollywood's biggest motion picture studios and home to the world's fastest single-car spinning roller-coaster. Lego fans should head to **Legoland Dubai**, with over 40 rides themed around the plastic building-block toys, or cool off at Legoland Waterpark's themed waterslides and attractions. When the weather is too hot, space-themed **Neon Galaxy** is an interactive indoor play zone geared for kids and teens. **Riverland Dubai** is the arena's waterside shopping and retail district where you can wander along the boardwalk or take a riverboat journey through various themed zones, including India Gate and the French Village. If one day isn't enough, make a night of it at **Lapita, Dubai Parks and Resorts**, a four-star Polynesian-themed hotel with two swimming pools, a lazy river and a spa for when the excitement gets a bit much.

ROVE EXPO 2020

As the only **hotel** at Expo City Dubai, this is the place to stay if you're heading here for an event or want to enjoy more than just one day exploring the surrounds. The funky hotel offers no-frills rooms that are are clean and comfortable and have views over Al Wasl Dome. There's plenty of co-working spaces, including phone boxes designed for hosting Zoom calls, and **The Daily** is a good place to have breakfast, lunch or dinner, whether you're spending the night or not.

Expo City Dubai

Urban parks, pavilions and more

What was previously undeveloped land on Dubai's southern edge was transformed into a megacity for Dubai Expo 2020. Today, it's **Expo City Dubai**, a place billed as the human-centric city of the future. Still in its infancy, the smart city will be home to residential communities, schools, hospitals and universities, as well as tech companies and green startups.

For now, Expo City is the place to go for quiet parks and green spaces, including a grassy shaded pavilion underneath **Al Wasl Dome**, a focal point of the Expo and now where several new high-profile events are being hosted, including **Untold**, Dubai's first mega music festival. A few country pavilions from the Expo itself remain, including from the UAE and Saudi Arabia. The **Garden in the Sky** observation tower that lifts visitors 55m above ground for epic views towards Dubai is also still here. **Terra Pavilion** is an immersive indoor and outdoor space exhibition space all about nature, and **Surreal** is a structure where a spectacle of music, water and fire combine. Designed by the same company responsible for the Burj Khalifa Fountain and the composer of the *Game of Thrones* score, Ramin Djawadi, it's a place to dip your feet in the water, watch it flow magically upwards and wonder at the flaming torches that periodically come alive – although the attraction does stop in summer time. The city's wide streets make it popular for bike-riding, roller blading and dog-walking, and there are handy water, snack and toilet stations setup for four-legged visitors.

Terra Pavilion

Last Exit

Last Exit

Pit-stop dining

Heading to or from Abu Dhabi? Break up your trip with a stop at the **Last Exit**. This funky food truck hub is found in a few spots around the city, but is most prominent on either side of Sheikh Zayed Rd. The Americano-inspired pit stops have drive-thru food trucks where you can order burgers, tacos, milkshakes, fried chicken and more. Eat on the go or head inside where picnic tables, convenience stores, toilets and arcade games sit beside monster trucks, traffic lights, used tyres and vintage motoring signs.

Outlet Village

Fashion on a budget

Touting itself as Dubai's first luxury discount mall, the **Outlet Village** next to Dubai Parks and Resorts is a sprawling Italian-style shopping centre where fashionistas can shop at over 100 shops including Armani, Michael Kors and Caroline Herrera. There's everything from fashion and beauty to sportwear and jewellery. Even if you're not a big shopper, it's worth visiting just to check out the Tuscan-inspired architecture that evokes San Gimignano, a hilltop Italian town that was earmarked as a Unesco World Heritage Site in 1990. Wander over arched walkways, walk cobbled paths and stroll past Gothic-style towers.

Outlet Village

JA The Resort

Dubai stalwart stay that remains a firm favourite

The drive to **JA The Resort** isn't Dubai's most scenic as the hotel lies beyond the city's industrial zone, but once you reach the sprawling coastal resort, it's all about the holiday vibes. First opened in 1981, it's one of the city's oldest and also Dubai's largest 'experience resort'. It's made up of three hotels: choose to stay at the original JA Beach Hotel, enjoy garden views at JA Palm Tree Court, or bed down at the recently opened and eco-minded JA Lake View hotel. No matter which property you stay in, there's access to all facilities across the resort including a sprawling private beach, seven swimming pools, 25 restaurants, a nine-hole golf course, horse-riding stables and more. Keep your eyes peeled for the resort's colourful roaming peacocks.

BAB AL SHAMS 2.0

An Arabian-style retreat in Dubai's Al Qudra area, **Bab Al Shams** is Dubai's longest-running desert resort and has recently undergone an extensive renovation. Almost 20 years since the hotel in Al Qudra first opened, it relaunched with a new lease of life in early 2023 and is a great place for a family escape surrounded by the wilds of the desert. Rooms and suites are inspired by Bedouin traditions and come with spacious terraces, overlooking uninterrupted sand-dune views. There's an Insta-worthy infinity pool and a host of desert-inspired activities including falcon shows, camel rides and safari drives.

Gazelle, Al Marmoom Desert Conservation Reserve

MORE IN SOUTH DUBAI

Back to Nature in Al Marmoom Desert Conservation Reserve

Indigenous wildlife and desert vistas

Swap urban sights for nature on Dubai's outskirts at **Al Marmoom Desert Conservation Reserve**. Encompassing 10% of Dubai as a whole, this desert reserve is the largest unfenced nature park in the country. It's open to the public and the perfect place to surround yourself with nature, especially in the winter months.

Abundant in native wildlife, the reserve is home to one of the city's largest populations of Arabian oryx and one of the biggest flocks of flamingos. The pink-hued birds aren't alone, and keen birders can look forward to spotting some 200 species of native birds, and up to 150 different types of migratory birds depending on when you visit.

One way to really embrace the charm of this vast desert space is to book the **Al Marmoom Bedouin Experience** from OceanAir Travels. Starting with a hotel pick-up from the city, the experience takes visitors to the nature reserve,

WHERE TO FIND DUBAI'S BEST LAKES

Al Qudra Lake
A shrub-surrounded desert oasis in Al Marmoom Desert Conservation Reserve.

Love Lake Dubai
Giant artificial lakes in the shape of two interconnected love hearts.

Moon Lake
Artificial lake styled as a crescent moon: poignant given the celestial symbol's importance in Islam.

passing desert flora and fauna, including the UAE's national ghaf trees. Experienced guides will point out falcons, deer, oryx and gazelle enroute to a traditional Bedouin village in the heart of the reserve. Get ready to discover the desert in the footsteps of the region's traditional tribes, with a morning camel caravan over dunes where the handlers will share more about the importance of the long-eyelashed creatures you're riding on. Post ride, enjoy Arabic coffee and dates back at the village, the traditional way that Bedouin tribes have started their days for time immemorial.

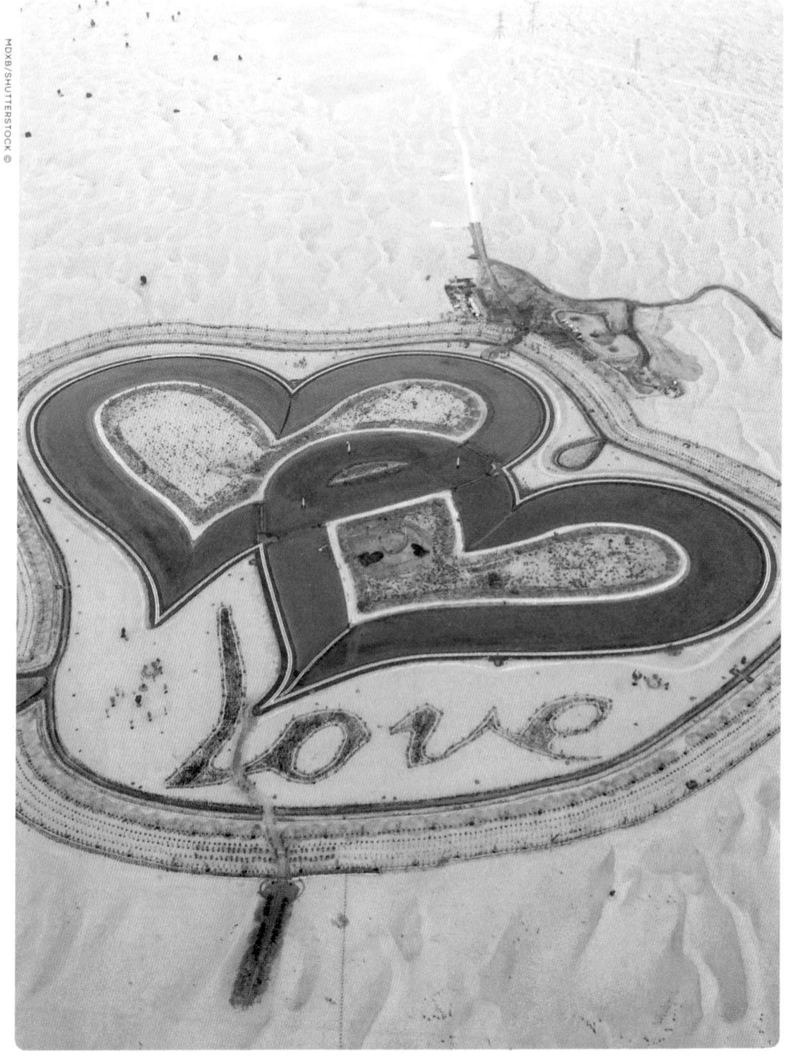

Love Lake Dubai

ABU DHABI

THE GUIDE

Chapters in this section are organised by hubs and their surrounding areas. We see the hub as your base in the destination, where you'll find unique experiences, local insights, insider tips and expert recommendations. It's also your gateway to the surrounding area, where you'll see what and how much you can do from there.

Downtown Abu Dhabi
p128

Breakwater & Around
p136

Al Zahiyah, Al Maryah Island & Al Reem Island
p146

Sheikh Zayed Grand Mosque & Around
p152

Al Mina & Saadiyat Island
p162

Yas Island & Around
p172

Sheikh Zayed Grand Mosque (p156)

Al Zahiyah, Al Maryah Island & Al Reem Island

NEW CENTRAL BUSINESS DISTRICT

Al Zahiyah has transformed through redevelopment while maintaining its vibrant and multicultural character. Nearby, Al Maryah Island boasts an international financial centre, five-star hotels, a luxurious shopping mall and upmarket dining options. Al Reem Island is home to residential apartments, leisure facilities and a cosmopolitan atmosphere.

p146

Al Mina & Saadiyat Island

CULTURAL STRONGHOLD

Close to the atmospheric markets of Mina Zayed, Saadiyat Island is home to the capital's most prestigious cultural attractions, including the Louvre Abu Dhabi and the upcoming Guggenheim Abu Dhabi. Nesting hawksbill turtles and dolphins are often spotted on the island's beautiful sandy beaches and turquoise waters.

p162

Downtown Abu Dhabi

COMMERCIAL HEART OF THE CITY

The neighbourhoods of Downtown Abu Dhabi trace the city's journey from a fishing and pearling coastal settlement to a thriving capital. Landmarks like Qasr Al Hosn showcase its rich culture, while shopping malls, parks and the Corniche reflect its modern lifestyle. The streets of Al Danah boast a diverse food scene.

p128

Breakwater & Around

ALL THE MAGNIFICENCE

This is where you get a palpable sense of Abu Dhabi's confidence as a leading capital city. On a stroll around the Breakwater area, the Qasr Al Watan and Emirates Palace impress with their regal architecture, while the Founder's Memorial honours Sheikh Zayed's visionary leadership.

p136

NEIGHBOURHOODS AT A GLANCE: ABU DHABI

Find the places that tick all your boxes.

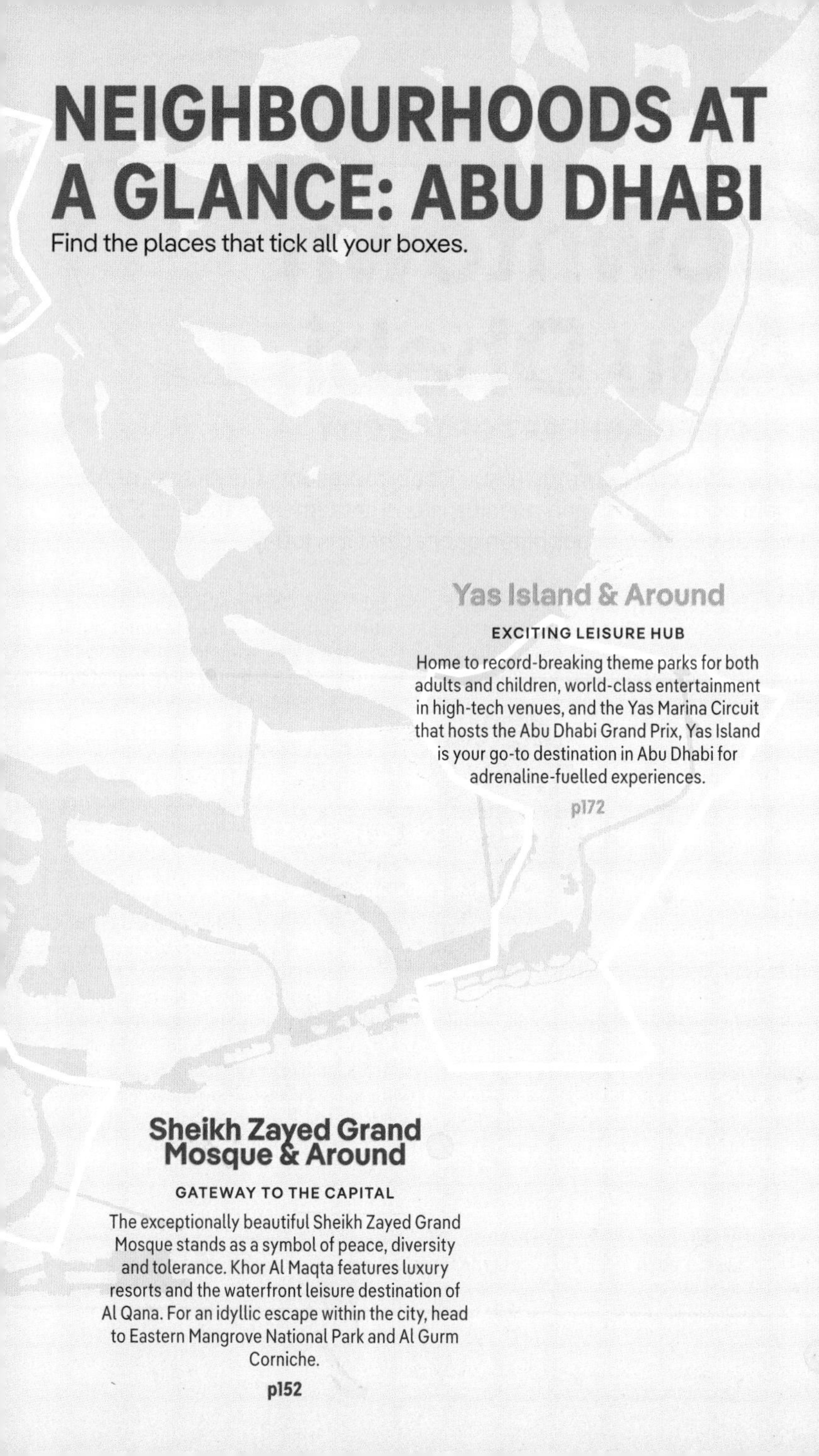

Yas Island & Around

EXCITING LEISURE HUB

Home to record-breaking theme parks for both adults and children, world-class entertainment in high-tech venues, and the Yas Marina Circuit that hosts the Abu Dhabi Grand Prix, Yas Island is your go-to destination in Abu Dhabi for adrenaline-fuelled experiences.

p172

Sheikh Zayed Grand Mosque & Around

GATEWAY TO THE CAPITAL

The exceptionally beautiful Sheikh Zayed Grand Mosque stands as a symbol of peace, diversity and tolerance. Khor Al Maqta features luxury resorts and the waterfront leisure destination of Al Qana. For an idyllic escape within the city, head to Eastern Mangrove National Park and Al Gurm Corniche.

p152

Downtown Abu Dhabi

COMMERCIAL HEART OF THE CITY

The evolution of Downtown Abu Dhabi represents the journey of Abu Dhabi from a fishing and pearling island settlement in the late 1790s to the culture-rich cosmopolitan capital that it is today.

This area spreads out around the Qasr Al Hosn, a fortress that houses Abu Dhabi's oldest structure, a coral and sea stone watchtower built in 1760 that provided a sense of security to the coastal settlement that was beginning to form on Abu Dhabi Island. Today, a visit next door to the Cultural Foundation, an impressive arts and culture centre with art exhibitions, workshops and events, offers a glimpse into the city's contemporary cultural scene.

It was here that the city's first central souq saw vendors sell sacks of onions, wooden chests and Wrigley's chewing gum from humble stalls in the late 1950s. Today, high-rise buildings and skyscrapers in the area house five-star hotels, shopping malls, high-end residences and some of Abu Dhabi's biggest corporations. The World Trade Center Souk and Mall are located on the site of the old souq. Within the same complex, the 92-floor, 382m-high Burj Mohammed Bin Rashid stands proudly as the city's tallest structure.

Running along the coastline is the Corniche with its manicured lawns, benches, jogging track and bicycle path. Numerous parks, including as the Lake Park, Formal Park, Capital Park and Family Park, dot the neighbourhood.

A hub of activity at all times of the day, the Al Danah neighbourhood offers plenty of opportunities to eat and shop, with reasonably priced restaurants, cafeterias and bakeries serving piping-hot *manakeesh* (baked flatbread with toppings like cheese and vegetables), Armenian kebabs, Pakistani biryanis and Chinese hotpots.

KHALDOUN_AZZAM/SHUTTERSTOCK ©

DON'T MISS...

QASR AL HOSN
This fortress houses an excellent museum that is a must-visit to learn about Abu Dhabi's history.
p130

CULTURAL FOUNDATION
Visit this impressive cultural centre for a look at the city's energetic contemporary art scene.
p131

WORLD TRADE CENTER SOUK
This modern reimagination of a traditional marketplace is a fantastic place to shop for souvenirs.
p134

TOP TIP

To explore this area, stroll or cycle along the Corniche to admire the scale of some of the remarkable skyscrapers. Then move inward to eat and shop your way around Al Danah. To get around by bike, use the Cyacle Bikeshare app.

Left: Lake Park (p134); Above: World Trade Center Souk (p134)

I LIVE HERE: UNDER THE RADAR IN DOWNTOWN ABU DHABI

Abdulrahman Alzaabi (@adaywithabdul on Instagram), Abu Dhabi-based engineer and passionate Emirati tour guide, shares his favourite spots in the area.

Zayed the 2nd Mosque

Before the Sheikh Zayed Grand Mosque, the Zayed the 2nd Mosque was where the city gathered for religious ceremonies. Built in 1969, its beautiful courtyard welcomes worshippers from around the world.

Urban Park and Etihad Square

Right next to towering buildings, the Urban Park and Etihad Sq offer a breath of fresh air and a look at the past through structures hinting at Emirati traditions.

Rain Cafe

Great espressos and lattes with seriously impressive latte art.

PRACTICALITIES

Scan this QR code for prices and opening hours:

TOP SIGHT

Al Hosn Site

Comprising an enlightening museum housed in a fortress that was once home to the ruling Al Nahyan family, a stone watchtower built in 1760, a traditional crafts exhibition and a contemporary cultural centre, a visit to Al Hosn is like flipping through the chapters in Abu Dhabi's intriguing story of transformation from a fishing and pearling village in the 18th century to today's powerful, forward-looking capital city.

DID YOU KNOW?
The seven-day **Al Hosn Festival**, held at Qasr Al Hosn each January, is a fantastic chance to learn about Emirati customs and handicrafts, watch cultural performances, sample Emirati fare, and shop for merchandise created by local artisans.

Qasr Al Hosn

A coral and sea stone watchtower, built in 1760 after freshwater was discovered on Abu Dhabi Island, still stands in the fortress complex at Qasr Al Hosn, hidden away among the area's high-rises. This is Abu Dhabi's oldest structure. With the Burj Mohammed Bin Rashid, Abu Dhabi's tallest building, rising in the background, it serves as a poignant reminder of the city's roots.

In 1793, the watchtower began to be expanded into a defensive fortress – the Inner Fort – which became the seat of government, military headquarters and a royal residence that would inspire confidence in the community on the island settlement. Between 1939 and 1945, on the orders of Sheikh Shakhbut bin Sultan Al Nahyan, the Outer Palace began to be constructed around the original fortress, tripling its area and showcasing Abu Dhabi's emerging power in the region after oil was found. After a long history that included housing a consultative council and a national archive, Qasr Al Hosn reopened as a museum in 2018, following nearly 11 years of conservation and restoration work.

Entering through the gatehouse, you'll find the old 1760-built round stone **watchtower** on your left located at the corner of the inner courtyard. Take your time to visit the exhibitions in the **Inner Fort** – these trace the history of Abu Dhabi from the journey of the Bani Yas from the oases of Liwa to Abu Dhabi Island and its rise as a pearling, fishing and trading town to its post-oil development, and, finally, its position as a global city.

Across the courtyard of the **Outer Palace**, in the arcaded residential wings, are rooms that house exhibits including furniture, jewellery, household items and clothing that bring to life the stories of the members of the ruling family that lived at Qasr Al Hosn. Notable among these are a set of rooms about the courageous and influential women that once lived here and were an active part of community life, including Sheikha Salama bint Butti, the mother of Sheikh Shakhbut bin Sultan Al Nahyan, and Sheikha Quot bint Shakhbout Al Nahyan, who not only learned to drive at a time when few cars and roads existed in Abu Dhabi but also supposedly taught this valuable skill to a few palace guards. Plan to spend at least 90 minutes visiting the exhibitions.

Cultural Foundation

Founded in 1981 and following a 10-year renovation, this beautiful cultural centre reopened in 2018 as a hub of the city's art and culture scene. The galleries here showcase the work of both local and international artists. Dedicated studios at **Al Marsam Al Hor** run workshops in painting, sculpture, jewellery design, pottery, fashion design and calligraphy, among other art forms. There's a 900-seat performing arts theatre that runs a full program of events throughout the year including ballet, theatre and concerts. The bright and colourful spaces and interactive experiences at the 5250-sq-metre **Abu Dhabi Children's Library**, located within the centre, are popular with families on the weekends. Notice the centre's contemporary Islamic architectural features such as blue-tiled arches, geometric patterns, fountains, courtyards and shaded walkways.

HOUSE OF ARTISANS

Emirati women in burkas chitchat while their fingers intertwine spools of thread to create silver *talli* (traditional embroidery). Pavilions showcase the crafts of Al-Sadu (weaving dyed wool yarn) and *khoos* (weaving or braiding palm fronds to create baskets).

TOP TIPS

- At Bait Al Gahwa in the House of Artisans, *gahwa* (Arabic coffee) demonstrations held every 30 minutes present the opportunity to sip on cardamom-infused Arabic coffee in a *majlis*. Take off your shoes before you enter.
- Refrain from photographing female artisans at work in the House of Artisans. If you're interested in photographing the crafts, ask for permission.
- General admission tickets include entry to Qasr Al Hosn, the House of Artisans and the *gahwa* demonstration.
- There is no entrance fee for exhibitions at the Cultural Foundation. Rates for workshops at Al Marsam Al Hor and performances at the Cultural Foundation vary.

HIGHLIGHTS
1 Qasr Al Hosn
2 World Trade Center Souk

SIGHTS
3 Abu Dhabi Beach
4 Al Danah
5 Capital Park
6 Etihad Square
7 Family Park 1
8 Formal Park
9 Lake Park
10 Zayed The 2nd Mosque

ACTIVITIES
11 House of Artisans

SLEEPING
12 Al Maha Arjaan by Rotana
13 Courtyard by Marriot World Trade Center
14 Le Royal Méridian Abu Dhabi
15 Millennium Downtown
16 Sofitel Abu Dhabi Corniche
17 Tryp by Wyndham Abu Dhabi

EATING
18 Al Ajaweed Restaurant
19 Al Ibrahimi Restaurant
20 Bait El Khetyar
21 Dampa Seafood Grill
22 Karam Al Sham
23 Lahmajoon

ENTERTAINMENT
24 Cultural Foundation

SHOPPING
25 Al Souk (Traditional Market)
26 Madinat Zayed Shopping & Gold Centre
27 Old Souq

STEPHEN BARNES/UNITED ARAB EMIRATES/ALAMY STOCK PHOTO ©

Madinat Zayed Shopping & Gold Centre

MORE IN DOWNTOWN ABU DHABI

Shopping at Madinat Zayed Gold Centre

All that glitters

Embroidered abayas, colourful kaftans, stylish men's leather sandals (referred to as 'Arab sandals'), lace scarves, perfumes and pearl-embellished purses are just some of the things that tempt you to loosen your purse strings at **Madinat Zayed Shopping & Gold Centre**, one of Abu Dhabi's oldest shopping malls. A local favourite thanks to its reasonable prices, this place with its keen shoppers and labyrinthine layout feels more like a souq in this city full of high-end shopping malls and is a good spot to shop for souvenirs. You might be surprised by the crowds at the Gold Centre, where extravagant tiered gold necklaces, dainty diamond bracelets and ruby- and emerald-encrusted bridal crowns seen in window displays are certainly not cheap, but showcase the region's love of gold.

BEST BUDGET RESTAURANTS IN DOWNTOWN ABU DHABI

Al Ibrahimi Restaurant
Since the 1980s, this famous Pakistani restaurant has drawn the city's carnivores for the mutton biryani, *harees* (a porridge-like stew made of cracked wheat and meat) and *mandi*, among other Pakistani and local dishes. $

Dampa Seafood Grill
This Pinoy restaurant is wildly popular for its seafeast dump – a heap of grilled shrimp, crab, mussels, clams and sweet corn cob on your table, with unlimited rice and a choice of five sauces. It serves two to three and is meant to be eaten by hand (you'll be given disposable gloves). $

Lahmajoon
This Armenian bakery and cafeteria is popular for its *lahmajoon* (flatbread with a variety of toppings) and Armenian *kibbeh* (deep-fried meatballs). $

WHERE TO STAY IN DOWNTOWN ABU DHABI

Courtyard by Marriott World Trade Center
Bright rooms with modern amenities, a fitness centre and pool, plus three restaurants. **$$**

Le Royal Méridien Abu Dhabi
Modern rooms in a centrally located high-rise in Al Danah. It has Stratos, Abu Dhabi's only revolving rooftop bar. **$$**

Millennium Downtown
Simple, classic-style rooms, a gym, a swimming pool, and two restaurants, within walking distance to the Corniche. **$$**

BEST SHAWARMA IN DOWNTOWN ABU DHABI

Bait El Khetyar
Choose from chicken or beef, sandwiched in *saj* (unleavened flatbread) or *kaak* (sesame-covered soft bread), or plated with fries. $

Al Ajaweed Restaurant
Both the beef and chicken shawarmas come in normal and spicy options, with the spicy meat packing a punch. $

Karam Al Sham
The flavourful shawarma, succulent kebabs and velvety hummus make for a satisfying meal. $

Parks Along the Corniche

Lakeside picnic

Grab a spot on one of the benches to watch the ducks or admire the 15m-high fountain in the lake at **Lake Park**, located between the Corniche and the residential and commercial district of **Al Danah**. A bridge allows you to cross over the lake. The kids' playground, walking paths and manicured lawns make this park popular with families in the evenings and on the weekends. At neighbouring **Formal Park**, stroll in the labyrinth, relax by the pond, or get a workout in at the outdoor gym and exercise track. There are designated BBQ areas if you want to picnic like the locals. Or step into one of the bakeries on Al Janayen St to pick up hot *manakeesh* (baked flatbread with toppings like cheese and vegetables) and spinach *fatayer* (stuffed pie) to enjoy on one of the picnic benches.

Shop at the World Trade Center Souk

A souq reimagined

Located on the site of Abu Dhabi's old central souq that was destroyed in a fire in 2003, the **World Trade Center Souk**, designed by British architect Norman Foster, pays homage to the past through architectural features such as lattice woodwork, rooftop perforations that stream dappled sunlight into narrow alleys, public squares and atriums to people-watch, and stained-glass windows with geometric patterns. A worthwhile spot for souvenir shopping, here you'll find shops selling frankincense, elegant hand-embroidered pashmina shawls, pearl chokers, traditional lamps, dried fruits and nuts, wool carpets and colourful *jalabiyas* (traditional kaftans worn in the Gulf). It's connected to the World Trade Center Mall by a bridge.

Sunbathe on Abu Dhabi Beach

Morning at the beach

One of the quieter stretches of sand along the Corniche, this **beach** opposite the Family Park is perfect for a relaxed morning of sunbathing. If you're feeling adventurous, parasailing flights and banana and doughnut rides can be booked with **Abu Dhabi Parasail**, located on the beach. Nearby, **Flatout Specialty Coffee** does delicious iced lattes. There's a lifeguard on duty and public toilets are available.

WHERE TO STAY IN DOWNTOWN ABU DHABI

Sofitel Abu Dhabi Corniche
Business hotel on the Corniche with sea-facing rooms and a spa. Has a jazz bar and a fantastic Korean restaurant. $$

Al Maha Arjaan by Rotana
Centrally located hotel apartment with spacious rooms, a gym, spa, restaurant and rooftop pool. $$

Tryp by Wyndham Abu Dhabi
Modern rooms, some with partial sea views, two restaurants and a pool bar, a gym and a swimming pool. $

SONIA ALVES-POLIDORI/SHUTTERSTOCK ©

World Trade Center Souk

Breakwater & Around

ALL THE MAGNIFICENCE

If there's one area in Abu Dhabi that visually showcases the capital's ambition and grandeur with unabashed confidence, it's the one around the Marina Breakwater.

Connected to the Breakwater is the south-western end of the 8km-long Corniche, a lively recreational hub thanks to its well-maintained waterfront promenade, beautiful parks, sandy beaches and cycling track.

On the peninsula of Al Ras Al Akhdar, the Qasr Al Watan stands within the compound of the working Presidential Palace, with its regal domes, exquisite white facade and landscaped gardens welcoming visitors keen to learn about the country's diplomatic relations, regional leadership and role in fostering a culture of tolerance and acceptance not only in the Gulf but also the world. Next door, the rose-hued Emirates Palace, built on 100 hectares of reclaimed land, is a magnificent palace hotel with a private marina, a 1.3km private beach and four helipads. It opened its doors in November 2005 in the run-up to the 26th Gulf Cooperation Council (GCC) Summit, which was being hosted by Abu Dhabi. Its stately suites have hosted heads of state and Hollywood celebrities, and its grand auditorium is the venue for concerts, opera and movie premieres.

Nearby, at the Founder's Memorial, a captivating three-dimensional portrait of the UAE's founding father, the late Sheikh Zayed bin Sultan Al Nahyan, sparkles celestially at night as a profound reminder of his values and vision, which continue to act as a beacon on Abu Dhabi's remarkable path of progress.

Across the street are Abu Dhabi's most impressive skyscrapers: the twin Nation Towers and the dazzling 342m-high ADNOC headquarters, the second-highest skyscraper in the city. Nearby, at the sleek Etihad Towers, a 74th-floor observation deck offers panoramic views of the Abu Dhabi coastline.

DON'T MISS...

FOUNDER'S MEMORIAL
This portrait of the late Sheikh Zayed bin Sultan Al Nahyan takes on a celestial appearance at night.
p139

QASR AL WATAN
A tour of this working palace is an insight into Emirati hospitality, diplomacy and intellectual heritage.
p140

OBSERVATION DECK AT 300
Head to the city's highest vantage point for incredible panoramic views of Abu Dhabi.
p142

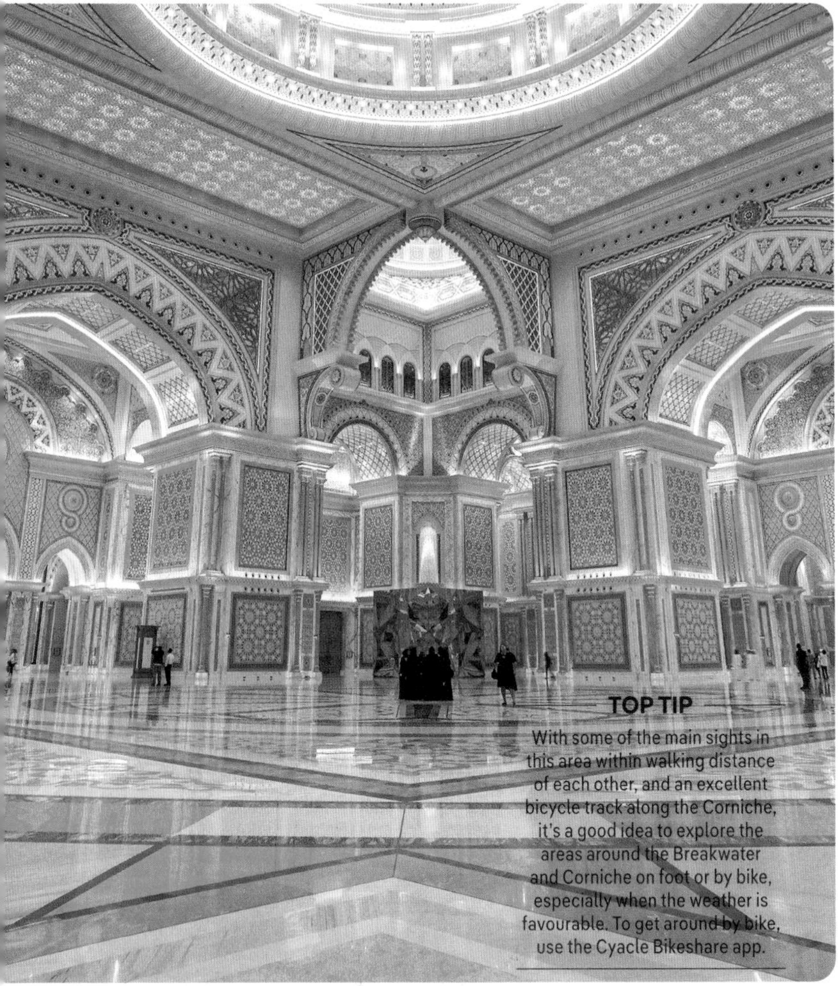

TOP TIP

With some of the main sights in this area within walking distance of each other, and an excellent bicycle track along the Corniche, it's a good idea to explore the areas around the Breakwater and Corniche on foot or by bike, especially when the weather is favourable. To get around by bike, use the Cyacle Bikeshare app.

Left: Founder's Memorial (p139); Above: Qasr Al Watan (p140)

I LIVE HERE: INSIDER FAVOURITES IN BREAKWATER & AROUND

Tanya Naveed (@tanleo_ on Instagram and tanleo.darkroom.com), an Abu Dhabi-based street photographer, shares her favourite spots around the Breakwater area.

Milestones Coffee
This cafe is a must-visit for its lovely ambience and view of Qasr Al Hosn.

A'l Bahar
Grab a coffee or ice cream, or ride a bike, all with a great sea view. An underground tunnel connects A'l Bahar to the Khalidiya parking lot with a food area that's great for families and kids.

Cultural Foundation
This is your one-stop for Emirati culture. There's always an exhibition, art gallery or event worth checking out. Definitely visit their secret prayer room outside.

BREAKWATER & AROUND

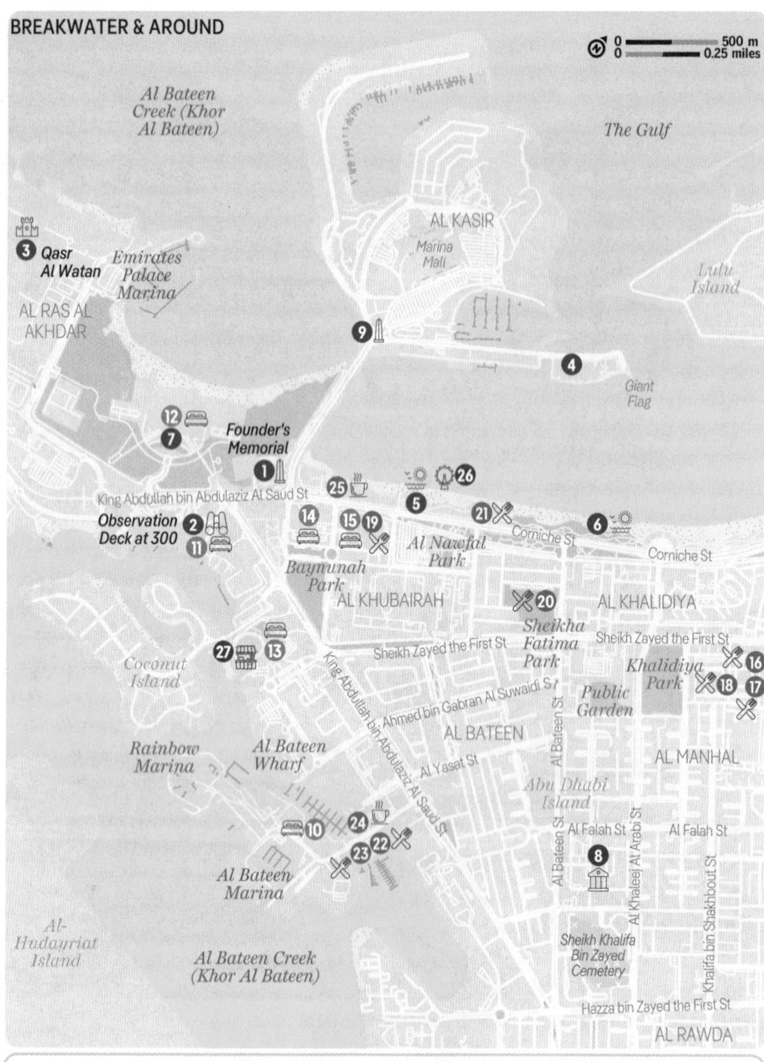

HIGHLIGHTS
1 Founder's Memorial
2 Observation Deck at 300
3 Qasr Al Watan

SIGHTS
4 Abu Dhabi Heritage Village
5 A'l Bahar
see 2 Avenue at Etihad Towers
6 Corniche Beach
7 Emirates Palace
8 Etihad Modern Art Gallery
9 Pearl & Ship Sculpture

SLEEPING
10 Abu Dhabi Edition
11 Conrad Abu Dhabi Etihad Towers
12 Emirates Palace Mandarin Oriental
13 Intercontinental Abu Dhabi
14 Radisson Blue Hotel & Resort Abu Dhabi Corniche
15 St Regis Abu Dhabi

EATING
16 Al Khayam Bakery & Sweets
see 8 Art House Cafe
17 Fatair Liwa
18 Kaak Bladna Sweets
see 2 Li Beirut
19 Mado
20 Mamafri
21 Patron Meat House
22 Saddle House Al Bateen
23 Tashas

DRINKING & NIGHTLIFE
24 Brunch and Cake
25 Em Sherif Cafe

ENTERTAINMENT
26 AquaDhabi Water Park

SHOPPING
27 Fishmarket

Emirates Palace Mandarin Oriental

Emirates Palace Mandarin Oriental MAP P138

Unmatched grandeur

Boasting incomparable opulence, this astounding palace hotel with 114 domes, 1002 crystal chandeliers, expansive manicured gardens, grand arches, gold-leaf interiors and 200 fountains is one of Abu Dhabi's most iconic landmarks. A good way to visit – if you're not staying in one of its stately rooms or dining at one of its restaurants – is on a private tour. You'll hear stories about the history, admire architectural highlights (like the 72.6m central dome adorned with gold, mother-of-pearl and crystals), peek into the remarkable Palace Suite, and finish with a gold-flecked Palace Cappuccino. Alternatively, book a day pass to enjoy the hotel's private 1.3km white-sand beach.

Founder's Memorial MAP P138

An ode to the Founding Father

A celebration of the life, achievements and values of the late Sheikh Zayed bin Sultan Al Nahyan, this larger-than-life public art installation was inaugurated in 2018 as a memorial to the revered founder of the UAE on the 100th anniversary of his birth. At its heart is the Constellation, a captivating three-dimensional portrait of Sheikh Zayed set in a 30m-high pavilion. It was designed by artist Ralph Helmick using 1327 hand-welded platonic solids, each representing a star, suspended on 1110 cables. Depicting the late ruler's values and teachings as the country's guiding light, the prismatic installation sparkles at night, taking on an ethereal appearance.

In a nod to the late Sheikh Zayed bin Sultan Al Nahyan's love for green spaces, also set within the memorial site is a beautiful garden with indigenous trees and medicinal plants, a *falaj* (irrigation channel), seating and an elevated walkway. The visitor centre screens a short film that documents the creation of the artwork. Complimentary 30-minute guided tours by knowledgeable Emirati cultural guides provide deeper context to Sheikh Zayed's legacy. These are available throughout the day during opening hours and can be booked online by email or on arrival at the visitor centre.

ASIFGRAPHY/SHUTTERSTOCK ©

PRACTICALITIES

Scan this QR code for prices and opening hours:

TOP SIGHT

Qasr Al Watan

Set in landscaped gardens within a 380,000-sq-metre complex that houses the offices of the president, vice president and crown prince of Abu Dhabi, Qasr Al Watan (the Palace of the Nation) was opened to the public in 2019 to shine the spotlight on the achievements of the UAE. This working palace formally hosts heads of state and dignitaries on state visits and is the official venue for summits.

DID YOU KNOW?

A series of three stunning sculptures by Emirati artist Mattar bin Lahej called *The Power of Words* feature inspiring quotes by the late Sheikh Zayed bin Sultan Al Nahyan. These include a spherical golden sculpture in the Great Hall as well as a pair of silver sculptures in the palace's garden.

Inside Qasr Al Watan

A contemporary interpretation of architectural traditions from the Gulf region, Qasr Al Watan is a breathtaking sight with its regal domes, white granite and limestone facade, hand-carved maple wood doors, and elaborate arcades that offer respite from the sun.

Crowned by a massive 60m high central dome with a diameter of 37m and stained-glass windows, the **Great Hall** is the epitome of splendour. A stunning visual feast, it features traditional design elements such as grand arches, detailed tilework, ornate domes, interwoven geometric patterns, vegetal and floral motifs, stylised lettering and crystal chandeliers. The colour palette of gold, white and blue that dominates the interior draws from the landscape of desert, sky and sea, while the white exterior of the palace signifies peace and purity.

Geometric patterns adorn the floors and the walls are decorated with latticed *mashrabiya* designs. Notice the recurrence of the eight-pointed star in the design – comprising two overlapping squares, it holds great significance in the Arab

Great Hall

world. Step into each of the four mirrored geometric cubes inside the Great Hall to learn more about the design elements, diversity of patterns, and detailed craftsmanship involved.

The Great Hall offers access to various rooms reserved for specific uses or housing exhibitions that highlight the country's diplomatic relationships and historical achievements.

In the **Presidential Gifts** room, a collection of diplomatic gifts presented to the UAE by visiting heads of state includes a handmade carpet from Turkmenistan, a porcelain tulip vase from the Netherlands, and several swords and daggers from countries such as Saudi Arabia, Kuwait and Oman. A magnificent 12-tonne chandelier with 350,000 crystals hangs from the gold-leaf-lined dome above a circular table in the **Spirit of Collaboration** room, which serves as the official venue for summits involving the Federal Supreme Council, the Arab League and the Gulf Cooperation Council.

In the **Presidential Banquet** hall, which hosts state banquets in honour of visiting dignitaries, take a peek at sumptuous custom-made silverware and perfectly set tables. The **House of Knowledge** is the most interesting of all the zones at Qasr Al Watan. It showcases artefacts and manuscripts that highlight the contributions of Arab scholars to the development of various fields like astronomy, science, art, mathematics, literature, exploration, cartography and medicine from the 8th century to the 13th century, during a period known as the Arab Golden Age.

Other rooms include the **Official Meeting Room**, used during official state visits, and **Al Barza**, the *majlis* (reception room) at Qasr Al Watan. The **Qasr Al Watan Library** houses a collection of over 50,000 books, including rare editions and manuscripts that advance the preservation of Arab culture and intellectual heritage.

VISUAL EXTRAVAGANZA

Post-sunset, an immersive light-and-sound show called **Palace in Motion** transforms the facade of the palace and tells the story of the UAE's inspiring journey. The price of the show is included in the ticket price for the day of your visit. Though it's only on for 15 minutes, this spectacular experience is worth revisiting the palace grounds for a second time if you've already toured it earlier in the day.

TOP TIPS

- Both men and women are advised to wear clothing that covers the knees and shoulders.
- Download the map available on the website to easily locate the different zones at the palace.
- The Palace in Motion show takes place nightly at Qasr Al Watan, 30 minutes after sunset. If you plan on watching it, it's best to check show times online as this can vary seasonally. The last entry for the show is 30 minutes before showtime.

Observation Deck at 300

MAP P138

Afternoon tea with a view

Located on the 74th floor of Tower 2 at the Conrad Abu Dhabi Etihad Towers, this elegant **observation deck** and cafe offers spectacular panoramic views of the city and outstanding service. At 300m, it's also Abu Dhabi's highest viewpoint. While visitors are free to choose from the cafe's à la carte menu of salads, sandwiches, pastries, tea and coffee, the award-winning Afternoon Tea is a worthwhile experience and an excellent excuse for a midday break. Nibble on six types of savoury tea sandwiches, eight kinds of delicious pastries and scones, and sip on a variety of teas and coffee, while admiring the skyscrapers, islands, marinas and sandy beaches that dot the Abu Dhabi coastline, through expansive floor-to-ceiling windows. Ask for a table with views over the Breakwater and Qasr Al Watan, but don't forget to stroll around the deck for other views. Tickets to the deck include a credit voucher of Dhs55 redeemable on food and beverages. Afternoon Tea packages include admission to the deck and must be booked at least a day in advance.

Observation Deck at 300

Mamafri

MAP P138

Food for the soul

Stepping into this stylish restaurant at the lively Sheikha Fatima Park feels like you've stumbled upon a real secret in Abu Dhabi. An undulating avant-garde installation hangs overhead, chefs theatrically flambé prawns behind a glass window, dinner tables are busy with Emirati patrons, even on a weeknight, and the buzz of conversations and deep house music fills the air. Various Southeast Asian cuisines make an appearance on the menu with dishes like chicken bao, Wagyu sando, ramen, kimchi fried rice and Malaysian curry. Whatever you pick, it's likely to be flavourful, generously portioned and deeply comforting.

Ways of the Past at Abu Dhabi Heritage Village

MAP P138

Life in an oasis village

If you're curious about life in the capital before the discovery of oil, a quick visit to this reconstructed fortified **village** with museums, exhibitions, a souq and a mosque is worth your time.

Museum collections that trace the history of Abu Dhabi include old photographs documenting life in the region, weapons, traditional clothing, footwear, silver jewellery, manuscripts, old coins and currency notes, and bronze *dallah* (coffee pots), among other household wares.

In the village, notice the tents made of goat hair – these were used by the Bedouins as shelter in winter, as they journeyed through the desert. In summer, people lived in *barasti* houses such as the one you'll find in the village. Built with wooden frames, their roofs were thatched with palm fronds to facilitate air circulation.

A boat exhibition displays the region's long maritime heritage and hints at the ingenious techniques of shipbuilding practised in the Gulf. On the beach behind the village, pearl diving dhows and traditional rowboats stand across the water from a stunning skyline of high-rises and skyscrapers.

A handicrafts souq showcases *khanjars* (curved daggers), rugs and traditional robes, while there are stalls selling kaftans, shawls, handmade soaps, henna, spices and touristy knick-knacks.

TREASURES OF THE SEA

A sculpture featuring a pair of sails and four oysters, each with a pearl inside, stands on the **Marina Breakwater** as a nod to Abu Dhabi's pearl diving heritage. Before the discovery of oil in Abu Dhabi, pearling was a major contributor to the economy. But this wasn't an easy profession for the divers who spent months at sea away from their families, enduring challenging weather and tough living conditions. However, the demand for natural pearls plummeted due to the Great Depression of the 1930s and the invention of mass-produced cultured pearls in Japan.

Lebanese Fine Dining at Li Beirut

MAP P138

A taste of Beirut

This plush **restaurant** at the Conrad Abu Dhabi Etihad Towers feels more like a lounge with its sleek black and red interiors, geometric screens, and Beirut-inspired photographs on the walls. The menu features traditional Lebanese dishes (including the chef's family recipes) with just the right amount of contemporary flair. It's a firm fine-dining favourite in the city, thanks to its sumptuous dishes, impeccable service and beautiful terrace views. Expect to dine on meze such as beetroot *moutabel* and spinach *fatayer*, *kunafa*-wrapped tiger prawns and mains like the *kebbeh bel laban* and chargrilled sea bass. Dessert is a highlight with options like pistachio *mohalabia* and labneh cheesecake.

WHERE TO EAT WITH A VIEW IN BREAKWATER & AROUND

Em Sherif Cafe
An elegant setting, top-notch service, delicious Lebanese meze and grills, and gorgeous views. **$$**

Patron Meat House
Stylish steakhouse on A'l Bahar Beach serving Turkish kebabs, grills and dry-aged steaks. **$$$**

Fishmarket
There's no menu at this iconic seafood restaurant. Pick from the display and choose your accompaniments. **$$$**

BEST BRUNCH IN BREAKWATER & AROUND

Brunch and Cake
Boho-chic interiors in a bright glasshouse setting on Al Bateen Marina. This brunch spot is known for friendly service, massive portions, and dishes such as lobster shakshuka and pistachio French toast. **$$**

Tashas
Warm farmhouse decor and breakfast dishes that range from healthy açai bowls to Spanish omelets and French toast, served till 6pm. **$$**

Mado
Along with fantastic views, this Turkish restaurant at the Nation Galleria mall serves delicious breakfast fare including cheese-stuffed Turkish bagels and *menemen* (eggs cooked with tomatoes and peppers). **$$**

NURPHOTO/GETTY IMAGES ©

Al Sahil Beach

Unwind at Conrad Spa

MAP P138

Mind and body

Setting foot into **Conrad Spa** at the high-end Conrad Abu Dhabi Etihad Towers is like entering a warmly lit marble, wood and stone sanctuary that promises the ultimate wellness for both mind and body. Begin by sipping on lime mint juice and nibbling dates, then deeply inhale a choice of three fragrances – lavender, ylang-ylang or lemongrass – to usher in a mode of relaxation. Then, centre your mind as you trace shapes with miniature toys on the coloured sand of a sand tray. Once you're visibly relaxed, a therapist leads you to a luxurious treatment room.

The 60-minute holistic massage involves a combination of massage techniques from around the world, while the hot stone massage uses heated stones on acupressure points to relieve tiredness. Heated beds and experienced therapists make this spa stand out in a city full of great spas. Besides two en suite couples suites (worth the splurge if you're visiting with a friend), the 1465-sq-metre spa has a sauna, steam room, steam showers, Himalayan salt room and plunge baths. The Hammam suite comes with a traditional heated marble *goebektas* (raised platform). A range of hammam treatments incorporate renowned Amra products such as those with crushed diamonds and pearls.

Get Some Sun at Corniche Beach

MAP P138

Sand in your toes

Between October and March, join Abu Dhabi residents to enjoy the pleasantly sunny weather at this 2km Blue-Flagged **public beach** that's split into various free and paid beaches

WHERE TO STAY IN BREAKWATER & AROUND

Emirates Palace Mandarin Oriental Stately suites, 24-hour butler service, a private beach, a luxurious spa and award-winning restaurants. **$$$**

St Regis Abu Dhabi
Glamorous rooms and suites offer sea views and butler service. Seven excellent restaurants and bars. **$$$**

Intercontinental Abu Dhabi
This family-friendly hotel has simple rooms and is home to some fantastic restaurants. **$$**

and has five volleyball courts, two football pitches and three playing fields. Bordered by palm trees, manicured lawns, a boardwalk and a bike track on one side and the cerulean waters of the Arabian Gulf on the other, this is the perfect spot for a laid-back few hours of swimming and beach activities.

On the western end is **A'l Bahar**, a free 600m public beach with cafes, restaurants, kiosks, a shaded kids' playground, volleyball and basketball courts, water sports, an outdoor gym, a climbing wall and the **AquaDhabi waterpark**. Loungers, umbrellas, kayaks and paddleboards are available to rent.

On the eastern end, **Al Sahil Beach** is divided into a free section and separate paid beaches meant for families (no single men) and mixed-use (singles and large groups), with sunbeds and umbrellas available for hire. Entry to the paid beaches is Dhs10.50 for adults and Dhs5.25 for children aged five and above. Toilets, showers and changing rooms are available.

Art at Etihad Modern Art Gallery

MAP P138

Art gallery and cafe

This **art space** in a villa in Al Bateen hosts temporary exhibitions that showcase the contemporary works of Emirati artists, both up-and-coming and established, in multiple galleries. The venue hosts art events, artist talks and poetry nights.

The gallery is attached to the **Art House Cafe**, a cheerful space decorated with painted plates, patterned tiles, vintage suitcases, upcycled oil barrels, tyres and colourful wooden benches that make you feel like you're visiting the eclectic home of an artist friend. It's a lovely spot for sandwiches, wraps, burgers, coffee and shakes.

Lunch at Saddle House Al Bateen

MAP P138

Gourmet meal on the marina

Stylish sunlit interiors and lush plants transport you into an urban oasis, and plate after plate of beautifully presented food attracts your attention at this chic restaurant in a glass house on the marina at Marsa Al Bateen. Suspended from the roof is a striking art installation by Emirati artist Mattar Bin Lahej. Outside, tables on the terrace offer views of the marina.

The fantastic ambience is just a bonus – the food at Saddle House alone is worth venturing out to this neighbourhood for. The menu has plenty of options for both breakfast and all-day dining, and the friendly staff are happy to share recommendations. You can't go wrong whether you're in the mood for a refreshing peach stracciatella salad, a rich pistachio pesto linguini, or a supremely satisfying crispy chicken burger.

BEST BAKERIES IN BREAKWATER & AROUND

Fatair Liwa
Regulars claim this place serves the best *manakeesh* in Abu Dhabi. You'll be inclined to believe them when you've had one bite of their cheese and *zaatar manakeesh*. **$**

Al Khayam Bakery & Sweets
Tea cakes, crispy rusk, jam-filled shortbread cookies, and puff pastry: this bakery's got plenty of delicious options for your mid-afternoon cravings. **$**

Kaak Bladna Sweets
The *kaak* (bagel-shaped sweetbreads), *maqroota* (pinwheel cookies) and pistachio *mamoul* cookies taste even better than they look. **$**

Conrad Abu Dhabi Etihad Towers Contemporary design, spectacular views, award-winning restaurants and bars, a private beach and a spa. **$$**

Abu Dhabi Edition Beautiful modern rooms at this design-forward hotel, plus six restaurants, a spa and fitness centre. Excellent location. **$$$**

Radisson Blu Hotel & Resort Abu Dhabi Corniche Comfy rooms, pools, a health club and spa, six restaurants, and a beach club. **$$**

Al Zahiyah, Al Maryah Island & Al Reem Island

NEW CENTRAL BUSINESS DISTRICT

Long-time residents still refer to today's Al Zahiyah neighbourhood as the 'Tourist Club area', named after a beachfront recreational complex popular with locals, expats and tourists in the 1970s that was eventually demolished.

This area witnessed a post-oil construction boom that led to the city's first high-rises. Much of this neighbourhood, renamed Al Zahiyah ('colourful' in Arabic) in 2014, has undergone redevelopment, with several of the old buildings having been razed or refurbished. Even today this working-class neighbourhood continues to be home to many communities from around the world. This vibrant diversity is reflected in its streets, where you'll find restaurants specialising in Egyptian *kushari* (a dish of macaroni, rice, lentils, fried onions and tomato sauce), sugary *kunafeh* (a syrupy cheese-based pastry), Pakistani biryani and Indonesian *nasi padang* (rice with an assortment of cooked dishes).

A five-minute drive away, Al Maryah Island is centred on the Abu Dhabi Global Market Square (formerly called Sowwah Square), where you'll find an international financial centre with over 50 companies, glossy skyscrapers home to luxurious five-star hotels, residences, high-end restaurants, the Cleveland Clinic Abu Dhabi, and the Galleria Al Maryah Island, a posh retail, dining and entertainment destination. Gourmets will love this area, where some of the most exciting names in the UAE's dining scene have set up shop in recent years.

Neighbouring Al Reem Island is home to a large number of expats and young families attracted to the high quality of residential apartments, communities with leisure facilities, cosmopolitan culture, international restaurants and cafes, parks, beaches and shopping malls.

TRABANTOS/SHUTTERSTOCK ©. OPPOSITE PAGE: ANAS YACOUB ALMAHARMEH/SHUTTERSTOCK ©

DON'T MISS...

EM SHERIF SEA CAFÉ
This Lebanese restaurant stands out for its creative flair and exceptional seafood dishes.
p149

GALLERIA AL MARYAH ISLAND
High-end shopping mall home to luxury brands, a cinema, restaurants and cafes.
p148

AL MARYAH ISLAND PROMENADE
Walk or jog to fabulous sea and skyscraper views along this 5.4km waterfront promenade.

HERITAGE PARK
On the weekends, join picnicking families at this public park along the corniche.

TOP TIP

A visit to Al Maryah Island is a good plan for a brutally hot summer afternoon when you don't want to be outdoors. Not only is there plenty to see and do at the Galleria Al Maryah Island, this shopping mall, a destination in its own right, is home to top restaurants and lovely cafes for a bit of people-watching.

Left: The Corniche; Above: Al Reem Island

I LIVE HERE: FAVOURITE HANGOUT SPOTS

Tia Mills (@tiatakesthe-world on Instagram) is an international educator and travel content creator based in Abu Dhabi. Here are her favourite spots in Al Zahiyah, Al Maryah Island and Al Reem Island.

Reem Central Park
Escape the city and take in the tranquil beauty of this park with a beautiful beach, skate park, sports courts and food trucks.

The Corniche
For a fun-filled outing at the Abu Dhabi's Corniche, lay beachside and enjoy the gorgeous views of the Gulf, try out water sports, take a stroll or have a picnic.

Abu Dhabi Global Market
Here you'll find stunning architecture, beautiful fountains and a lively atmosphere filled with entertainment and dining options.

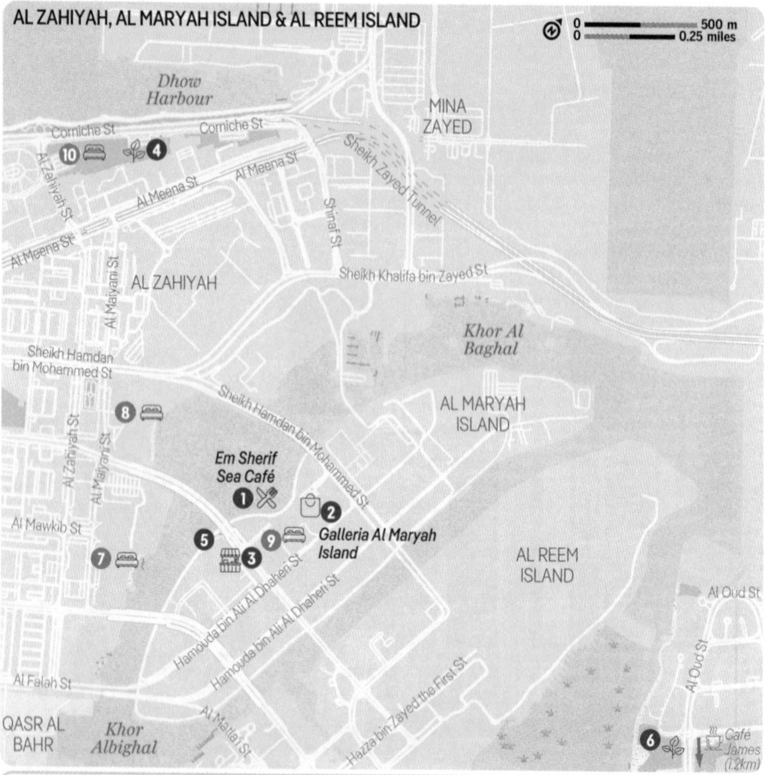

AL ZAHIYAH, AL MARYAH ISLAND & AL REEM ISLAND

HIGHLIGHTS
1 Em Sherif Sea Café
2 Galleria Al Maryah Island

SIGHTS
3 Abu Dhabi Global Market Square
4 Heritage Park
5 Promenade - Al Maryah Island
6 Reem Central Park

SLEEPING
7 Beach Rotana Abu Dhabi
8 Le Méridien Abu Dhabi
9 Rosewood Abu Dhabi
10 Sofitel Abu Dhabi Corniche

EATING
see 9 Dai Pai Dong

DRINKING & NIGHTLIFE
see 9 Dragon's Tooth
see 9 Hidden Bar
see 9 La Cava

Galleria Al Maryah Island

Shop till you drop

This **shopping mall**, the centrepiece of the **Abu Dhabi Global Market Square** on Al Maryah Island, is an upmarket dining, retail and entertainment destination. With Italian marble walkways, skylights, floor-to-ceiling glass walls and serene water features, everything here feels luxe. In addition to over 300 brands including the likes of Valentino, Bottega Veneta and Boucheron, there are nearly 100 restaurants and cafes, including Taiwanese favourite **Din Tai Fung**, **Magnolia Bakery** and speciality cafe **Maison Samira Maatouk**. A cinema, kids play areas, indoor climbing and trampoline park, VR gaming centre and three rooftop parks mean you could easily spend an entire day here.

Em Sherif Sea Café

Lebanese Mediterranean dining with sea views

At this sophisticated Lebanese-Mediterranean restaurant, the brainchild of celebrated Lebanese restaurateur Mireille Hayek, hand-painted Portuguese Azulejo tiles adorn the walls, an 8m-long chandelier with 300 brass pots and baskets hangs from the ceiling, and the use of rope, wood, marble and rattan decor sets the tone for an elaborate seaside meal. Floor-to-ceiling windows offer views of the turquoise waters around Al Maryah Island.

The menu features an elevated take on Lebanese dishes and seafood is clearly the star here. Begin with meze such as *kibbet samak* (seabass and bulgur pie) or calamari *bil kuzbara* (sautéed calamari with coriander, garlic and lemon). Mains include flavourful grilled butterfly fish topped with greens and tomatoes. There's a seafood bar displaying the fresh catch of the day, and a beef bar with premium grilled meats.

The wine list has a variety of wines from Lebanon and elsewhere. As the meal progresses, it's only natural to find your feet tapping to the catchy Middle Eastern music being played by the resident DJ. A must-visit for its sumptuous dishes, lively ambience and impeccable service.

Galleria Al Maryah Island

MORE IN AL ZAHIYAH, AL MARYAH ISLAND & AL REEM ISLAND

BEST BARS IN AL ZAHIYAH, AL MARYAH AND AL REEM ISLAND

La Cava
This stylish wine cellar is a sophisticated setting for an evening of premium wines, charcuterie and good conversation. There's a cigar room with an impressive whisky selection in the basement.

Dragon's Tooth
Go to this speak-easy-style bar inside Dai Pai Dong for saké or cocktails infused with lemongrass, green tea and coconut purée.

Hidden Bar
A buzzing gin bar where you'll find over 230 of the world's best gins plus delicious gin cocktails and a seriously good Negroni.

Cantonese Street Food at Dai Pai Dong

Dim sum, hotpot and barbecue

Seemingly busy every night of the week, this Cantonese **restaurant** located at the Rosewood Abu Dhabi transports you to a secret alleyway in Hong Kong where only those in the know gather to feast on what might just be the best Chinese street food in the capital. Dark-wood furniture and mellow lighting create an air of mystery, bottles of soy sauce line the walls and steam rises dramatically behind a glass window in the open kitchen where chefs stuff dim sum and toss noodles in large woks.

It's best to approach a meal here with a sharing mindset because there's so much you'll want to try. Begin with the dim sum menu where the *xiao long bao* (chicken soup dumplings) and crispy mango shrimp roll are excellent choices. On the à la carte menu, crispy duck salad, wok-fried Szechuan prawns and braised eggplant are the kind of dishes you'll think about afterwards.

Finish with jasmine tea, crème brûlée and Hong Kong egg tarts. The Friday night hotpot brunch, where you cook your choice of meats, seafood and noodles in a hotpot on your table, and multi-course weekend brunch are also popular.

An Exquisite Meal at Café James

Where food looks like art

It's hard to define the cuisine on the menu at this casual but stylish bistro on Al Reem Island helmed by American-South Korean chef James Soo Yong Kim. What matters though is that most dishes, from snow crab raviolo and salmon with gnocchi to cuttlefish cascarecce and quail-egg-topped steak tartare, are a testament to his brazen creativity. A must-visit for its exceptional food.

WHERE TO STAY IN AL ZAHIYAH, AL MARYAH ISLAND & AL REEM ISLAND

Rosewood Abu Dhabi
Sleek design, bright modern rooms and brilliant sea views, plus luxurious spa, rooftop pool and eight stellar restaurants and bars. **$$$**

Le Méridien Abu Dhabi
Modern rooms, a pool with a swim-up bar, a private beach, a host of fitness offerings and five restaurants. **$$**

Beach Rotana Abu Dhabi
A good choice for families: a private beach, infinity pool, beach club, water-sports centre, kids clubs and 12 restaurants. **$$**

Beach Rotana Abu Dhabi

Sheikh Zayed Grand Mosque & Around

GATEWAY TO THE CAPITAL

Abu Dhabi Island, home to Abu Dhabi's oldest neighbourhoods, has a history dating back to the 1700s when it was first settled after freshwater was discovered on the island.

Separated from the mainland by Khor Al Maqta, a narrow strait that once could only be crossed safely during low tide, today the island is linked to it via three bridges. The oldest of these, Al Maqta Bridge, opened in 1968, followed by the Musaffah Bridge in 1978, and finally the iconic Sheikh Zayed Bridge, designed by Iraqi-born British architect Zaha Hadid, in 2010. When you cross this historic waterway on any of these bridges, the resplendent marble domes and slender gold-glass-mosaic-topped minarets of the Sheikh Zayed Grand Mosque make for a fitting introduction to the capital.

Luxury resorts and fine-dining restaurants dot the shores of Khor Al Maqta. The 146,000-sq-metre waterfront development Al Qana – where you'll find restaurants and cafes, an indoor adventure park, a VR and gaming complex, a cinema, wellness space, a marina and the National Aquarium – is set to become a major leisure destination.

A 10-minute drive from Sheikh Zayed Grand Mosque, the Eastern Mangrove National Park is a protected forest home to diverse aquatic species and rich birdlife. The reserve, along with neighbouring Al Gurm Corniche, is an idyllic pocket of the city that's worth exploring.

Also nearby is Capital Centre, a business district home to the Abu Dhabi National Exhibition Centre, an exhibitions, conferences and events venue; five-star hotels; and Capital Gate, Abu Dhabi's very own 'Leaning Tower'. The world's furthest leaning building, as per the Guinness World Records, this 160m-high, 35-floor skyscraper leans 18 degrees westwards. The Andaz Capital Gate, Abu Dhabi hotel is located here. The residential neighbourhood of Al Mushrif, 7km away, is home to parks such as the community favourite Umm Al Emarat Park.

DON'T MISS...

SHEIKH ZAYED GRAND MOSQUE ABU DHABI
This magnificent mosque is open to both worshippers and visitors.
p156

WAHAT AL KARAMA
Memorial built to honour the Emirati national heroes who sacrificed their lives in service of the UAE.
p158

UMM AL EMARAT PARK
This beautiful park has contemporary installations, cafes, a botanic garden and an amphitheatre.
p155

EASTERN MANGROVE NATIONAL PARK
A favourite of bird-watchers as well as wildlife photographers in Abu Dhabi.
p159

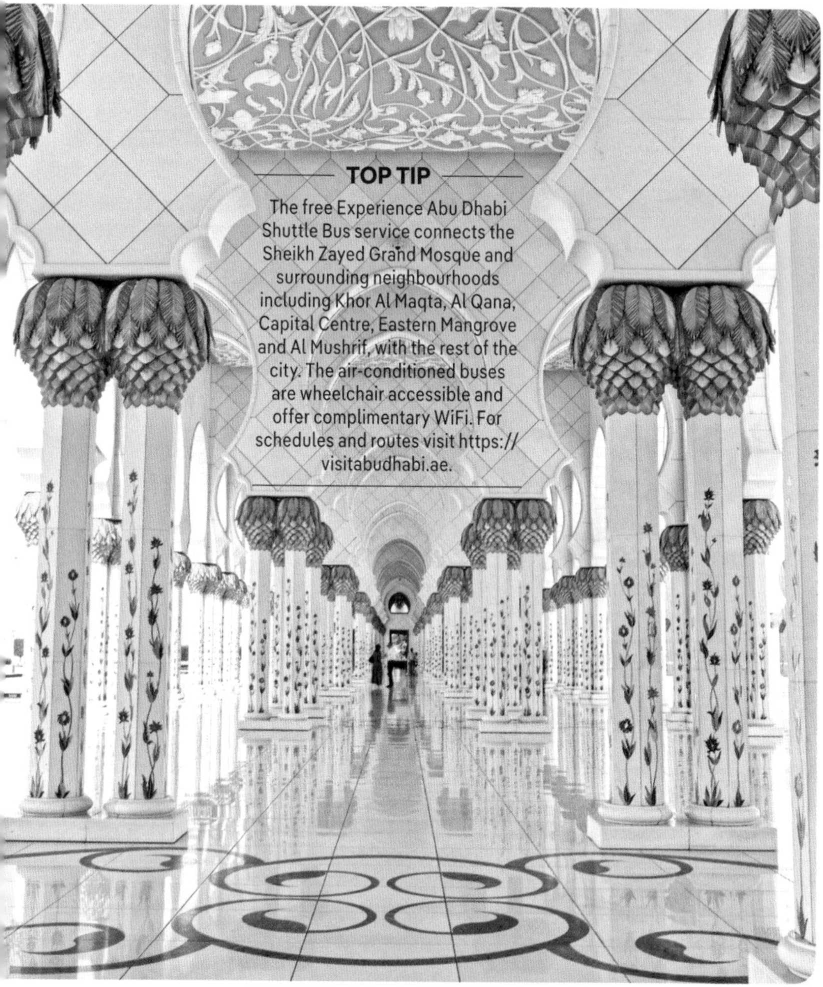

TOP TIP

The free Experience Abu Dhabi Shuttle Bus service connects the Sheikh Zayed Grand Mosque and surrounding neighbourhoods including Khor Al Maqta, Al Qana, Capital Centre, Eastern Mangrove and Al Mushrif, with the rest of the city. The air-conditioned buses are wheelchair accessible and offer complimentary WiFi. For schedules and routes visit https://visitabudhabi.ae.

Left: Eastern Mangrove National Park (p159); Above: Sheikh Zayed Grand Mosque (p156)

I LIVE HERE: OFF THE BEATEN PATH

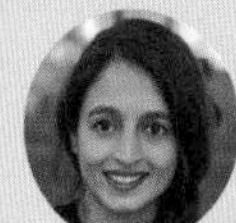

Arpita Soni (@foodlore uae on Instagram), Abu Dhabi–based food blogger and culinary critic, shares some favourite under-the-radar places in the area.

DRVN Coffee
Famous for its speciality coffee, authentic Neapolitan pizza and its impressive collection of racing cars from marques including Ferrari and Aston Martin. A unique experience that combines fine cuisine with a thrilling motorsports atmosphere.

Madinat Zayed Gold Centre
The Madinat Zayed Gold Centre (also called the Gold Souk) is a popular shopping destination boasting bespoke gold and jewellery pieces.

Ushna Restaurant
Enjoy the tantalising flavours of Ushna's Indian cuisine, paired with the breathtaking backdrop of the iconic Sheikh Zayed Mosque.

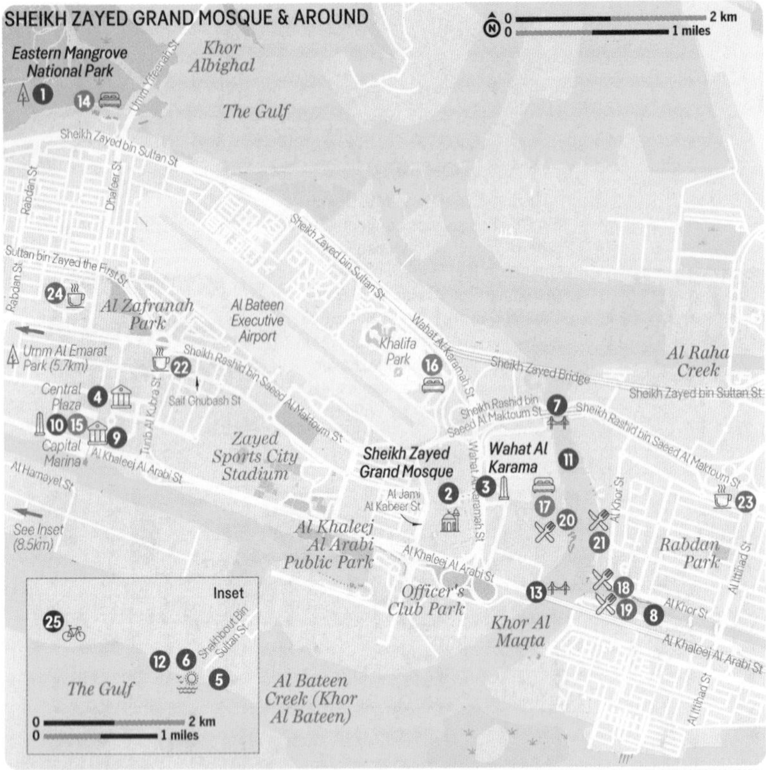

SHEIKH ZAYED GRAND MOSQUE & AROUND

HIGHLIGHTS
1 Eastern Mangrove National Park
2 Sheikh Zayed Grand Mosque
3 Wahat Al Karama

SIGHTS
4 Abu Dhabi National Exhibition Centre
5 Al Hudayriyat Beach
6 Al Hudayriyat Island
7 Al Maqta'a Bridge
8 Al Qana
9 Artbooth Gallery
10 Capital Gate
11 Khor Al Maqta
12 Marsana Beach
13 Musaffah Bridge

ACTIVITIES, COURSES & TOURS
see 8 National Aquarium Abu Dhabi

SLEEPING
14 Anantara Eastern Mangroves Abu Dhabi
15 Andaz Capital Gate
16 Park Rotana
17 Ritz-Carlton Abu Dhabi Grand Canal

EATING
18 Mado Al Qana
19 Otoro
20 Punjab Grill
21 Ushna

DRINKING & NIGHTLIFE
22 DRVN Coffee
23 House of Tea Cafeteria
24 Yadoo's House

TRANSPORT
25 Circuit X

Jubail Mangrove Park (p170)

Umm Al Emarat Park

Al Mrzab Traditional Restaurant

A traditional feast

Wildly popular for lunch, this **traditional restaurant** dishes out delicious home-style Emirati and Kuwaiti dishes. For the full experience, skip the dining tables and ask to be seated *majlis*-style at one of the low tables with colourful floor cushions. Traditional dark-wood furniture and old photos of Abu Dhabi on the walls offer a sense of the emirate's past. The Emirati chicken *machboos* (a meat and rice dish), fish curry, Kuwaiti lamb *machboos,* and *murabyan* shrimp (rice with shrimp) are all excellent choices. Save space for desserts such as the sticky sweet *luqaimat* (deep-fried dough balls drizzled with date syrup).

Umm Al Emarat Park

Park strolls and community events

Formerly known as Mushrif Park, this beautiful public **park** is among the city's oldest and was opened in 1982 as a women's-only garden. Today, this massive green space, which was renovated with contemporary design features, welcomes all visitors who come to stroll along its fountains and palm-tree-lined promenade, attend open-air concerts, pop-up markets or movie nights in its amphitheatre, or get breakfast at one of the cafes in the park, including the popular **Home Bakery**.

The **Botanic Garden** is home to over 200 regional plant species, and others from around the world. Marble slabs in the **Wisdom Garden** feature inspiring quotes by His Highness the late Sheikh Zayed bin Sultan Al Nahyan. The 30m-high **Shade House** offers respite from the sun thanks to a design that incorporates passive cooling. There are brilliant views of the park from the two decks on the upper levels. Children can keep busy between the dedicated children's park, playgrounds, and an animal barn with ponies, baby goats and tortoises.

ALEXEY STIOP/SHUTTERSTOCK ©

PRACTICALITIES

Scan this QR code to check opening hours, mosque etiquette and dress code, and book your visit and a cultural tour.

TOP SIGHT

Sheikh Zayed Grand Mosque

You might think that the most remarkable thing about the Sheikh Zayed Grand Mosque is its transcendent beauty or its monumental scale. Yet it is the symbolism of this architectural wonder that has elevated it to the status of a cultural icon. The melange of Islamic architectural styles represents diversity, peace and tolerance. The vision of the UAE's founding father, His Highness the late Sheikh Zayed bin Sultan Al Nahyan, the mosque is also his final resting place.

DID YOU KNOW?
While His Highness the late Sheikh Zayed bin Sultan Al Nahyan did not live to see the completion of the mosque's construction in 2007, his mausoleum is located next to it. mausoleum.

Architecture

Integrating traditional Mamluk, Ottoman, Andalusian, Moorish and Fatimid influences and modern designs, the Sheikh Zayed Grand Mosque is one of the greatest examples of contemporary Islamic architecture in the world. Open to non-Muslim visitors, it presents an opportunity to learn about the Islamic faith.

The mosque's 82 **marble domes**, the largest of which crowns the main prayer hall, are adorned with gold-glass mosaic finials. While walking from the main entrance to the main prayer hall through one of two foyers – the South Foyer or the North Foyer – glancing up at the interior of the domes reveals Moroccan artwork and verses from the Holy Quran in Glass Reinforced Gypsum (GRG).

Each of the four 106m-high **minarets** combines three geometric shapes in a nod to the different Islamic architectural styles. The white Macedonian marble that dominates the exterior creates a sense of purity and reverence. Stunning floral designs adorn the marble floor of the 17,400-sq-metre courtyard, which can accommodate nearly 31,000 worshippers.

The external **arcades** are supported by 1096 marble columns featuring intricate floral designs inlaid with semi-precious stones such as lapis lazuli, red agate, amethyst, abalone shell and mother-of-pearl. These are said to have been hand-carved by artisans descended from those who crafted the columns of the Taj Mahal, India's legendary Mughal monument. A date-palm-inspired golden aluminium crown adorns each column.

Prayer Halls

An active mosque that can accommodate 50,000 worshippers (across its prayer halls and courtyard), the Sheikh Zayed Grand Mosque houses three prayer halls. The **main prayer hall** has a capacity of over 7000 worshippers, while two smaller prayer halls each have a capacity of 1500 worshippers.

As you step into the main prayer hall in the interior of the mosque, expect to be dazzled by the sight of three **chandeliers** made of gilded stainless steel and gilded brass, and adorned with Swarovski crystals. The one in the centre is the largest and weighs approximately 11 tonnes, while the ones on each side weigh approximately 7.25 tonnes each. Look carefully and you'll realise their design is reminiscent of an upturned palm tree, their sparkling red, green and yellow crystal balls like clusters of dates.

Beneath your feet lies the world's largest **hand-knotted carpet**, featuring a medallion design and floral motifs. Made of wool and cotton, this 5700-sq-metre masterpiece, which took two years from ideation and design to completion, was handcrafted by nearly 1200 artisans. Delicate mother-of-pearl vines adorn the 96 marble columns that support the three domes over the main prayer hall.

The design of the gold-glass mosaic **mihrab** (a vaulted niche in a mosque wall showing the direction of Mecca) is inspired by a reference in the Holy Quran to a river of honey and milk, among the abundant rivers of heaven. This wall, known as the **Qibla Wall**, is illuminated with the 99 names of Allah in the Kufic style of Arabic calligraphy. To its right is the minbar (pulpit) made of carved cedar wood inlaid with mother-of-pearl, glass mosaic and white gold.

Lunar Lighting

By evening, the mosque transforms into an ethereal sight, thanks to a cleverly designed lighting system that reflects the phases of the moon. The mosque is surrounded by 22 light towers that project light and wispy drifting clouds onto the facade and domes. The light shifts gradually from blue to white according to the lunar cycle, reaching peak brilliance on the night of the full moon and turning a deep blue to represent darkness.

Visitors on the guided tour who walk through the North Foyer can see the mausoleum of His Highness the late Sheikh Zayed only from a distance. Only sitting presidents are permitted to enter. Visitors are not allowed to photograph the mausoleum.

TOP TIPS

- To enter, visitors must wear long-sleeved, loose-fitting, ankle-length opaque clothing. Women must wear a headscarf. Buy a reasonably priced headscarf, *abaya* or *kandoura* at one of the shops in Souq Al Jami'.
- Insightful, free, 45-minute guided cultural tours of the mosque are held daily every hour from 10am to 8pm (except Fridays between noon and 4pm).
- When having photos taken around the mosque, pose formally and maintain distance with companions. Displays of affection and hand gestures are prohibited.
- The best time to visit is 30 minutes before sunset. Stay longer to admire the lunar lighting in the evening.

Wahat Al Karama

MEMORIAL TO THE HEROES

Wahat Al Karama ('Oasis of Dignity' in Arabic) is a memorial to the Emirati martyrs who gave up their lives in service of their nation. Spread over 46,000 sq metres, the site consists of the Memorial, the Pavilion of Honour, the Memorial Plaza and a Visitors' Centre. It was inaugurated on Commemoration Day in 2016 in honour of the UAE's national heroes, including soldiers, police, diplomats and civilians.

The memorial, designed by British artist Idris Khan, consists of 31 colossal aluminium-clad tablets that lean on each other, representing the unity, solidarity and mutual support between the leaders of the UAE, its citizens and residents, and those who protect them through service. The tablets are engraved with poems and quotations by the rulers of the UAE, including His Highness the late Sheikh Zayed bin Sultan Al Nahyan. The Pledge of Allegiance of the UAE Armed Forces is inscribed on the long spine at the base of the Memorial.

Inside the polygonal **Pavilion of Honour**, a circular internal wall is clad with over 2800 aluminium plates, reclaimed from military vehicles, bearing the names of the UAE's martyrs. The eight slabs on the roof represent each of the UAE's seven emirates and the UAE's heroes. The centrepiece is made of seven glass panels with the Pledge of Allegiance on both sides. A pool of water surrounds this central structure, creating a sense of calm.

DON'T MISS

The galleries at the **Visitors' Centre** with interactive exhibitions offer information about the site and the UAE's diplomatic and humanitarian programs around the world. Also worth a read is the letter written by His Highness Sheikh Mohammed bin Rashid Al Maktoum, vice president and prime minister of the UAE and Ruler of Dubai, on the International Day of Tolerance in 2017 offering insight into the legacy and significance of tolerance in Emirati culture.

There is a nice view of the Sheikh Zayed Grand Mosque from the rooftop.

PETER JESCHE/SHUTTERSTOCK ©

Wahat Al Karama

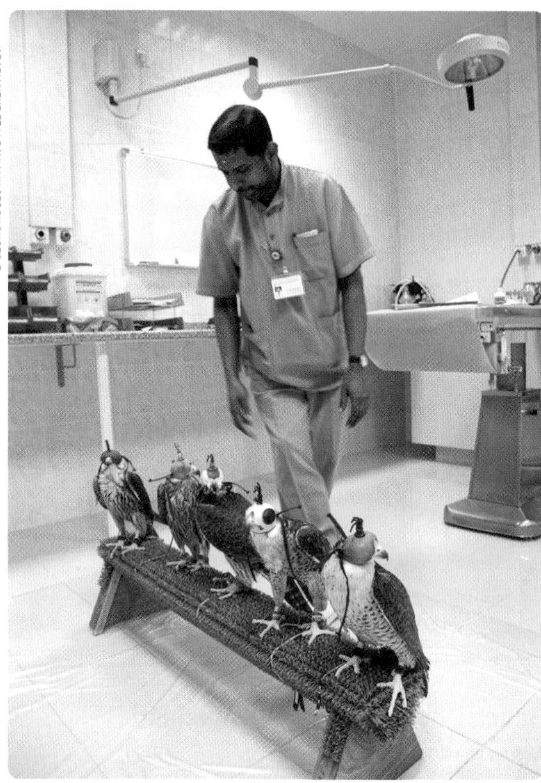

ARABIANEYE FZ LLC/ALAMY STOCK PHOTO ©

Abu Dhabi Falcon Hospital

Abu Dhabi Falcon Hospital

SYMBOL OF HERITAGE

Perhaps no other place in the emirate offers a deeper insight into the cultural significance of the falcon, the UAE's beloved national bird, as the **Abu Dhabi Falcon Hospital**. The world's first and largest falcon hospital, this world-class facility treats thousands of falcons from across the UAE and the region every year.

Daily two-hour tours involve a visit to the museum to learn about the heritage of and techniques involved in falconry, followed by a stop at the examination room to see feather repairs and talon trims. Watching these magnificent birds in free flight at the aviary is a memorable experience.

Eastern Mangrove National Park

SWATHES OF GREEN

At the **Eastern Mangrove National Park**, mottled crabs scurry in and out of sandbars, western reef herons fish in tidal lagoons, and turtles gently swim in the narrow channels between lush mangrove vegetation. A hot spot for biodiversity, this protected reserve attracts the city's bird-watchers, nature photographers and others looking for a reprieve from city life.

The best way to experience this stunning landscape is on a guided two-hour kayak tour with local operators **Sea Hawk Watersports and Adventures** or **Noukhada Adventure Company**. Rental kayaks are also available. If you're lucky, you might also spot a dolphin or dugong in the waters.

Alternatively, head to **Al Gurm Corniche**, which has a 3.5km walkway and cycling track just across the water from the mangrove park. With its viewing terraces, shaded picnic spots, outdoor gym and wellness platforms, it offers plenty of opportunities to admire the mangroves and bird-watch or exercise outdoors. For a meal or coffee with mangrove views, sit down at one of the restaurants on the **Eastern Mangroves Promenade** close to the Anantara Eastern Mangroves hotel.

BEST KARAK SPOTS

House of Tea Cafeteria
Locals sing praises of the milky *zafran* tea (saffron tea), caramelly biscuit tea (karak topped with biscuits) and sweet karak tea at this no-frills cafeteria. $

Yadoo's House
You can't go wrong with the karak at this Emirati restaurant, whose name translates to 'grandmother's house'. Also does great Emirati breakfast. $

Filli Cafe
The *zafran* tea is an insider favourite, as are Indian teatime snacks like the *vada pav* (deep-fried potato dumpling in a bun). $

Al Hudayriyat Beach

MORE IN SHEIKH ZAYED GRAND MOSQUE & AROUND

Beach Day on Al Hudayriyat Island

Active seaside getaway

A morning or afternoon on the beach at **Al Hudayriyat Island**, just a 10-minute drive from Al Bateen, is a splendid idea if you're visiting Abu Dhabi during the relatively cooler months from October to April. While the sun-drenched shores and beautiful cerulean waters of **Marsana Beach** and neighbouring **Al Hudayriyat Beach** are reasons enough to visit the island, a host of activities means you can easily make a (very active) day of it.

Besides food trucks and cafes, at these public beaches you'll find a kids playground, an outdoor gym, courts for football, volleyball, basketball and tennis, water sports, running trails, and separate cycling tracks for road and mountain bikes. Adventure park **Circuit X** is home to a skate park, a BMX park, a three-level ropes obstacle course, a 100m zipline, a 50ft climbing wall and a kids splash park. Grab a coffee or a bite

WHERE TO GO FOR CASUAL EATS

Salt
Outside Umm Al Emarat Park, this food truck does juicy grilled beef sliders and crispy chicken sliders with Cheetos crumbs. $

Home Bakery
Inside Umm Al Emarat Park, this bakery is wildly popular for its velvety milk cake and delicious breakfast dishes. $$

Lgymat & Rgag
A neighbourhood favourite for *luqaimat* (doughnuts) and crispy *raqaq* (traditional Emirati bread). $

at one of the fantastic cafes in the area such as DRVN Coffee, Saddle Cafe or Rain.

The island is set to become a major sports destination, with plans to open a world-class surfing attraction, a velodrome, an urban park and several new beaches in the near future.

Art Exhibitions at Artbooth Gallery

Art in the city

Located in the Centro Capital Centre hotel, this new **art gallery**, founded to promote artistic exchange and collaboration between Beirut and the UAE, showcases the work of Lebanese, Emirati and other regional and international artists in a variety of mediums. Exhibitions are free to enter and most of the art is available for sale.

Wildlife Wonders at the National Aquarium

Aquatic museum with a rescue program

Opened in 2021 in Al Qana, a new waterfront leisure and dining hub, the **National Aquarium Abu Dhabi** houses over 46,000 marine and terrestrial animals and over 330 species, including sand tiger sharks, barracudas, lobsters, stingrays, super snakes and puffins. Interactive exhibits in 10 themed zones educate visitors about the UAE's heritage of pearl fishing, the biodiversity of the country's mangroves and coral reefs, and the marine ecosystems of the Atlantic, Pacific and Arctic Oceans. Free-flying birds and a 115kg reticulated python, believed to be the world's largest living snake, are found in the aquarium's rainforest zone.

The largest aquarium in the region as of June 2023, it claims to source its animals responsibly and ethically and runs a wildlife rescue, rehabilitation and release program in partnership with the Environment Agency – Abu Dhabi. Under this initiative, sea turtles found in a poor or distressed state are housed at the aquarium where they undergo a one-year rehabilitation program before being released into the sea. Other rescued residents include an abandoned African grey parrot and a loggerhead turtle found entangled in a fishing net.

A general admission ticket allows access to the 10 zones, while the behind-the-scenes tour includes a visit to the rehabilitation centre. Diving and glass-bottomed-boat tours of the aquarium are also available.

BEST WATERFRONT RESTAURANTS

Mado Al Qana Fabulous views over the Al Qana waterfront and mouthwatering Turkish *menemen* (eggs with peppers and tomatoes), kebabs, pide (flatbread) and lamb tandir (slow-cooked lamb). **$$**

Punjab Grill Enjoy a contemporary take on Indian dishes such as salmon tikka and butter chicken, alongside gorgeous canal views at this award-winning Indian restaurant. **$$$**

Otoro The sushi, Wagyu burger and *kushiyaki* grills at this Japanese restaurant in Al Qana make it a firm favourite among foodies in the know. **$$**

WHERE TO STAY AROUND SHEIKH ZAYAD GRAND MOSQUE

Ritz-Carlton Abu Dhabi Grand Canal Five-star beach resort with a Venetian village–style layout, manicured gardens, pools and restaurants. **$$$**

Anantara Eastern Mangroves Abu Dhabi Luxurious rooms with views of Eastern Mangrove National Park, plus restaurants and an exceptional spa. **$$**

Park Rotana A modern city hotel with five restaurants, a fitness centre, a swimming pool and views over Khalifa Park. **$$**

Al Mina & Saadiyat Island

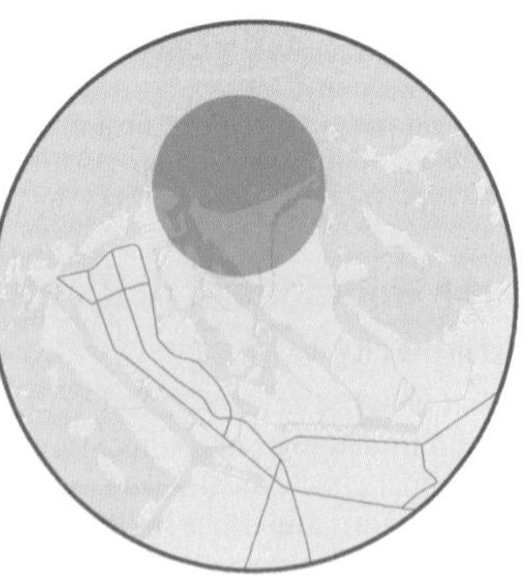

CULTURAL STRONGHOLD

Opened in 1972 in Al Mina, Mina Zayed, Abu Dhabi's central port, became the heart of the capital's commercial activity and ushered in an era of cultural exchange, as trade so often does.

The area around the dhow harbour was being redeveloped in June 2023, but as seen with the opening of the new Fish Market, its wealth of diversity and openness remains much the same. A Syrian salesman sells you Omani prawns at the fish market, a Bangladeshi shows you indoor plants at the Plant Souk, and a Keralite vendor offers you Lebanese apricots at the fruit and vegetable market.

The port's significance is so deeply embedded in the city's heritage that it continues to spark the imagination of nostalgic artists who organise art projects and exhibitions in and around repurposed warehouses in Al Mina.

A 10-minute drive from Mina Zayed takes you to Saadiyat Island (Island of Happiness), where cultural institutions such as Louvre Abu Dhabi, Abrahamic Family House, Manarat Al Saadiyat and the upcoming museums Guggenheim Abu Dhabi and the Natural History Museum Abu Dhabi, both set for completion in 2025, hint at Abu Dhabi's ambition to solidify its position as a cultural powerhouse in the region in the near future.

The architecture in this area, known as the Saadiyat Cultural District, is nothing short of astonishing, from the gigantic perforated dome of Louvre Abu Dhabi and the dune-like undulating exterior of the UAE Pavilion (home to Berklee Abu Dhabi) to the dramatic wing-shaped towers of the Zayed National Museum (under construction in 2023).

Elsewhere on this natural island, hawksbill turtles nest on dunes along the 9km beach from March to June, thanks to a government-run conservation program, humpback dolphins are often seen in the cerulean waters, and Arabian gazelles are spotted on the lush grounds of resorts and the Saadiyat Beach Golf Club. The slow rhythms of Saadiyat Island call for a relaxing beach holiday.

DON'T MISS...

LOUVRE ABU DHABI
A must-visit for its unique architecture and to see masterpieces from around the world.
p166

MANARAT AL SAADIYAT
Mingle with art enthusiasts at this cultural centre that hosts contemporary exhibitions and community events.
p169

ABRAHAMIC FAMILY HOUSE
Visit this complex with a church, mosque and synagogue to understand the UAE's culture of tolerance, diversity and peaceful coexistence.
p165

TOP TIP

To go from the past to the present, begin at the markets around Mina Zayed. The new Fish Market is a good place to start your day with lively banter and a delicious meal before exploring other markets in the area. Then head to Saadiyat Island where world-class museums offer a contemporary cultural experience.

Left: New Fish Market (p168); Above: Eminence Ahmed El-Tayeb Mosque, Abrahamic Family House (p165)

I LIVE HERE: AL MINA & SAADIYAT ISLAND MUST-SEES

Ebrahim Alharbi, founder and CEO of Golden Link Travel & Tourism (www.goldenlinktravel.com) and certified Emirati tour guide shares some of his favourite sights.

Dates, Fruits & Vegetables Market
From local to imported produce, everything is available. One area is dedicated to date varieties. Sample Colombian mangoes and 'banana grapes'.

Fish Market
The new Fish Market is a modern form of the traditional fish trade. Buy the seafood of your choice and get it cooked at one of the market restaurants.

Drive by Saadiyat Golf Club
A scenic drive starting at the roundabout in front of the Golf Club, this road is full of greenery and wildlife.

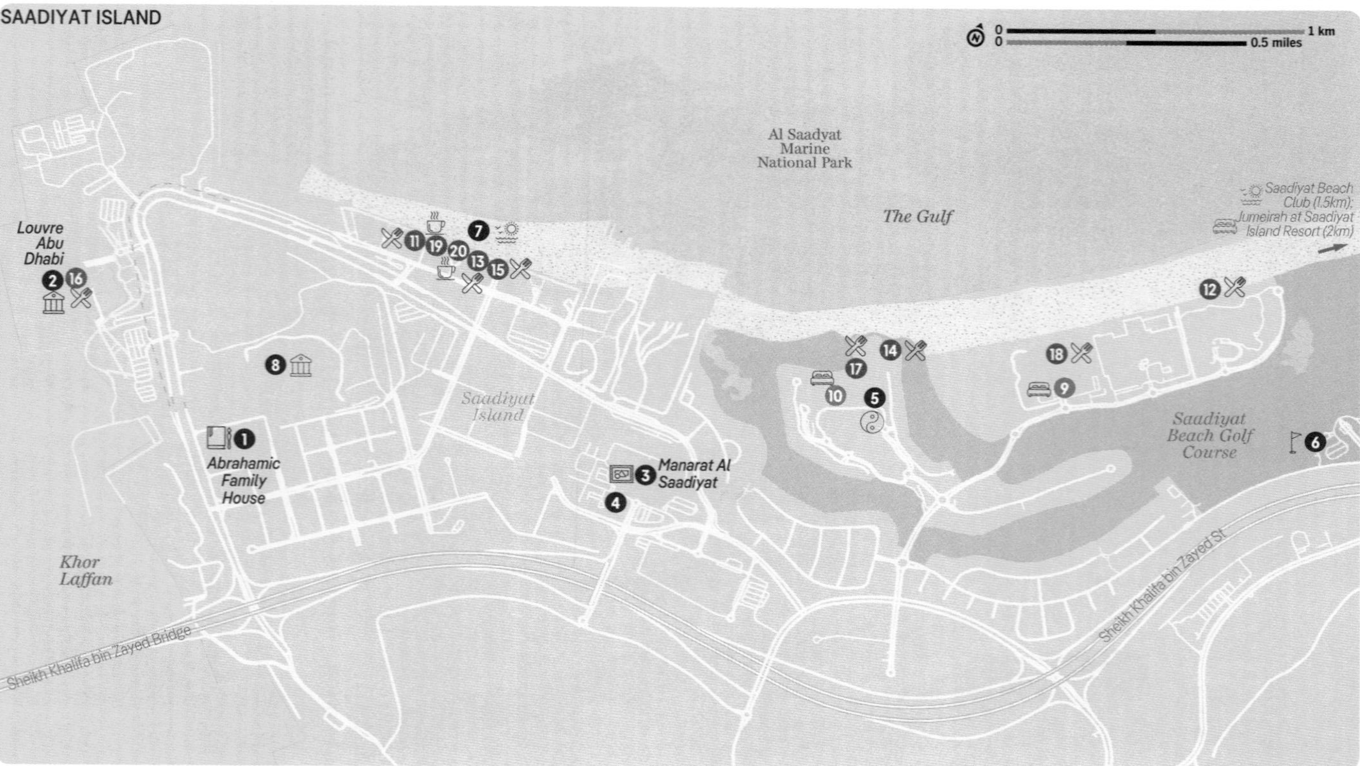
SAADIYAT ISLAND
0 1 km
0 0.5 miles
Al Saadyat Marine National Park
The Gulf
Saadiyat Beach Club (1.5km);
Jumeirah at Saadiyat Island Resort (2km)
Louvre Abu Dhabi
2
16
8
1
Abrahamic Family House
7
11
19
20
13
15
Saadiyat Island
3
Manarat Al Saadiyat
4
17
14
10
5
18
9
12
Saadiyat Beach Golf Course
6
Khor Laffan
Sheikh Khalifa bin Zayed Bridge
Sheikh Khalifa bin Zayed St

Abrahamic Family House

MAP P164

An ode to peaceful coexistence

A visit to this **complex**, home to a church, a mosque and a synagogue, offers a palpable sense of the UAE's culture of tolerance, diversity and peaceful coexistence. The three houses of worship welcome worshippers and visitors of all faiths. Designed by Ghanaian-British architect Sir David Adjaye, the site's architecture is full of religious symbolism.

Inside the **Eminence Ahmed El-Tayeb Mosque**, which faces the holy city of Mecca, sunlight streams in through *mashrabiya* (latticework) panels on the windows. The vault in the **St Francis Church**, which faces the east, is comprised of timber battens that represent the divine light. The bronze chainmail and skylight inside the **Moses Ben Maimon Synagogue**, which faces Jerusalem, reference a sukkah, a traditional tent used during the Jewish festival of Sukkot.

While you're free to walk around on your own, complimentary guided tours, held every 20 minutes, offer deeper context to the architectural significance and symbolism.

KNOW BEFORE YOU GO

Each of the buildings is in use for worship. While photography for personal use is permitted, it must not feature other visitors without their consent. To be allowed entry, both men and women must wear appropriate clothing that covers the arms and legs. Women should carry a scarf to be allowed entry into the mosque. Scarves and robes may be borrowed at the visitor centre but are subject to availability.

HIGHLIGHTS
1 Abrahamic Family House
2 Louvre Abu Dhabi
3 Manarat Al Saadiyat

SIGHTS
4 Berklee Abu Dhabi
5 Iridium Spa
6 Saadiyat Beach Golf Club
7 Soul Beach
8 Zayed National Museum (under construction)

SLEEPING
9 Saadiyat Rotana Resort
10 St Regis Saadiyat Island

EATING
11 Alkalime

see 2 Art Lounge Louvre Abu Dhabi
12 12 Beach House
13 Beirut Sur Mer
14 Buddha-Bar Beach
15 Ethr
16 Fouquet's Abu Dhabi
17 Sontaya
18 Turtle Bay Bar & Grill

DRINKING & NIGHTLIFE
19 LOCAL Mamsha
20 Mamsha Al Saadiyat
see 2 Marta Bar
see 2 Museum Café

HAMADALZAABI/SHUTTERSTOCK ©

Abrahamic Family House

MOHAMED SOMJI/LOUVRE ABU DHABI ©

PRACTICALITIES
Scan this QR code for prices and opening hours:

TOP SIGHT

Louvre Abu Dhabi

MAP P164

Having opened its doors in 2017, Louvre Abu Dhabi is the first museum of its kind in the region and an iconic piece of contemporary architecture in Abu Dhabi. Inside the museum's 23 galleries are art, artefacts, sculptures, manuscripts and exhibits that showcase cultural achievements by civilisations around the world, spanning thousands of years of human history.

DID YOU KNOW?
The mammoth dome that appears to float above the buildings at Louvre Abu Dhabi not only significantly shades the buildings and outdoor plaza, but also reduces the overall energy consumption of the museum.

Architecture

An astounding architectural masterpiece by Pritzker Prize-winning architect Jean Nouvel, the museum's most arresting feature is the gleaming 7500-tonne geometric steel dome that hovers over a medina-like cluster of 55 low-rise buildings, including 23 that house galleries. Comprising 7850 stars, the eight-layered, perforated dome creates a sublime pattern of dappled sunlight in the outdoor plaza, reminiscent of light filtering in through palm fronds. To fully admire this effect, known as the 'rain of light', spend some time on the steps on the terrace that lead to the pools. Inspired by early coastal settlements, the museum is surrounded by water on three sides.

Museum Galleries

In acknowledgement of the shared humanity of civilisations, the museum's galleries are organised chronologically into 12 chapters from the prehistoric age to the present day. These showcase over 600 art pieces, including statues, religious texts, pottery, paintings and other exhibits from the museum's permanent collection, as well as artworks on loan from museums such as the Musée d'Orsay, Centre Pompidou and Department of Antiquities of Jordan. The emphasis on universal themes and idiosyncrasies in creative expression, rather than geography or isolated histories, lies at the core of the museum's ethos.

Beginning at the **Grand Vestibule**, it's best to visit the galleries, spread over four wings, in order. The galleries in **Wing 1** tell the story of the first settlements and how the emergence of agricultural lifestyles shaped the concept of power, kingdoms, and eventually vast empires and civilisations. The galleries in **Wing 2** document the rise of religions such as Buddhism, Christianity and Islam over 2000 years and the emergence of trade routes which fuelled creativity, innovation and cultural exchange.

The four galleries in **Wing 3** are focused on navigation and cosmography, territorial, economic and military expansion, the early effects of globalisation, and the impact of manufacturing on societies and cultures. Finally, the galleries in **Wing 4** showcase the effects of the Industrial Revolution, colonialism and technological advancement on artistic expression, and the reinvention of art in the contemporary age.

In addition to the permanent collection, the museum also hosts temporary exhibitions. For those short on time, 45-minute guided express tours led by museum educators are available daily at noon. Alternatively, download the museum's multimedia guide, available on the App Store and Google Play, in English, Arabic, French, Mandarin, Russian, German and Hindi.

Highlights

Some highlights of the collection include a sculpture of Roman emperor Augustus from 27 BCE to 100 CE, a Bodhisattva statue dating from 100 CE to 300 CE, an 18th-century brass astrolabe by Muhammad ibn Ahmad Al-Battuti, Jacob Jordaen's 17th-century painting *The Good Samaritan*, Rembrandt's 17th-century painting titled *Head of a Young Man with Clasped Hands, Study of the Figure of the Christ*, and Georges de La Tour's 17th-century artwork *A Girl Blowing on a Brazier*.

Dining at Louvre Abu Dhabi

At **Aptitude Café**, enjoy breakfast, salads, sandwiches and mains. The **Museum Café** is a decent choice, but pricier. The rooftop **Art Lounge**, open during cooler months, is a good place for a sundowner. At **Fouquet's Abu Dhabi**, expect a Parisian brasserie–style fine-dining experience created in collaboration with notable chef Pierre Gagnaire. For a nightcap, head to the sumptuous **Marta Bar**.

CHILDREN'S MUSEUM

Spread across three floors, the **Children's Museum** engages young children from ages four to 10 through fun interactive elements and immersive exhibitions.

TOP TIPS

- Visiting several galleries within a few hours can get overwhelming. The outdoor walkways are a calm space for when you need to step outside.
- Download the incredibly helpful multimedia guide on your smartphone before you visit and use your earphones to do a self-guided tour and hear the stories behind the artworks and architectural features.
- End your visit with a guided 60-minute kayaking tour around the museum, offered by **Sea Hawk Water Sports & Adventures**. Book one around sunset for the best views and bring an extra pair of clothes to change into later.
- Wheelchairs and strollers are available for use on a complimentary basis.

Mina Markets

MAP P168

Market hopping in Mina Zayed

The markets around Mina Zayed, Abu Dhabi's main port, are a delightful treat for the senses.

At the **New Fish Market**, vendors eagerly point to rows of wild Omani lobsters, giant tiger prawns, pink Sultan Ibrahims and glossy white calamari. Pick your seafood of choice, then take it to the cleaning stations to be gutted and filleted. Bring it to one of the restaurants in the market to be grilled or fried, or order directly from their menus. The friendly vendors are willing to bargain and happy to let you take photos (but it's always nice to ask).

At the **Fruit & Vegetable Market**, a 10-minute walk away, buy Moroccan blueberries, Turkish grapes and Indian mangoes. Next door at the **Dates Market**, sample date varieties such as medjool, khalas, dabbas and shishi. Prices vary according to the origin, sweetness and texture. Some vendors will offer you *gahwa* (Arabic coffee) while you choose. It's not just dates – also consider *mamoul* (date cookies), date ketchup and dried figs.

At the **Carpet Souk**, every shop is a riot of colour where Afghani salesmen proudly unfurl rug after rug made of silk or wool in Afghanistan, Kashmir, Turkiye, Morocco or Iran. Handwoven rugs, some of which take two years to craft, are pricier than machine-made rugs. The folks at **Al Ghouth Carpet Shop**, in the business for generations, will offer tea while you choose. Bargaining is the norm, though prices are reasonable to begin with.

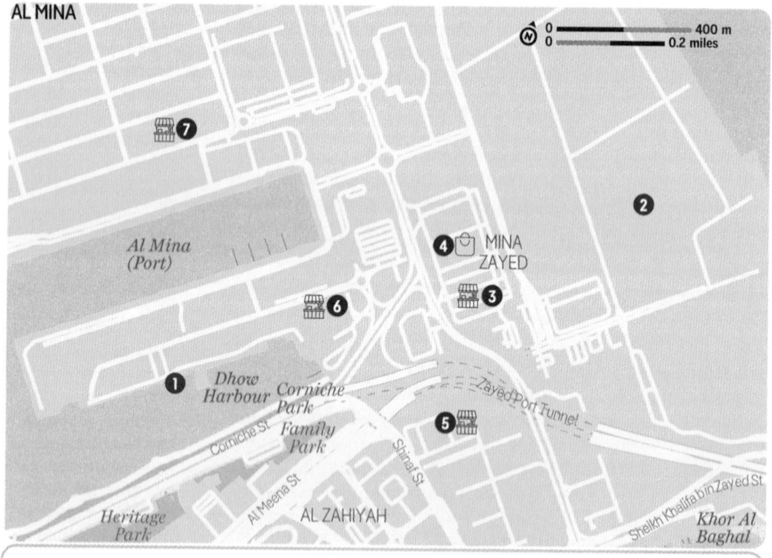

AL MINA

0 400 m
0 0.2 miles

SIGHTS
see 7 421
1 Dhow Harbour
2 Mina Zayed

SHOPPING
3 Abu Dhabi Dates Market
see 6 Bu Tafish Mina Fish Market
4 Fruit & Vegetable Market
5 Mina Carpet Market
6 New Fish Market
7 Warehouse 421

Manarat Al Saadiyat

MORE IN AL MINA & SAADIYAT ISLAND

Contemporary Culture at Manarat Al Saadiyat

MAP P164

Art, culture and community

One of a handful of venues at the heart of Abu Dhabi's exciting culture scene, **Manarat Al Saadiyat** plays host to art and culture exhibitions and community events throughout the year. Free to visit, the space hosts temporary exhibitions across three galleries and an atrium. Dedicated art and photography studios offer workshops and drop-in classes in art, sculpture, pottery and photography for both adults and children.

Mingle with like-minded folks at the centre's community events that include comedy nights, yoga and sound healing sessions and artist talks. The event schedule is regularly updated online. The centre also hosts **CineMAS**, an alternative

ABU DHABI ART FAIR

An annual five-day art showcase held in November at the Manarat Al Saadiyat, the **Abu Dhabi Art Fair** celebrates the works of local and international artists, both established and emerging. Widely attended by regional artists, art lovers and collectors, the fair involves exhibitions, commissions, curations, installations, performances, art talks and other events. The venue also exhibits artworks for sale, sourced from galleries around the world.

WHERE TO STAY ON SAADIYAT ISLAND

St Regis Saadiyat Island
Elegant rooms with butler service, a white-sand beach, outdoor pools, a spa, tennis courts and restaurants. **$$$**

Jumeirah at Saadiyat Island Resort
Sustainability-minded resort with luxe rooms, seven restaurants, pools, a private beach and a spa. **$$$**

Saadiyat Rotana Resort
Families will love the padel courts, football pitch, mini golf and fantastic kids club at this beach resort. **$$$**

JUBAIL MANGROVE PARK

A 10-minute drive from Saadiyat Island, **Jubail Mangrove Park** is not just a blissfully green pocket of the emirate; this carbon dioxide-absorbing mangrove forest also highlights Abu Dhabi's commitment to restoring its natural mangrove habitats in the fight against climate change. Turtles, crabs, herons, mangrove gastropods and various species of fish and migratory birds thrive in this ecosystem of grey mangroves, salt marshes and tidal lagoons.

Stroll along the park's 2km long boardwalk with information boards, viewpoints, a viewing tower, a beach platform and other points of interest. One-hour guided tours by kayak and electric boat are available (during high tide). To avoid disappointment, call and confirm tour timings before you visit.

film festival that screens movies by indie filmmakers from around and beyond the region and features director talks.

The outdoor park, **MAS Space**, is popular with residents who come to hang out, play basketball and table tennis, or practise kickflips on the skate ramp. Others discuss art over coffee or pizza, depending on the time of day, at the on-site Italian cafe and restaurant **L'Arte**.

Art Scene at 421

MAP P168

Abu Dhabi for art lovers

An arts and community space, located in a renovated warehouse in the Mina Zayed neighbourhood, **421** offers a closer look at the evolution of Emirati culture and society in the contemporary context through the lens of art. It regularly hosts art and photography exhibitions by artists from the UAE and around the region and encourages dialogue through special events, talks and film screenings. There's a quiet co-working space and library, a small courtyard, and a cafe if you want to linger after you've seen the exhibitions. The space is free to enter but requires you to register online before visiting.

Cafe Scene at Mamsha Al Saadiyat

MAP P164

Coffee and concept stores

Homegrown cafes, shops and restaurants dot the beachfront promenade at **Mamsha Al Saadiyat**, set across from the lively Soul Beach on Saadiyat Island.

At Emirati-owned cafe and concept store **Ethr**, grey floors, off-white ceiling drapes, wood furniture and indoor plants create a sanctuary-like space to escape the afternoon sun. Besides speciality coffee, try one of the locally inspired items on the menu such as the orange fig cake or the dates and sandalwood tea. Inspired by Emirati heritage, the merchandise around the cafe is crafted in their studio and includes keychains and necklaces with cultural motifs, fragrances, minimalistic leather wallets and laptop sleeves. Other branches are at the Abrahamic Family House (p165) on Saadiyat Island and at Al Ain Oasis.

At cafe, lifestyle store and barbershop **LOCAL Mamsha**, you'll find street-style clothing and merchandise sourced from around the world. Regulars come here to work while enjoying views of the beach and sipping on speciality coffee.

BEACH CLUBS ON SAADIYAT ISLAND

St Regis Saadiyat Island
A day pass offers access to three outdoor pools, including an adults-only and a kids pool, and the private white-sand beach.

Saadiyat Beach Club
Has a 650-sq-metre infinity pool set on a Blue Flag beach, live music, pool bar, three restaurants, Jacuzzi and padel tennis courts.

Soul Beach
Affordable access that includes a sunbed and umbrella as well as toilets and showers on a 1km-long public beach.

Play Golf at the Saadiyat Beach Golf Club

MAP P164

Golf with beach views

Designed by legendary golfer Gary Player, the award-winning par 72 course at the **Saadiyat Beach Golf Club** is the first beachfront golf course in the region. Set among three saltwater lakes and sand dunes, it's a stunning setting in which to practise your game. In the clubhouse, the restaurant **Hawksbill** serves Mediterranean fare. Tee times can be booked online on the Viyagolf website.

A Thai Feast at Sontaya

MAP P164

Robust flavours

Every dish at **Sontaya**, an elegant Thai restaurant located in the St Regis Saadiyat Island, is a celebration of flavours and textures. From satisfyingly crunchy panko-crumbed spring rolls and perfectly tangy papaya salad to flavoursome seafood, comforting pad thai and hearty curries, there are no wrong choices. Wash it all down with one of their signature cocktails or fruity mocktails. The service is top-notch, with the staff happy to make recommendations when you can't decide. The outdoor terrace, which includes poolside seating on what appear to be floating pavilions, is perfect for an intimate dinner date. It's a popular spot on the weekends, so make reservations.

Rejuvenate at Iridium Spa

MAP P164

Reason to relax

With a nod to the original Iridium Room that opened its doors in 1938 at the St Regis New York, **Iridium Spa** at St Regis Saadiyat Island offers plenty of reasons to swap a few hours of exploration for an invigorating massage or body treatment in one of its luxurious treatment rooms. Beyond traditional Thai, Balinese and Swedish massages, the menu features spa experiences that combine modern techniques with the region's wellness heritage, such as the Turkish Bath and the Royal Hammam, which incorporates a honey and royal jelly mask. Try the Moroccan Tekmida Ritual, which involves the application of an amber body scrub followed by a tension-relieving massage using hot wet towels. Arrive 30 minutes early to take advantage of the plunge pool and sauna facilities, which are complimentary for spa guests. If you're visiting with a significant other, the couples' spa suite comes with a private Jacuzzi and is worth the splurge.

WHY I LOVE SAADIYAT ISLAND

Natasha Amar, writer

Saadiyat Island feels like a special part of Abu Dhabi. It's where I most experience a tangible sense of Abu Dhabi's cultural evolution through sites that are an important representation of the emirate's self-identity. Whether it's wandering the galleries of Louvre Abu Dhabi, watching indie films at the Manarat Al Saadiyat or shopping heritage-inspired streetwear in Mamsha Al Saadiyat, I'm always reminded of how masterfully Abu Dhabi balances the past and the future. Then there's the work of Emirati and UAE-based artists, exhibited at venues such as Manarat Al Saadiyat, that offers a powerful lens through which everyone is invited to take a look.

WHERE TO EAT ON SAADIYAT ISLAND

Alkalime
Seasonal menu featuring açaí bowls, salads, bean burgers, dairy- and sugar-free desserts, and healthy juices and smoothies. **$$**

Beirut Sur Mer
Go here for their take on the Lebanese breakfast such as fig jam-topped grilled halloumi and *zaatar*-spiced scrambled eggs. **$$**

Buddha-Bar Beach
Alfresco beachfront dining on Japanese-Peruvian cuisine including tempura, ceviche and sushi, as well as delicious cocktails. **$$$**

Yas Island & Around

EXCITING LEISURE HUB

Just two years after the foundation stone was laid in 2007 on what was then a barren desert island, Yas Island welcomed thousands of F1 fans and spectators from around the world as host of the first Abu Dhabi Grand Prix, showing off its impressive 5.5km Hermann Tilke-designed race track – the Yas Marina Circuit.

Glowing above the race track stood the futuristic LED-lit colour-changing canopy of the only hotel in the world located on an F1 race track – today, the W Abu Dhabi Yas Island.

For petrolheads, there were more reasons to visit when Ferrari World Abu Dhabi opened its doors in 2010, welcoming supercar enthusiasts to a host of exhilarating experiences that had until then only been accessible to professional race-car drivers. Even today, over a decade later, hordes of visitors patiently queue up for a spot on Formula Rossa, still the world's fastest roller-coaster.

Since then, Yas Island has grown to become Abu Dhabi's biggest leisure and entertainment hub, and a must-visit for those looking to throw in a whole bunch of pulsating adventures on their Abu Dhabi holiday. With theme parks such as Yas Waterworld, Warner Bros World Abu Dhabi and SeaWorld Abu Dhabi, there's never a dull moment on the island.

Located on Yas Bay, alongside some of the island's best restaurants, cafes and nightlife venues, the spectacular 18,000-capacity Etihad Arena has seen the likes of Sting, Backstreet Boys, Maroon 5, Kevin Hart and AR Rahman perform to packed audiences. For those who want to take it easy, Yas Beach and luxurious beach clubs such as Café del Mar Abu Dhabi offer plenty of reasons to relax.

DON'T MISS...

YAS BAY WATERFRONT
For Japanese street food or a fun evening of live music, the bars at this waterfront promenade do not disappoint.
p177

FERRARI WORLD ABU DHABI
Visit this indoor theme park to be able to tick the world's fastest roller-coaster off your bucket list.
p176

YAS WATERWORLD
The UAE's best waterpark offers fun and adventure in equal doses, and plenty of ways to cool off.
p175

TOP TIP

The complimentary air-conditioned Yas Express shuttle bus stops at all the sights, attractions and hotels on Yas Island and is an excellent way to get around.

Left: W Abu Dhabi Yas Island (p178); Above: Ferrari World Abu Dhabi (p176)

I LIVE HERE: YAS ISLAND'S COOLEST SPOTS

Tamara Clarke (@iamtamaraclarke on Instagram), an American expat, freelance journalist and author living in Abu Dhabi, shares some of her favourite spots on Yas Island.

Yas South and Yas West Skateparks

Yas Island is Abu Dhabi's top destination for entertainment, but lesser-known venues, such as Yas South and Yas West skate parks, pack big fun, too. Overhead coverings help skaters keep it cool.

Central

The good times continue to roll at Central on Yas Bay with an arcade, bowling alley, and some of the best burgers on offer in the capital under one roof.

Yas Links

Zone out with stunning views of the Abu Dhabi skyline and the Arabian Gulf from Yas Links, an 18-hole golf course set alongside the water's edge.

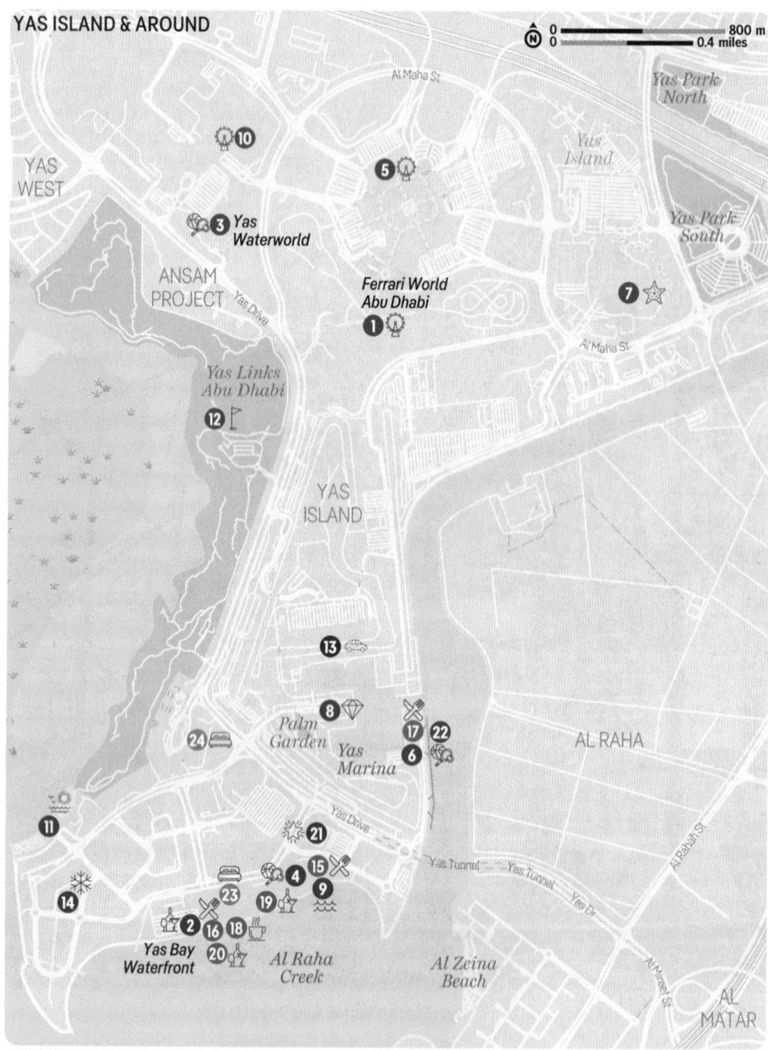

HIGHLIGHTS
1 Ferrari World Abu Dhabi
2 Yas Bay Waterfront
3 Yas Waterworld

SIGHTS
4 Etihad Arena
5 Fun Works
6 Musical Fountain
7 SeaWorld Abu Dhabi
8 Spa at W Abu Dhabi Yas Island
9 The Emerging Man
10 Warner Bros World Abu Dhabi
11 Yas Beach
12 Yas Links
13 Yas Marina Circuit
14 Yas South Skate Park

EATING
see 8 Angar
15 Art Market Yas Bay
16 Asia Asia
17 Cipriani

DRINKING & NIGHTLIFE
18 Cafe del Mar Beach Club Abu Dhabi
19 Lock, Stock & Barrel
see 21 Mad on Yas Island
20 Siddharta Lounge by Buddha-Bar
see 8 W Lounge

ENTERTAINMENT
21 White Abu Dhabi

SPORTS & ACTIVITIES
22 Seawings

SLEEPING
23 Hilton Abu Dhabi Yas Island
see 8 W Abu Dhabi Yas Island
24 Yas Island Rotana

Warner Bros World Abu Dhabi

World's largest indoor theme park

This record-setting indoor **theme park**, set over 153,000 sq metres, promises to bring out your inner child while you go on 29 fun and high-tech rides, attractions, roller-coasters and games, themed by iconic characters such as The Flintstones, The Jetsons, Scooby-Doo, Batman and Superman. Besides rides spread across six themed lands, there are 15-minute shows at the Warner Bros Plaza to keep you entertained, and plenty of restaurants and ice-cream shops to grab a bite at.

TOP RIGHT: RZULEV/SHUTTERSTOCK ©, BOTTOM LEFT: VLADIMIR ZHOGA/SHUTTERSTOCK ©

Warner Bros World Abu Dhabi

Yas Waterworld

Take the plunge

Slide into a day of adventure with Emirati character Dana on a quest for a pearl at the UAE's most exciting water-park. There are over 40 thrilling rides and slides, including the world's largest six-person tornado water coaster, a high-intensity looping waterslide, and the world's largest surfing sheet wave on a massive double-hump speed slide. Those not quite as keen on stomach-lurching adventures can take it easy in the wave pool, lazy river and 5D theatre.

Yas Waterworld

Yas Beach

Relaxed vibe and mangrove views

This beautiful palm-fringed sandy beach with calm, shallow waters is ideal for an afternoon of sun-soaking and dips in the infinity pool. If you're feeling active, play a game of volleyball or padel, ride a jet ski, or kayak around the mangroves across the shore. A beachfront restaurant serves salads, sandwiches, pizzas and seafood mains, plus smoothies and cocktails.

Weekends are upbeat with pool parties and live DJs. Entrance includes towels and sun loungers with parasols. Private air-conditioned chalets and poolside cabanas are also available to rent. The Ladies Day package (on Wednesday) offers good value for money for women planning to spend the day. If you're staying at a hotel on Yas Island, ask if they offer complimentary access to Yas Beach.

Ferrari World Abu Dhabi

High-octane thrills

Housed in a striking red structure inspired by the classic double curve side of the Ferrari GT chassis, this indoor **theme park** offers over 40 dizzying Ferrari-themed experiences. The biggest draw here is **Formula Rossa**, the world's fastest roller-coaster that surges from 0 to 240km/h in a heart-pounding 4.9 seconds while reaching a height of 52m. If you've ever wondered what it's like to drive an F1 racing car, the Formula Rossa is your answer.

Other exhilarating rides include **Flying Aces**, where you'll ascend to 63m reaching speeds of up to 120km/h on the world's highest roller-coaster loop, and **Turbo Track**, which propels you through the roof and brings you back down in a dramatic zero gravity fall.

For an additional Dhs895, the **Ferrari Driving Experience** lets you zip around Yas Island in a Ferrari, accompanied by an instructor. The park's 290m go-karting track is the UAE's first electric go-kart circuit.

Experiences for younger kids and families include remote-controlled boats and cars, a tyre-changing challenge and an immersive 4D theatre.

Ferrari World Abu Dhabi

Yas Marina Circuit

Need for speed

This Hermann Tilke-designed track made its F1 debut as the host of the Abu Dhabi Grand Prix in 2009. Outside of race season, the **Yas Marina Circuit** offers guided tours of the venue and a host of exciting motorsports experiences. Get behind the wheel of an Alfa Romeo Giulia Quadrifoglio and feel the power of its 510 BHP Twin Turbo or sign up for a 10-minute drive in the single-seat Formula Yas 3000 with its quick F1-style paddle shift gear changes and a 0 to 100km/h acceleration in a mere 2.8 seconds. Go drag racing in a Chevrolet Camaro SS, sharpen your drifting skills in a Polaris RZR RS1, or hit the 1km track at Yas Kartzone.

Cipriani

YAS BAY SCULPTURES

The waterfront promenade at Yas Bay is dotted with a dozen fascinating **art installations** and **sculptures** by talented artists from around the world. These include *The Emerging Man*, a giant 8m-high bronze-coloured head wearing a diving mask, and two enormous hands emerging from the water; a 10m-high golden flower sculpture called *Flower Parent and Child* by Japanese artist Takashi Murakami; and four giant *Astrocat* sculptures by CoolRainLabo.

MORE IN YAS ISLAND & AROUND

Bar-Hopping at Yas Bay Waterfront

Nightlife central on Yas Island

You'll find the best new restaurants, bars and cafes at this lively waterfront promenade. Come evening the 3km boardwalk becomes the hangout spot for those looking to party, plus holidaying families and stylish locals. Go to **Akiba Dori** for Japanese street food, groove to live bands at **Lock, Stock & Barrel** and dance the night away at **White Abu Dhabi**. Have the ultimate pool day in cabanas and villas with private Jacuzzis at the award-winning floating beach club **Café Del Mar**.

Also here is **Etihad Arena** with a capacity of 18,000, which hosts big-name concerts, sporting events, stand-up comedy and musicals. Check the website for event schedules.

SeaWorld Abu Dhabi

Marine theme park

The experiences here include live shows, rides, games, rollercoasters and animal encounters. Other than 68,000 marine animals in the aquarium, expect to see sealions, dolphins,

WHERE TO EAT ON YAS ISLAND

Art Market Yas Bay
Cool, arty vibe, good coffee, healthy bowls and salads, and delicious toasts and sandwiches. **$**

Asia Asia
Maki rolls, robata grills, curries, and cocktails infused with wasabi and saffron, plus a buzzing atmosphere. **$$$**

Cipriani
Fine-dining Italian restaurant serving dishes like ricotta gnocchi, pan-seared scallops, and Chilean sea bass. **$$$**

flamingoes, walruses, macaws, puffins, seals, sea otters, sharks and rays in captivity. Animal encounters (termed 'expeditions') and presentations involve walruses, sealions, sea otters, seals, dolphins, and an underwater walking tour in the aquarium.

From all this, the jugglers, stilt walkers and live shows (with human actors and themes around pearl diving and polar exploration) are a welcome distraction. Visitors can also peek into the in-house veterinary facility. SeaWorld Abu Dhabi runs research, rescue, rehabilitation and education programs and claims to be committed to marine conservation work. The theme park is certified by Global Humane.

BEST BARS ON YAS ISLAND

Lock, Stock & Barrel
Energetic crowds, live music and four-hour-long happy hour (up to eight hours on the weekends) at this edgy industrial bar.

W Lounge
You'll want to dress up to match the glamour at this stylish lounge that serves excellent cocktails and also offers views over Yas Marina.

Siddharta Lounge by Buddha-Bar
Tapas and cocktails with views over Yas Bay. On the weekends, the party continues late into the night with visiting Buddha-Bar DJs, dancers and acrobats.

Recharge at the Spa at W Abu Dhabi Yas Island

Restful downtime

Take a break from chasing thrills at the award-winning **Spa at W Abu Dhabi Yas Island** with massages, body and facial treatments, and deeply cleansing hammam treatments to leave you feeling brand new. Try the 60-minute Abu Dhabi Soul, which involves a thorough exfoliation using a rich scrub followed by a rejuvenating massage with aromatic essential oils.

Indian Feast at Angar

A taste of India

The chefs in the kitchen at this restaurant at the W Abu Dhabi Yas Island sure know how to cook up a storm, evident by how full the place is even on a weeknight. Go straight for the juicy tandoor grills such as the melt-in-your-mouth saffron herbs chicken tikka and the spicy lamb chops. The coconutty fish curry is flavourful and the butter chicken, as the name suggests, is 'Old Delhi' level delicious indeed.

Golf At Yas Links

Swing into scenic surrounds

The region's first links course, this gorgeous Par 72 championship course designed by Kyle Phillips is a must for keen golfers. Set among rolling hills and mangroves on the western shore of Yas Island, it currently ranks 48th in Golf Digest's Top 100 courses in the world. Besides the 18-hole course, there's also a nine-hole par 3 academy course, as well as a clubhouse, swimming pool, fitness centre and a men's spa.

WHERE TO STAY ON YAS ISLAND

W Abu Dhabi Yas Island
The world's only hotel located on an F1 racetrack. Avant-garde design, award-winning restaurants and bars, and an exceptional spa. **$$$**

Hilton Abu Dhabi Yas Island
Bright and modern rooms with waterfront views, five restaurants and a massive outdoor pool at this luxurious hotel. **$$$**

Yas Island Rotana
Spacious and modern rooms, six restaurants, a fully equipped gym, outdoor pool and complimentary access to Yas Beach. **$$**

W Abu Dhabi Yas Island

Day Trips from Dubai & Abu Dhabi

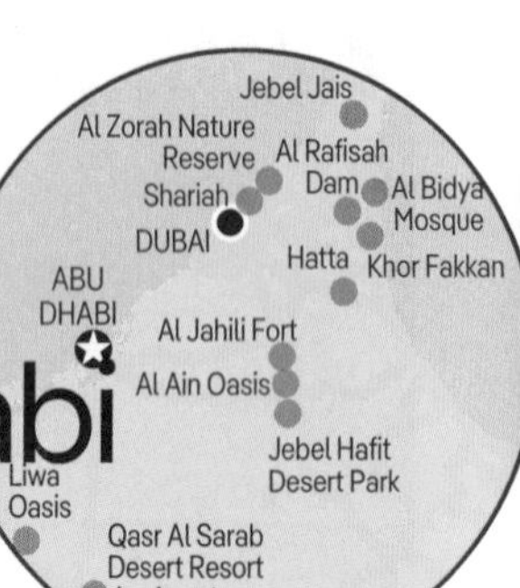

Venture beyond Dubai and Abu Dhabi to see sublime deserts, verdant oases, craggy mountains and fortresses that nod to the region's past.

If you're after deeper context about the UAE's history, culture and people, then leave the cities behind for its surprisingly diverse landscapes. The rippled orange-red dunes of the Empty Quarter, sun-dappled emerald oases of Liwa and Al Ain, and jagged peaks of the Hajar Mountains aren't just stunning landscapes that make for pretty pictures – their stone fortresses, ancient tombs, palace museums and laid-back villages chart the UAE's journey since the beginning of human civilisation in the region – as far back as the Neolithic period. Meanwhile, the emirate of Sharjah invites you to immerse yourself in the region's art and culture – both traditional and contemporary – through its impressive museums and vibrant festivals.

TOP TIP

While public transport links the cities of Dubai and Abu Dhabi to some day-trip destinations such as Hatta, Ajman and Al Ain, renting a car reduces travel times significantly.

Dhafeer Fort

PHILIP LANGE/SHUTTERSTOCK ©

Rub' al Khali

Dramatic Landscapes of Liwa Oasis

Dunes, oases and forts

Some of the most captivating landscapes in the UAE lie in Abu Dhabi's Al Gharbia region, a 2½-hour drive from the city. Here, gargantuan dunes turn a deep orange-red as you get closer to **Rub' al Khali**, the world's largest continuous sand desert. Also known as the Empty Quarter, most of it lies in Saudi Arabia, with parts spread across the UAE, Oman and Yemen. Traversed by nomadic Bedouin tribes such as the Bani Yas (ancestors of the current rulers of the UAE) for thousands of years, it is one of the harshest environments in the world.

To its north stands the crescent-shaped **Liwa Oasis** with quiet villages, date plantations and forts. Most of the forts were built in the 19th century to defend the settlements' farms and water sources, but were rebuilt after they fell into disrepair. Some worth visiting are **Al Yabbana**, rebuilt in the early 2000s, **Al Meel Fort** and **Mezaira'a Fort**, both rebuilt in the 1980s, and **Dhafeer Fort**, which was reconstructed in 1996. Entry is free. Expect to spend 10 minutes at each one. Climb up to the watchtowers for views.

FRUIT OF THE OASIS

The **date palms** of Liwa Oasis are a precious resource for the region, where traditionally the trunk, fronds and fibre have been used in construction and handicrafts, among other uses. Perhaps no other part of the date palm is as culturally significant as its sweet, caramelly fruit. Prized for their nutritional value, dates are an integral part of the Emirati diet. Harvested until autumn, dates are also an important source of income for local producers. The **Liwa Dates Store** in Mezaira'a is worth a visit to buy dates, date jams and date *mamoul* (cookies). Check if your visit coincides with the annual **Liwa Date Festival**, which involves dates competitions and auctions.

WHERE TO GRAB A BITE IN LIWA OASIS

Liwa Dates Cafe Stop for iced coffee, milkshakes or date ice cream at this cafe in Mezaira'a. $

Amber Rolls Restaurant and Grill Portions are generous at this restaurant that serves hearty Pakistani meat dishes, *mandi*, grills and kebabs. $

Liwa Alhaditha Markets & Bakery Fuel up on your Liwa road trip with fresh baklava, *fatayer* and *kunafeh* at this bakery that also does pizza. $

BACK FROM THE BRINK

The **Qasr Al Sarab Protected Area** is a 308-sq-km reserve home to several species of birds, reptiles and desert mammals. A remarkable success story of conservation is that of the Arabian oryx, a desert antelope with a white coat and ringed horns, declared extinct in the wild in the 1970s. Thanks to a 50-year conservation project that began in 1968 with a captive breeding program and the Sheikh Mohamed Bin Zayed Arabian Oryx Reintroduction Programme in 2007, the species was reintroduced in the wild by the Environment Agency Abu Dhabi. At the end of 2022, the UAE was home to the largest population of Arabian oryx (about 1595) reintroduced in the wild.

Qasr Al Sarab Desert Resort by Anantara

From Mezaira'a, continue south to **Tel Moreeb**, a 300m-high dune and the tallest in the UAE. The annual **Liwa International Festival**, held in December, features motorsport racing events that see the region's daredevils drive up its steep slope in modified 4WDs, motorbikes and UTVs while thousands of spectators cheer on. While you might not have similar aspirations, it's worth renting a car to do the spectacular drive to the main car park. This paved road snakes past staggering dunes with lay-bys to stop and admire the landscape, which becomes especially stunning around sunset. A 4WD is not necessary.

Buses on the X60 line run from Al Nahyan, Abu Dhabi Bus Station to Mezaira'a Bus Station (Dhs32.50, 3½ hours).

Dine Among Dunes at Qasr Al Sarab

A meal to remember

Surrounded by enormous dunes, the **Qasr Al Sarab Desert Resort by Anantara** with its bubbling fountains and palm-tree-lined walkways stands like a magnificent fortress at the edge of the astounding desert expanse that is the Rub' al Khali. A meal at one of the restaurants, also open to day visitors with reservations, means you'll be admiring rippled dunes right from your table indoors, poolside or on a rooftop terrace

WHERE TO STAY A NIGHT IN THE DESERT

Qasr Al Sarab Desert Resort by Anantara Stately rooms and pool villas, six restaurants, pool, fitness centre, and a range of desert experiences. **$$$**

Bab Al Nojoum Bateen Liwa Comfortable villas with private pools and firepits set among the dunes. Pool, fitness centre and desert activities. **$$$**

Liwa Hotel Classic rooms and villas, an outdoor pool and a restaurant, set on a hilltop in Mezaira'a. **$$$**

while enjoying some of the best food in the oasis. At **Ghadeer**, open for lunch and dinner, choose from Mediterranean salads, meze, seafood, pasta and pizza. At steakhouse **Suhail**, open for dinner only, the menu features prime steaks and an award-winning wine list, best enjoyed on the rooftop terrace.

A Deeper Desert Experience

Sand beneath your feet

While a meal or sunset among the dunes is a good enough reason to visit Qasr Al Sarab, the resort also offers **guided desert experiences** to those who want to venture deeper. These should preferably be booked in advance by day visitors. Explore the dunes on soft desert drives, fat bikes, Polaris buggies or camelback. For a more tranquil experience, there's nothing like a stargazing session in the heart of the desert. Learn about celestial bodies as the resident adventure guide animatedly points out constellations, tells stories of Arab astronomers, and invites you to appreciate the night sky through a telescope.

CULTURAL HERITAGE OF AL AFLAJ

Al Ain Oasis is a good place to see ***aflaj*** (plural of *falaj*) at work, and this 3000-year-old method of irrigation using a network of hand-dug underground and surface channels continues to be an effective means of irrigating arable land. The two types of *falaj* systems in use in Al Ain are known as Al Aini and Dawood. The water comes from mother wells sunk into the water table and from seasonal streams in the Hajar Mountains. The evidence of *falaj* from the Iron Age in the nearby Hili Oasis is indicative of the region's long agricultural history. Al Aflaj is on Unesco's Representative List of the Intangible Cultural Heritage of Humanity.

Wander Through Al Ain Oasis

A canopy of palm fronds

A 90-minute drive from the city of Abu Dhabi, **Al Ain**, whose name translates to 'the spring', surprises with its verdant oases, leafy parks, historic forts, archaeological sites and relaxed pace of life. Begin your exploration of Abu Dhabi's 'green city' with a leisurely wander or bicycle ride at **Al Ain Oasis**, the largest of the six oases in the city to be included in the Unesco World Heritage Cultural Sites of Al Ain.

Rent a bike or buggy at the main entrance at the West Gate, or set off on foot on the shaded pathways that lead visitors past thousands of date palms and fruit-bearing mango, orange, banana and sidr trees. Narrow *falaj* irrigation channels, unique to the region, feed hundreds of farms in the oasis around the year. Even with the crowds on the weekends, it's easy to get wonderfully lost so that your only company in this labyrinthine oasis are the birds chirping among the palm fronds. **Ethr**, a cafe (closed in summer) in the oasis, serves iced drinks and coffee. An **eco-centre** offers information about the history of the oasis.

Buses on the X90 line run from Al Nahyan, Abu Dhabi Bus Station to Al Ain Central Bus Station (Dhs27, 2¼ hours). From Dubai's Al Ghubaiba Bus Station, regular buses run on the E201 route to Al Ain Central Bus Station (Dhs25, 2¼ hours).

WHERE TO EAT IN AL AIN

Al Fanar Restaurant & Cafe
Wooden tables in a leafy courtyard surrounded by arched columns transport you to a traditional Emirati home. **$$**

Zaher El Laymoun
Regulars love this restaurant in Al Jahili for its shawarma and grills, generous portions and friendly service. **$$**

Golden Sheep Restaurant
You can't go wrong here with the kebabs, Jordanian *mansaf*, and grilled seafood and meats. **$$**

Visit the Historic Al Jahili Fort

Stories of the desert and oases

During its existence, the mud-brick **Al Jahili Fort**, built in 1898 on the orders of Sheikh Zayed bin Khalifa Al Nahyan (also known as Zayed the First), has served as a royal residence and the military headquarters of British forces. After being restored a few times, it now houses a cultural centre with multimedia exhibits and a gallery with a permanent exhibition centred on the travels of British explorer Sir Wilfred Thesiger in the region, which notably include crossing the Empty Quarter twice in the 1940s, with the help of his Bedouin companions.

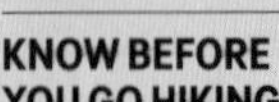

KNOW BEFORE YOU GO HIKING

It's best to go hiking in Hatta from October to April, when the temperatures are lower and the afternoon sun isn't quite as harsh. Don't underestimate the heat from June to September, when the heat and humidity can leave you feeling dizzy without warning. With scree and loose rocks, the rough terrain isn't exactly a walk in the park – wear hiking shoes with good grip to avoid slips and ankle injuries.

Carry at least 3L of water per person (4L for longer hikes) to prevent dehydration.

Ancient Tombs at Jebel Hafit Desert Park

A piece of history

Located at the foot of Jebel Hafit, the **Jebel Hafit Desert Park** in Al Ain is a 20-minute drive from the city. Part of the Unesco World Heritage Cultural Sites of Al Ain, this fascinating archaeological site is home to remains that indicate the presence of nomadic pastoral communities in the area during the Neolithic period. Scattered around the park are over 500 beehive tombs dating to the Bronze Age, nearly 5000 years ago. Discovered during excavations in 1959, some of these circular single-chamber tombs have been restored. To explore this rugged landscape on a guided hike, mountain bike, buggy or camel ride, visit the park's activity hub (open from September to May).

Watch the Sunset at Jebel Hafit

Sublime views

From Jebel Hafit Desert Park, a 30-minute drive, half of which involves an 11.6km ascent up the mountain via the excellent winding Jabal Hafeet St, takes you to the summit viewpoint at **Jebel Hafit**. At 1249m, Jebel Hafit is Abu Dhabi's highest peak (and the second highest in the UAE), and offers spectacular panoramic views over the rocky landscape and the city of Al Ain, making it a fantastic spot to watch the sunset. There are car parks and viewpoints to stop at along the way, but the best views are from the top. There's ample parking, along with a children's playground, toilets and two cafeterias (closed in summer). Bring a picnic blanket and a jacket if you're visiting from November to February.

BEST PARKS IN AL AIN

Al Jahli Park
Large park with walking paths, playgrounds, and lawns where groups play football.

Green Mubazzarah Park
Beautiful park surrounded by Jebel Hafit. BBQ areas, hot springs, a lake (with kayaking) and public pools.

Al Wadi Park
Lovely park with shaded seating, playground, outdoor gym and sports courts.

Tombs, Jebel Hafit Desert Park

AMONG THE UAE'S OLDEST SETTLEMENTS

Formerly Omani territory, Hatta became an exclave of the emirate of Dubai around 1850. Archaeological excavations in the region, including tombs and petroglyphs, have unearthed evidence of settlement here since the Early Bronze Age. It is believed that villages in this region, then called Al Hajareen, were settled by communities who would move between the mountains and fertile valleys seasonally, practising agriculture and animal husbandry.

Mountain Adventures in Hatta

Highlands of Dubai

A 90-minute drive from Dubai, the town of **Hatta**, 130km southeast of the city at the foot of the Hajar Mountains, is a gateway into a landscape of craggy peaks, wadis (valleys or riverbeds), lakes, natural springs, fertile valleys and farmland where glimpses of village life abound.

The temperatures here are a few degrees lower than in Dubai year-round, making it a popular weekend getaway for Dubai residents. The sights around Hatta include conservation areas, fortresses, mosques, farms, dams, a heritage museum, an apiary and an activity centre.

The town sits just north of the **Hatta Mountain Reserve**, a protected reserve inhabited by indigenous wildlife such as the endangered Arabian tahr, Arabian leopard and Egyptian vulture, along with other species of birds, fish and amphibians.

Several marked hiking and biking trails crisscross these dry wadis and dusty peaks, passing fruit orchards, lakes and farms along the way and presenting the opportunity to explore this stunning landscape and possibly spot some of the area's wildlife. For hikers, there are approximately

WHERE TO STAY IN AL AIN

Al Ain Rotana
Modern and spacious rooms, swimming pools, padel courts, a fitness centre, a spa, and six restaurants. **$$**

Radisson Blu Hotel & Resort, Al Ain With three outdoor pools, tennis courts and five restaurants, this is a good affordable choice for families. **$**

Aloft Al Ain
Comfortable rooms, a rooftop pool, a gym, an international restaurant and a sports and cocktail bar with live music. **$**

WHY I LOVE HATTA

Natasha Amar, writer

This scenic mountain town is only a 90-minute drive from Dubai, but feels like a world away from its fast-paced lifestyle and offers a much-needed getaway for nature-loving city-dwellers like me. There's a raw quality and a calm quietness to the beauty of this rugged landscape dotted with emerald date farms and bright blue lakes. Between the cooler months of October and March, Hatta is full of opportunities to get (and stay) outdoors, whether it's kayaking on the calm waters of Hatta Dam or scrambling up one of its many trails with mountain goats for company. Staying overnight, or long enough to see the night sky light up with stars, is always worth it.

SARATH MAROLI/SHUTTERSTOCK ©

Kayaking, Hatta Dam

32km of trails, while cyclists can set off on nearly 50km of bike trails, all colour-coded according to varying difficulty and distance.

The trails are open year-round (6am to 6pm) and begin near the **Hatta Wadi Hub** (limited operating hours from May to October), where you can also find trail maps and information, and rent mountain bikes and e-bikes.

Hatta is set to become a major outdoor adventure destination in the next few years, with plans for the addition of an inland beach, a funicular railway, a lake, a souq and 120km of bicycle paths.

Hatta Express buses run on the H02 route from the Dubai Mall Bus Station to Hatta Bus Station (Dhs25, two hours, six daily). The Hatta hop-on, hop-off H04 bus operates on a circular route that begins and ends at Hatta Bus Station and stops at Hatta Wadi Hub, Hatta Hill Park, Hatta Dam and the Heritage Village (Dhs2 per stop, every 30 minutes).

WHERE TO GO GLAMPING IN HATTA

Sedr Trailers Resort
Air-con Airstream trailers on the banks of Hatta Dam. Comfy beds, TVs, wi-fi and a minibar plus bathrooms. **$$$**

Hatta Caravan Park
Air-con campers with en suite bathroom, living area, wi-fi, TV, kitchenette and outdoor terrace. **$$$**

Hatta Dome Park
Spacious air-conditioned dome tents with bathrooms, TV, wi-fi, and a terrace with BBQ and fire pit. **$$$**

Kayaking at Hatta Dam

Teal waters and jagged peaks

Built in the 1990s to provide a sustainable source of water to the area's residents, **Hatta Dam** is one of Dubai's most popular kayaking spots. With jagged peaks rising around the calm teal waters of the lake, the setting is quite dramatic. It's easy to spend a few hours paddling on the water, especially between October and May when the weather is pleasant. Kayaks, water bikes, pedal boats, donut boats and more can be rented at **Hatta Kayak**. Expect reduced operating hours on weekdays from mid-May to October.

Hatta Dam is also the site of a hydroelectric power plant being built by the Dubai Electricity and Water Authority. The first of its kind in the region, it is expected to be completed in late 2024 and is part of a larger strategy to derive most of Dubai's power from clean energy sources by 2050.

Action-Packed Experiences at Wadi Hub

Thrills for all ages

This activity centre runs the gamut of adventures in Hatta, from wall climbing, archery and axe-throwing to tube-sliding, ziplining and a dizzying human slingshot experience that reaches nearly 100km/h. A net walkway with lookouts, a multipurpose ropes course, zorbing, gel ball, and trampolines for both children and adults means there's something for every age group. A good way to cool off on a hot afternoon? One of the steep slides at Wadi Hub that drop you right into a plunge pool at nearly 80km/h. The centre closes for the summer, generally from mid-May to the end of September, but season opening dates can vary depending on the weather.

Explore Hatta Heritage Village

A wander through the old days

Under restoration in early 2023, the **Hatta Heritage Village** is a reconstructed mountain village that lets you peek into village life nearly 3000 years ago. For a glimpse of rural life in the old days, wander through reconstructed stone houses, courtyards, a *majlis* and a museum exhibiting traditional tools, handicrafts, clothing and weapons. The restored mud-brick and stone-built **Hatta Fort** dates to 1896 and was used for both defensive and residential purposes. Two round watchtowers, built in the 1880s, offer views over verdant farms. Visit the nearby **Al Sharia** farm to stroll under the shade of palm trees and see a working *falaj* (p183).

RESPECTFUL BEHAVIOUR OUTSIDE OF CITIES

In smaller, more conservative, towns and villages around the eastern coast of the UAE, pay special attention to being respectful towards the locals. For women, that means dressing in loose, comfortable clothing that covers the shoulders and knees. Both men and women intending to visit a mosque should wear clothing that covers the arms and ankles. Additionally, women also need to cover their heads with a scarf.

You might notice some Muslim women dressed more conservatively here, whether local residents or fellow tourists. Many wear a *niqab* (a veil that covers the face except for the eyes) and will not interact with men outside of family members. It should be obvious that photographing them, or anyone else, without their consent is inappropriate.

WHERE TO EAT IN HATTA

Tanoor Restaurant
This Hatta restaurant is famous for its juicy lamb, slow-cooked underground and served with rice. **$$**

Al Hajarain
From quesadillas and pizza to kebabs, this restaurant at the Hatta Heritage Village has something for everyone. **$$**

Janam Restaurant
Middle Eastern, Turkish and Indian fare such as kebabs and biryani at this traditional restaurant. **$$**

Visit the Hatta Honeybee Garden

Get buzzy

At the **Hatta Honeybee Garden and Discovery Center**, the UAE's first queen bee-rearing facility that's home to nearly 300 beehives, slip into a protective beekeeper's suit and veiled hat and get ready for an immersive masterclass in beekeeping. Besides learning about the significance of bees in the natural ecosystem, you'll see the bees at work in the beehives in this beautiful 16,000-sq-metre bee garden with indigenous honey-producing ghaf and sidr trees. Afterwards sample varieties of fresh honey, spiced honey fusions, nutritious raw honeycomb and propolis.

ENCLAVE WITHIN AN ENCLAVE

Madha is an Omani enclave in the UAE with low-rise houses, narrow roads and farms. The modernised village of **Nahwa** lies within Madha as an enclave of Sharjah (UAE territory). Look at it on a map to see why Madha is nicknamed the 'Oman Donut'. This double enclave dates to the 1930s when this region was the Trucial States. When asked to choose from the four dominant clans, the villagers of Madha pledged allegiance to the Sultan of Oman, hoping that his military prowess would protect their freshwater well – precious in the pre-oil era – while Nahwa pledged allegiance to the Qasimis, the current rulers of Sharjah and Ras Al Khaimah.

Scenic Views at Al Rafisah Dam

Nature and history in Wadi Shie

From Dubai, a 90-minute drive towards Khor Fakkan (easiest by rental car) brings you to **Al Rafisah Dam**. Built in the 1980s, the dam, which is part of the emirate of Sharjah, was developed as a recreational area. From the terrace, there are gorgeous views of turquoise waters set against the Hajar Mountains.

To get close to the lake's resident ducks, rent a kayak, pedalo or donut boat at **Al Khor Kayak**. There's a restaurant (under renovation at the time of research), while shaded picnic spots offer opportunities to enjoy a packed lunch. A constructed waterfall and kids play area make this spot popular with families.

A 1km-long walkway, signposted as The Walk, follows the bridge over the dam and continues along the mountain's edge. It leads to **Najd Al Maqsar Heritage Village**, an archaeological site within Wadi Shie where petroglyphs indicate the presence of settlements in the area dating to 2000 BCE. Here, restored 100-year-old houses built of mud, stone and palm fronds surround a 300-year-old fortress. The hilltop watchtower offers views over Khorfakkan. There are plans to develop the village into a heritage hotel in the near future.

If you're after a bigger challenge, **Al Rafisah Hiking Trail** winds up the mountain steeply after the bridge and leads to stunning views from the summit. It can also be experienced as a three-hour rerturn hike if you continue further up to **Al Suhub Rest Area**, also famous for panoramic views over Khorfakkan.

Next to the visitor centre at Al Rafisah Dam is a mosque, an ice-cream shop and a supermarket. Toilets and parking facilities are open year-round, but expect reduced operating hours at the restaurant, kayak rental and shops from May to October.

WHERE TO STAY IN HATTA

JA Hatta Fort Hotel Spacious rooms and villas with stunning mountain views. There's a pool, archery, padel tennis, mini-golf, a spa and more. **$$$**

Damani Lodges Resort Cosy air-con mountain lodges with wi-fi, TVs and private terraces overlooking Hatta Wadi Hub. **$$**

Hatta Terrace Stylish three-bedroom villa with a heated pool, kitchen and BBQ area. Fantastic views from the pool terrace. **$$$**

Al Rabi Tower

Coastal Charms in Khor Fakkan

Gateway to the east coast

A 90-minute drive from Dubai on the S142 Khor Fakkan Rd, **Khor Fakkan** is an excellent introduction to the UAE's eastern coast. Here, the Hajar Mountains rise majestically over date plantations and vast sandy beaches hug the Gulf of Oman. The largest town on the Fujairah coast, this exclave of the emirate of Sharjah attracts weekend visitors for its laid-back vibe.

For spectacular views over Khor Fakkan, head to **Al Rabi Tower** on a hill above the town. Dating to 1915, this watchtower was among the first built in the area to spot trespassers. The easy, well-marked 5.3km-long **Al Rabi Tower Trail** begins and ends here, with even better panoramic views from the summit at 395m.

A wander at the **Old Souq**, built like a traditional marketplace, reveals shops selling spices, pickles, coffee, dates and handicrafts, and a smattering of cafes. Within the restored houses is **Hisn Khor Fakkan**, a museum that showcases village life in the old days and speaks of its history. An important trading port, Khor Fakkan was invaded by the Portuguese and other regional powers in the 16th century.

UNDER THE SURFACE

At Khor Fakkan Beach (p190), expect boat operators to approach you for a 10-minute trip to the nearby **Shark Island**, where shallow waters, coral gardens and diverse marine species offer ideal conditions for snorkelling and diving. While the island is named after the blacktip reef sharks that are found east of the island from November to April, you're more likely to spot moray eels, rays, barracuda, mackerel, turtles, Arabian angelfish and tube-dwelling anemones.

Rates vary seasonally, but range from Dhs100 to Dhs300 per boat for a return trip, and are higher if you want to charter the boat for a few hours. Bring your passport to present to the port authority. **Freestyle Divers** and **Nemo Diving Center** offer guided dives in the area.

WHERE TO EAT IN KHOR FAKKAN

Husn Khorfakkan Restaurant
Jars of pickles and spices line the walls and every corner evokes nostalgia. Don't leave without trying a *namlet*. **$$**

The View by Wave
Stunning views over Khor Fakkan. Everything from Turkish eggs to fried chicken sandwiches. **$$**

Ahl Al Daar Pastry Bakery
For crispy *raqaq* (Emirati bread) and *karak* tea, head to this cafe-bakery in the Old Souq. Good for Emirati breakfast. **$**

STAY OVERNIGHT AT SIX SENSES ZIGHY BAY

A 40-minute drive from Dibba Al Fujairah, the **Six Senses Zighy Bay** feels like an Omani village in the Musandam Peninsula. The resort's stone villas, each with a private pool, stand along the turquoise Zighy Bay. From paragliding to diving, there's plenty to do. Otherwise, the resort's sandy beach, saltwater pool and spa are valid reasons to do less. Dining experiences include a beachfront feast of Omani *shuwa* (lamb slow-cooked underground) and seafood.

Embedded into every aspect of operations, the resort's commitment to sustainability is exceptional. On a sustainability tour, guests learn about their work in waste and water management, recycling, energy conservation, organic farming and community development.

HABIBULLAH QURESHI/SHUTTERSTOCK ©

Resistance Monument

At the **Resistance Monument**, which is hard to miss thanks to its striking geometric design and golden dome overlooking Khor Fakkan Sq, a museum uses augmented reality to bring to life the town's resistance against the Portuguese invasion of 1507. To learn more, make a quick stop at the **Portuguese Fort**, which dates to 1620.

The 3km-long **Khor Fakkan Beach** has a jogging track, play areas, toilets and changing facilities. Parasailing, jet-ski and boat rides can be booked at **Al Marjan Marine Amusements**.

Buses on the E700 route link the Union Square Bus Station in Deira, Dubai, to Fujairah city (Dhs25, 2½ hours).

WHERE TO EAT IN DIBBA AL FUJAIRAH

Murheb Mandi
A no-frills restaurant that serves delicious kebabs, grills and *mandi*, a meat and rice dish. $

Al Hamoor Indian
Grilled seafood, *mandi*, kebabs, biryani and South Indian-style fish curries are on the menu at this popular spot. $

Rumailah Farms Coffee Shop
Cool off with a milkshake, iced coffee or ice cream alongside a dates pudding or milk cake. $

The Oldest Mosque in the UAE

Historical architecture in Fujairah

The oldest mosque in the UAE still in use for daily prayers, the 1446-built **Al Bidya Mosque** in Fujairah, a 15-minute drive from Khor Fakkan along the coast, is notable for its distinct architecture and square shape. Multiple domes sit upon its four unequal domes and it's all supported by a single central pillar. Within the mud and stone walls are the mihrab and a minbar. Non-Muslims can enter but must wear clothing that covers the arms and ankles. Women must cover their heads with a scarf. Walk up to the two watchtowers behind the mosque for nice views of the farms and mountains.

High-Altitude Adventures at Jebel Jais

Highest mountain in the UAE

A two-hour drive from Dubai, **Jebel Jais**, the UAE's highest peak, stands at a height of 1934m in the Hajar Mountains in the emirate of Ras Al Khaimah. For striking panoramic views of the craggy desert mountain, rocky cliffs, hairpin roads, abandoned villages and arid wadis, take the 30km Jais St to the **Jais Viewing Deck Park**, located 1250m above sea level. Equipped with binoculars, the viewing decks offer a pleasant way to enjoy the scenery, and there's also two cafes, toilets and a children's playground.

For even more dramatic views, head up the signposted hiking trail that begins here to reach the **Viewing Deck Park Summit** at 1415m, marked by a large UAE flag. With a steep ascent, scree and rocky stairs, this 30-minute hike is a bit of a scramble, so try this only if you're wearing hiking shoes. The hike continues further to the **South Summit** at 1640m. Local operator **Adventurati Outdoor** offers guided hikes in Jebel Jais.

Those keen to admire this landscape from a heart-pounding perspective should head to **Jais Adventure Center** to fly across the valley superhero-style on Jais Flight, the world's longest zipline, which spans 2.83km, launching you from 1680m at speeds of 120km/h to 160km/h.

If that sounds easy, consider the two-hour Jais Sky Tour, where you'll soar over canyons and roads across a series of six ziplines covering 5km, linked by nine platforms including a terrifying sky bridge.

An equally fun but considerably shorter alternative is the Jais **Sledder** – the UAE's longest toboggan ride. This sled, with a rider-operated brake, twists and turns up and down the slopes at 40km/h, covering 1.84km in eight minutes.

BEAR GRYLLS SURVIVAL ACADEMY

In addition to a ropes course, rock climbing and guided hikes, the nearby **Bear Grylls Survival Academy** offers four-hour and 24-hour survival courses in Jebel Jais. You'll learn survival skills such as how to make a fire, build an emergency shelter and navigate a challenging terrain. To stay overnight, book a cabin at **Explorer Camp** (air-conditioned, with private toilets and showers, no wi-fi).

WHERE TO EAT IN JEBEL JAIS

1484 by Puro
The menu at the UAE's highest restaurant features salads, burgers, pizzas, and mains such as salmon teriyaki. $$

Puro Express
Snack on pizzas, burgers and waffles, and cool off with a slushy on the outdoor terrace at the Jais Viewing Deck Park. $$

The Muse Cafe
Decent hot and iced coffees, cakes and Nutella crêpes at this cafe at the Jais Viewing Deck Park. $$

WHERE TO EAT IN AJMAN

The Grove
This bright and modern restaurant serves a variety of cuisines, from delicious kebabs, Jordanian *mansaf*, Emirati *machboos*, and biryani to pasta and butter chicken, but the highlight is the mangrove view from the terrace. **$$**

Shakespeare and Co.
This cafe is a worthwhile choice for breakfast with a view of the mangroves. Its sandwiches, salads and wraps are also perfect for a summer day's lunch. **$$**

Sandwich Khas
Don't be fooled by the name of this unassuming restaurant that serves some of the best shrimp burgers, seafood sandwiches and salt-baked fish in Ajman. **$**

URBANMYTH/ALAMY STOCK PHOTO ©

Sharjah Calligraphy Museum

Kayaking at Al Zorah Nature Reserve

Idyllic mangrove forest

At **Al Zorah Nature Reserve**, a 50-minute drive from Dubai (easiest by taxi or rental car), pink flamingoes gracefully perch on one leg in a tidal creek and the only sounds are of birdsong and the swish of kayakers' paddles on the water. Located in the emirate of Ajman north of the city, this protected nature reserve consists of 1 million sq metres of natural mangrove forest where bird and marine life thrive and the surrounding urban life all but disappears. To get up close with the reserve's flamingoes, cormorants and egrets, join a guided kayak or electric canoe tour with **Quest for Adventure**. The only operator in the reserve, the company does significant conservation work in the mangroves and organises beach and ocean clean-ups in the area.

As the mangrove forest is a protected area, you can only visit with a guide. Guided kayak tours last for approximately two hours. The best chances of spotting flamingoes are during tours around high tide. Sunset tours present the opportunity to enjoy orange-pink skies over the mangroves from a kayak.

From Dubai buses on the E400 route link the Union Square Bus Station to Ajman's Al Musallah Bus Station (Dhs12, 50 minutes).

WHERE TO STAY IN AJMAN

Oberoi Beach Resort, Al Zorah Spacious rooms and suites with terraces and gardens, pool villas, a world-class spa and restaurants. **$$$**

Zoya Health & Wellbeing Resort Programs incorporate nutrition, yoga, detox, meditation, physiotherapy and aesthetic medicine. **$$**

Radisson Blu Hotel, Ajman Elegant rooms with modern amenities and six restaurants plus a glamorous 1920s jazz lounge. **$$**

Explore Sharjah's Heritage District

Cultural powerhouse

Located 30km from Dubai, **Sharjah** has a decidedly low-key vibe, but once you begin to explore the city and encounter its many museums, mosques, souqs and cultural sites, it quickly becomes obvious that this is a city whose identity is strongly rooted in its heritage and culture. The city was recognised by Unesco as the Cultural Capital of the Arab World in 1998 and the Capital of Islamic Culture in 2014.

A wander through the quiet alleyways of the heritage district **Heart of Sharjah** reveals restored coral stone buildings, most former Emirati residences, that house cultural institutions, cafes and boutique hotels. At the restored 1823-built fortress **Al Hisn** (also Sharjah Fort), once the seat of government and the residence of the ruling Al Qasimi family, exhibits tells the story of early life nearly 200 years ago and the history of governance in the emirate. At the **Sharjah Heritage Museum**, themed galleries showcase crafts, tools, clothing, jewellery and photographs that offer insight into traditional life and society.

Nearby, at the 19th-century **Bait Al Naboodah**, a traditional house formerly owned by a pearl merchant, admire designs and ingenious architectural elements typical of affluent houses in Sharjah. Excellent value for money, the joint Heritage Ticket (Dhs20) includes admission to the above museums and Al Hisn, as well as **Al Eslah School Museum**, Sharjah's oldest school and now museum (under restoration in June 2023), and **Sharjah Calligraphy Museum**, where you can admire stunning calligraphic artworks on canvas, paper, ceramics and wood.

A 10-minute walk along the Al Majarrah waterfront, the **Sharjah Museum of Islamic Civilization**, housed in a stately gold-domed building, exhibits a vast collection of over 5000 artefacts that showcase the contributions of Islamic culture and Muslim scholars across various fields including religion, sciences, technology, art and astronomy.

In the heart of Sharjah, the **Sharjah Art Museum** showcases the work of Arab artists from around the world through temporary exhibitions and a permanent collection featuring contemporary paintings and sculptures by established artists such as Abdulqader Al Rais, Louay Kayali and Bashir Sinwa.

From Dubai, there are buses on the E306 route from Al Ghubaiba Bus Station and E303 route from the Union Square Bus Station in Deira to Al Jubail Bus Station in Sharjah (both Dhs10, 45 minutes).

CONTEMPORARY CULTURE SCENE

Sharjah nurtures an exciting contemporary art and culture scene with an events calendar that's packed with interesting festivals and events. Most notable among these is the **Sharjah Biennial** (February to June), which sees exhibitions, artists talks, film screenings, performances and other community events take place in venues around Sharjah. Check if your visit coincides with the 10-day **Sharjah Light Festival** (February), when high-tech lights, sounds, projections and installations turn the city's architectural gems into a canvas for creative storytelling.

WHERE TO EAT IN SHARJAH

Arabian Tea House This quaint Emirati restaurant serves home-style dishes including a fantastic Emirati breakfast tray. **$$**

Restaurant at the Chedi Al Bait Feast on flavourful sea bass *sayadieh* (spiced rice), baked eggplant and butter chicken. **$$$**

Kabab Bombay Cafeteria What this no-frills spot lacks in ambience, it makes up with its delicious street-style chicken malai *boti* and chicken tikka. **$**

TOOLKIT

The chapters in this section cover the most important topics you'll need to know about in Dubai & Abu Dhabi. They're full of nuts-and-bolts information and valuable insights to help you understand and navigate Dubai & Abu Dhabi and get the most out of your trip.

Arriving
p196

Getting Around
p197

Money
p198

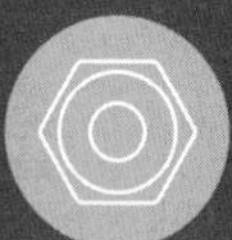

Nuts & Bolts
p199

Accommodation
p200

Food, Drink & Nightlife
p202

Family Travel
p204

Accessible Travel
p205

Responsible Travel
p206

Health & Safe Travel
p208

Language
p210

Travelling to the UAE during Ramadan
p212

Conrad Abu Dhabi Etihad Towers (p145)

Arriving

Dubai and Abu Dhabi's international airports continue to serve as the primary entry point for travellers into the UAE; there are also limited daily flights from Sharjah, Fujairah and Ras Al Khaimah. Many visitors also arrive daily via the many land border checkpoints shared with Sultanate of Oman and Saudi Arabia. Major cruise line routes also pass through Dubai and Abu Dhabi.

Visas

A 30-day visa on arrival is free only to limited nationalities; check your passport status before your trip. An e-visa can be obtained at gdrfad.gov.ae for Dhs300 or via airlines and travel agents.

SIM Cards

Etisalat and du are the two main ISPs in the UAE. Du offers free tourist SIM cards at Dubai Airport. Data packages range from Dhs49 for 2GB to Dhs189 for 20GB of data for 28 days.

Border Crossings

The UAE shares several land border crossings with Saudi Arabia and the Sultanate of Oman. A departure fee of Dhs35 must be paid by every traveller leaving the UAE.

Wi-Fi

Free wi-fi is available at all airports and across public transportation in the UAE. Wi-fi hot spots are easy to find in restaurants, cafes and malls across the country.

Public Transport from Airport to City Centre

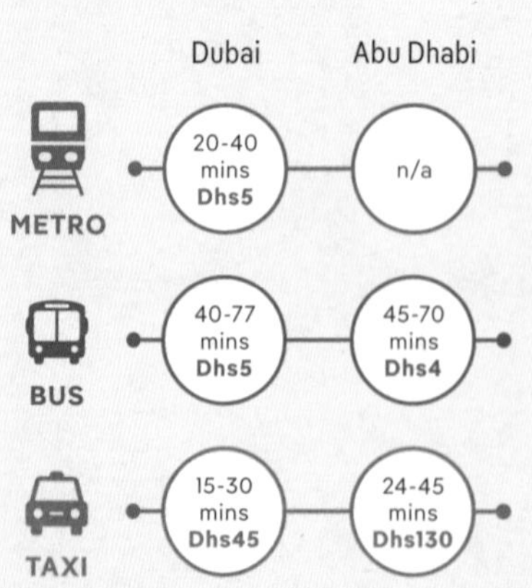

TRAVELLING BETWEEN DUBAI & ABU DHABI

Two daily intercity shuttle routes (E100 and E101) make travel between Dubai and Abu Dhabi relatively easy for just Dhs25. Trips from Abu Dhabi start at the Central bus station in the city centre and take approximately two hours to get to Dubai's Ibn Battuta bus station or Al Ghubaiba bus station.

There's also a 24/7 express shuttle from Abu Dhabi International Airport to Ibn Battuta bus station in Dubai. A one-way ticket costs Dhs30 and can be booked online or at the airport. Free shuttles are also available to and from Dubai when flying Etihad or Emirates.

Getting Around

Despite their expansiveness, Dubai and Abu Dhabi's key sites are relatively close together. Navigate them via taxis, buses and Dubai's metro and tram. In Abu Dhabi, ferries and abras offer scenic routes.

TRAVEL COSTS

Nol Red Ticket day pass
Dhs20

Intercity shuttle
Dhs25 one way

Taxi
From Dhs12

TRANSPORT ESSENTIALS

Trip planning apps Darbi for navigating Abu Dhabi's bus system and S'Hail for Dubai's public transport are two must-have apps; the latter allows you to also top up your Nol card, book a taxi and look up intercity bus schedules.

Rent a car in advance Avoid airport surcharges and book your car rental in advance – you're more likely to get a better daily rate. Insurance is mandatory when driving in the UAE; opt for comprehensive coverage as minor incidents are common. Certain nationalities require a valid international driving permit at the time of reservation, so secure one in advance if you do.

Tickets and passes If you plan on only using Dubai metro for a handful of trips, get a Nol Red Ticket. It costs Dhs2 and can be recharged 10 times. The Nol Silver Card offers better value if you're visiting for a couple of days. It costs Dhs25 with Dhs19 of credit, and fares start at Dhs3 for one zone. You can use the same card on Dubai's buses and trams. In Abu Dhabi, the Hafilat smart card (Dhs5 for the card only) provides access to the city's intercity bus system. A weekly pass offers unlimited bus trips within the city and costs Dhs30.

Pink taxis Available exclusively for women, with women drivers. Call 80088088 (Dubai) or 600535353 (Abu Dhabi) to book.

CAR RENTALS

Driving in the UAE is not for the faint of heart. However, the country's low cost of petrol makes car rentals an attractive budget option for day trips out of the city. To rent a car, you need to be over the age of 21, and have a valid driving licence and credit card; some nationalities need an international driving permit.

DRIVING ESSENTIALS

Drive on the right

Seatbelts are compulsory for all passengers.

Running a red light in Dubai will result in a Dhs50,000 fine and the confiscation of your vehicle.

Engaging in aggressive gestures or swearing at other drivers could result in imprisonment or possible deportation.

Public Transport

A vast bus network makes it possible to get around on a budget – bus fares in the capital begin at Dhs2. In Dubai, metro, tram, water taxi, ferry and abra are all operated by the Roads & Transport Authority (RTA). Download the RTA S'Hail app or visit www.rta.ae for maps, timetables and fares.

Tickets & Passes

Dubai's RTA transit system is split into seven zones. Purchase a rechargeable Nol card (nol.ae) beforehand and tap the card reader upon entry/exit. In Abu Dhabi, a rechargeable Hafilat card (hafilat.darb.ae) is required to use the bus. Purchase or refill your card at the airport or central bus station.

Rideshare Apps

Ride-hailing apps like Uber (uber.com), Careem (careem.com) and XXRide (xxride.com) operate here. While taxis can often end up being cheaper, rideshare apps offer convenience, a much better selection of cars and a pre-mapped route to your final destination.

Money

CURRENCY: **UNITED ARAB EMIRATES DIRHAM (DHS)**

Credit Cards

Visa and Mastercard are widely accepted throughout the UAE, including in taxis; many retailers and restaurants do not accept American Express.

Digital Payments

Digital wallets like Apple Pay and Google Wallet on phones and smart watches are popular payment methods in the UAE, with most places having tap-and-pay POS facilities.

Taxes & Refunds

Since January 2018, a 5% VAT has been added to almost all goods and services in the UAE. Tourists can claim back the VAT from registered outlets – keep a copy of all tax invoices for purchases over Dhs250. Refunds are processed on departure at the airport, seaport or land port.

Tipping

Hotels Porters Dhs5 to Dhs10, room cleaners Dhs5 to Dhs10 per day

Restaurants 10% to 15% of the bill. Cash is preferred so it goes directly to the servers.

Taxis Dhs5 to Dhs10, or letting them keep the change

Tour guides 10% to 15%

HOW MUCH FOR...

discount card for attractions
From Dhs229 (Dubai) or Dhs99 (Abu Dhabi)

buses Abu Dhabi to Dubai
Dhs25 with a precharged Nol card

museum entry
Dhs25–149

HOW TO... Save Some Dirhams

For budget travellers, the best time to visit the UAE is during the off-season, roughly April to September. This means reduced airfares, deals on hotel stays and plenty of sales, including Dubai's second-largest shopping festival, Dubai Summer Surprises, which runs from June to September. Even though the temperatures are high outside, most of the UAE's top attractions are located indoors.

LOCAL TIP

Download apps like Entertainer, Groupon and Cobone before your visit. They offer plenty of budget-friendly deals on popular tourist activities, hotels, dining, spas and health and fitness in the UAE.

THE HIGH COST OF LIVING

The discovery of oil in the 1960s forever changed the trajectory of the UAE's economy. Thanks to the reinvestment of wealth generated from the oil industry, you'll find Dubai and Abu Dhabi to be thriving hubs of international tourism, finance, technology, trade and transport. Prices reflect this prosperity, from luxury hotels and Michelin-starred restaurants to high-end malls. The high cost of doing business, including salaries for expat workers, also contributes to the UAE's reputation as an expensive tourist destination.

Nuts & Bolts

OPENING HOURS

Opening hours vary depending on the season and public holidays.

Banks 8am to 3pm Monday to Thursday, 7.30am to 12.30pm Friday

Government offices 7.30am to 3.30pm Monday to Thursday, 7.30am to noon Friday

Shopping malls 10am to 11pm Monday to Thursday, 10am to midnight Friday to Sunday

Bars 5pm to 1am

Restaurants noon to 3pm and 6pm to midnight

Smoking

Smoking is banned in all public spaces in Dubai and Abu Dhabi, except for bars and nightclubs. Shopping malls and hotels often have designated smoking areas.

Weights & Measures

The UAE uses the metric system. Litre is the official unit of measurement for fuel.

GOOD TO KNOW

Time zone
GMT/UTC+2

Country code
971

Emergency number
999

Population
9.28 million

PUBLIC HOLIDAYS

There are seven public holidays in the UAE. Islamic holiday dates are dependent on the sighting of the moon.

New Year's Day
1 January

Eid Al Fitr

Eid Al Adha

Islamic New Year

Prophet Muhammad's Birthday
29 September

Commemoration Day
30 November

National Day
2 December

Electricity 220V/50Hz

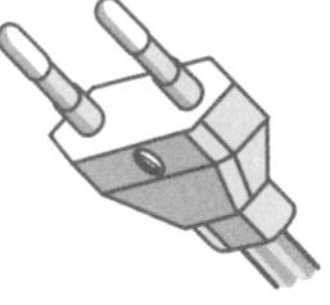

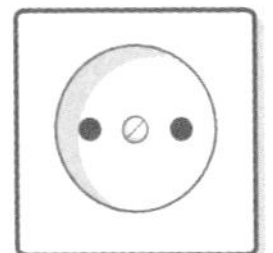

Type C
220V/50Hz

Type G
230V/50Hz

Accommodation

From 24-carat gold spa offerings and Michelin-starred dining to round-the-clock butler service and underwater suites, there's no denying that the UAE sets the standard for high-end hospitality. Apart from luxe lodgings, Dubai and Abu Dhabi also have accommodation to suit a variety of budgets, including hotel apartments, heritage B&Bs and even hostels. With over 120,000 hotel rooms in Dubai alone, you're never at a loss for somewhere to stay in the UAE – make sure you book ahead to get the best deal.

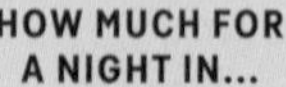

HOW MUCH FOR A NIGHT IN...

a heritage hotel **Dhs440**

a hostel dorm **Dhs55**

a hotel apartment apartment **from Dhs250**

Beach Resorts

Plenty of beachside resorts dot the UAE's coastline, ranging from ultra-luxe properties like Atlantis The Royal in Dubai to midrange options like the Sheraton Hotel & Resort in Abu Dhabi. These properties often feature private beach access, rejuvenating spa services and numerous dining and drinking options; many also offer water sports like paddleboarding, jet skiing and sailing.

Boutique & Heritage Hotels

Travellers searching for immersive cultural experiences when visiting the UAE will find that and more at Dubai's charming heritage hotels. Located in Deira and Bur Dubai, these boutique properties (often B&Bs) offer a unique blend of Arab hospitality and modern amenities, showcasing local architecture, design and customs.

Hotel Apartments

While hotel apartments are typically meant for extended stays, they can be a budget-friendly option for families or large groups visiting the UAE. Accommodation ranges in size from studios to three-bedroom apartments and often feature fully equipped kitchens and housekeeping, along with access to on-site gyms and pools.

Apartment Rentals

Not only are short-term apartment rentals a great way to get a more localised experience, but they're also an excellent option for groups. Check minimum-stay requirements and available amenities before you book – many provide parking and access to pools and gyms. A cleaning fee is typically charged at the end of your visit.

Hostels

Hostels may seem like an unlikely possibility in a country that has a reputation for luxury accommodation. However, there are a growing number of hostels across the region for visitors on a budget. They typically offer shared dormitory-style rooms (sometimes gender-separated), free wi-fi, lockers, shared bathroom facilities, and common areas for socialising. Some also provide breakfast.

ROOM RATES

Room rates in Dubai and Abu Dhabi vary widely based on hotel category and time of year. Prices usually peak from November to March due to pleasant weather or during popular holidays like Eid. Summer boasts the best deals, with hotels often including enticing incentives like free entry to the top city sights or free dining for kids. Top accommodation gets booked quickly, so make reservations in advance. Most properties can be booked online, often offering a best-price guarantee.

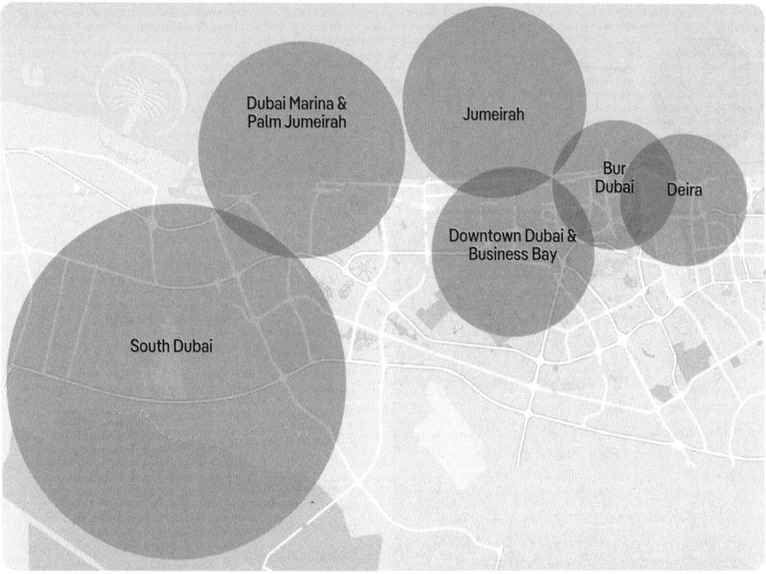

NEIGHBOURHOOD	ATMOSPHERE
Deira	Near the Creek with exceptional water views. Easy Metro access but difficult parking in peak hours; budget properties may also be brothels.
Bur Dubai	Several heritage hotels and boutique properties to choose from near the Creek; affordable hotel apartmes are behind Bur Juman shopping centre.
Downtown Dubai & Business Bay	Surrounded by some of Dubai's key attractions. Expect high-end hotels, fine dining and a thrilling nightlife scene.
Jumeirah	The neighbourhood for beach vibes. Hotel apartments are located by Mall of the Emirates. Most properties require a taxi journey to the nearest metro station.
Dubai Marina & Palm Jumeirah	Luxury hotels with private beach access dominate the Marina and Palm Jumeirah areas. Palm resorts are remote; budget options are scarce.
South Dubai	More residential; it's also out of the way from most Dubai sights and requires a taxi ride to the nearest metro.
Downtown Abu Dhabi	There are plenty of hotels to choose from for budgets of all sizes. For water views, stick to resorts that dot the Corniche.
Breakwater & Around	Emirates Palace is the key attraction here. There's plenty to see and do, including bird's-eye views from the Etihad Towers' observation deck.
Al Zahiyah, Al Maryah Island & Al Reem Island	Commonly known as the Tourist Club Area, Al Zahiyah is one of the city's oldest neighbourhoods and a direct contrast to the glitzy properties on Al Maryah and Al Reem islands.
Al Mina & Saadiyat Island	For a glimpse of old Abu Dhabi head to Al Mina, where souqs, art galleries and dhow harbours await. Saadiyat Island is where one goes to see and be seen in the capital; pricey.
Yas Island & Around	A family-friendly neighbourhood. Several hotels to choose from; can be pricey. There are daily shuttles to take you around the island.

Food, Drink & Nightlife

TOOLKIT

Restaurant Rules

Smoking Be warned: smoking cigarettes, cigars and shisha is only allowed in designated areas in many restaurants, pubs, bars and lounges.

Table manners Anti-social conduct, such as lewd language and evident drunkenness, is an offence.

Timings Typically, breakfast is served from 7am to 11am, brunch and lunch between noon and 4pm, and dinner from as early as 6.30pm, particularly in upmarket venues running two sittings per night.

Where to Eat

Hole-in-the-wall cafes Usually found in 'Old Town' neighbourhoods; expect fast, no-frills servings of snacks such as shawarma or stuffed paratha bread.

Food trucks Like hole-in-the-wall cafes, but with wheels. Find food trucks at Last Exit, Kite Beach and Khalifa City.

Unlicensed restaurants Restaurants outside of hotels, from beachside cafes to mall eateries, are typically unlicensed and family-friendly.

Licensed restaurants Only licensed restaurants, mainly found inside hotels, can serve alcohol. Children are usually welcome without set curfews.

MENU DECODER

Fattoush Salad made with crispy pita bread and pomegranate molasses

Kibbeh Fried rugby-ball-shaped patties of spiced ground beef or lamb and cracked bulgur wheat

Laban Strained yogurt drink

Labneh Thicker, creamier version of laban used as a savoury dip

Moutabel Baked and mashed aubergine seasoned with garlic, lemon and tahini

Shawarma Meat wrap made with thin cuts of chicken, lamb, mutton or beef stacked in an inverted cone and cooked on a vertical rotisserie, then sliced and served in flatbread

Shish tawook Kebab made with cubes of chicken breast meat

Sumac Zesty spice used to flavour kebabs and salads, such as fattoush

Toum Garlic cream served as a dip

HOW TO...

Share a Shisha

Smoking shisha is part of Arabian culture. The apparatus comprises a water-filled vase fitted with a bowl of fruit-flavoured tobacco, a tray of burning coals and a hosepipe. When users inhale through the hose, the suction forces air past the coal, heating the tobacco, which produces smoke. The smoke then travels down the stem, through the water and into the base, allowing the water to cool the smoke before it's inhaled.

Typically passed clockwise, shisha is shared with family and friends, the high levels of nicotine delivering a mild buzz, like an alternative to alcohol. Disposable plastic mouthpieces are provided to cover the end of the hose. However, in the post-pandemic world, there are concerns about the transfer of germs from respiratory tract fluid reaching the pipe. Smoke the pipe for just two to three minutes before passing it on. When everyone has finished, wrap the hose around the vase.

HOW MUCH FOR A...

glass of wine
Dhs40–200

pint of beer
Dhs40–70

coffee
Dhs30

shawarma
Dhs30

pub lunch
Dhs150–250

ice cream
Dhs25–50

all-inclusive brunch
Dhs250–700

Michelin-star restaurant dinner
Dhs600–2000

HOW TO... Drink Arabian Coffee

In the UAE, coffee is a symbol of hospitality. In the past, Bedouins brewed coffee over a firepit in the sand. Today, coffee-brewing apparatus is at the centre of Emirati kitchens. Brewing Arabian coffee is a process and each family has its own cherished recipe. The coffee pot is called a *dallah* and there are three types: the largest is used for brewing the coffee with flavourings, cardamom being the key ingredient; the medium-sized one is used for filtering; and the smallest one is used for serving. The server must hold the *dallah* with their left hand, with their thumb pointing to the top, and pour the coffee into the small cup *(finjal)*, which must be held in their right hand. If you're offered a cup of coffee, it's also polite to accept it in your right hand. Historically, in Islamic culture, right hands are used for eating and drinking, while left hands are reserved for personal hygiene. If you're pouring the coffee, serve the most important or oldest guest first. The pour should only fill around a quarter of the cup. Drink one to three cups. Tip the cup left to right a few times to signify when you've had enough.

Gahwa

In 2015, the custom of drinking Arabian coffee (*gahwa* in the Emirati Arabic dialect) was added to the UNESCO Representative List of the Intangible Cultural Heritage of Humanity.

BRUNCH UAE-STYLE

In most other parts of the world, brunch is a relaxed meal enjoyed between breakfast and lunchtime (the word is a portmanteau of the two meals' names). In the UAE, brunch is one of the biggest parties of the week, taking place at the same time as lunch and usually lasting a lot longer, around three to four hours.

It's typically held in five-star hotel restaurants at weekends, and Saturday plays host to the liveliest brunches, akin to a Friday night out in the West. All-inclusive packages include bottomless drinks, vast buffets or set menus, and a mix of entertainment, from bouncy castles, cartoon screenings and face-painting at child-friendly brunches to live bands, provocative dance acts and DJs spinning tunes at adults-only brunches.

Brunches should be booked in advance, especially around key holidays such as Christmas and New Year. The most popular ones sell out quickly. Decide if you want to sit inside or out; many places offer a choice and anyone with sensitive skin should avoid being seated outdoors. Parasols will be provided but the sun will shift throughout the brunch.

Brunch buffets are often a cornucopia of Middle Eastern meze, Mediterranean canapés, artisan bread, cheeses and cold cuts, shellfish, whole baked fish, roast meats, pasta, pizza, curries, salads, vegetables and an obscene array of desserts. Some brunch buffets are so big that hotels provide guests with maps. The more expensive ones feature oysters, caviar, king crab and steak, washed down with premium champagne. Pace yourself.

Family Travel

From aquatic adventures to thrilling theme park rides, there's no shortage of family-friendly activities in the UAE. Whether you choose to spend the day kayaking in Hatta or immersed in art in the children's museum at the Louvre Abu Dhabi, both Dubai and Abu Dhabi offer a wealth of experiences that can be enjoyed with the kids in tow.

Sights

Most attractions in the UAE offer children's tickets that are slightly cheaper than the adult rate; some even provide free admission for younger kids. In Abu Dhabi, for example, those under the age of 18 can visit the Louvre Abu Dhabi for free. Keep the budget in check by buying tickets online in advance.

Facilities

- Many beach resorts feature kids clubs and kid-friendly activities. Popular choices include Sandcastle Club at the St Regis Saadiyat Island in Abu Dhabi and Club Mina at the Le Méridien Mina Seyahi.
- While car rental agencies offer car seats for a fee, it's best to bring your own, along with strollers.
- Diapers and baby formula can be found at most pharmacies and supermarkets in the UAE.

Dining Out

Many large restaurants in the UAE offer children's menus. Some feature dedicated play areas, while others, like The Scene in Dubai Marina, have special days where kids dine for free. High chairs are often available if you ask.

Getting Around

Kids under the age of five can ride public transport for free in Dubai. In Abu Dhabi, the buses are free to ride for children under the age of 10.

KID-FRIENDLY PICKS

Dubai Parks and Resorts (p119)

A thrilling experience is in store at this Jebel Ali theme park.

Dubai Aquarium & Underwater Zoo (p79)

Rare aquatic life awaits at this popular Dubai Mall attraction.

Water parks

Choose from wave pools, slides or lazy rivers at Aquaventure on Palm Jumeirah, Wild Wadi Waterpark or Yas Waterworld in Abu Dhabi.

Ski Dubai (p91)

Learn how to ski on perfect snow at this indoor ski resort.

A SUMMER OF DEALS

Summertime provides some of the best deals for families visiting the UAE. With school out of session, kids have plenty of free time to pursue their hobbies and spend quality time with their families – it's also not unusual to see children at social and family gatherings that last well into the night.

Top sights like Dubai Parks and Resorts and Burj Khalifa's At the Top observation deck feature free entry for kids when accompanied by an adult during the summer months. And it doesn't stop there. Many hotels across the UAE, such as Jumeirah Emirates Towers, have 'kids go free' summer deals where children get to stay and, many times, also eat for free.

Accessible Travel

Government initiatives like the Dubai Disability Strategy 2020 have made the UAE more accessible for people with disabilities (officially known as people of determination). The level of accessibility can vary depending on where you are – for example, drop-down curbs are rare in older neighbourhoods.

Public Transport

Dubai metro stations include audio announcements and tactile floor paths for the visually impaired. Each metro compartment has designated spaces for wheelchairs. Taxis with special lifts for wheelchairs can be booked in advance.

Accommodation

Most international hotel chains in the UAE are equipped for people of determination. Accessible guest rooms have extra-wide doors and adapted bathrooms with roll-in showers and grab rails. Almost all hotels, including budget properties, have lifts.

Airport

Both international airports feature accessible check-in counters, automatic doors and lifts. Dubai International Airport also offers a dedicated check-in gate for travellers with special needs. In Abu Dhabi, there are e-gates with wheelchair access.

RESOURCES

Wings Of Angelz (instagram.com/wingsofangelz) A nonprofit focused on making public spaces in Dubai wheelchair-friendly, spreading awareness and providing help to people of determination.

Zayed Higher Organization for People of Determination (zho.gov.ae) Abu Dhabi's official umbrella organisation for providing education, therapeutic assistance and information to people of determination residing in the capital.

What to Wear

While the UAE is a tolerant country, it's also a Muslim one – and dressing modestly in public is a sign of respect. While women don't have to cover their hair, it is recommended to cover the shoulders and knees when spending the day at cultural sites or historic parts of town.

Women Travellers

Travelling solo to Dubai as a woman is generally safe – the UAE ranks high on the list of world's safest countries. It's safe for women to take taxis, stay alone in hotels and walk around town.

BEACHES

Kite Beach was one of the first beaches in Dubai to have a wheelchair-accessible walkway that leads directly to the beach. Umm Suqeim Beach, Al Mamzar Beach and Jumeirah Beach are all accessible as well.

MUSEUMS & SIGHTS

Popular sights such as the Burj Khalifa, Dubai Frame, Emirates Palace and Sheikh Zayed Grand Mosque are all wheelchair-accessible.

Malls in the UAE typically have wheelchair ramps at entrances and exits; lifts are readily available for easy access to different floors. Newer restaurants and bars are almost always wheelchair-accessible. However, accessibility might be more of a challenge in older parts of the city – make sure to call ahead.

Responsible Travel

Climate Change & Travel

It's impossible to ignore the impact we have when travelling, and the importance of making changes where we can. Lonely Planet urges all travellers to engage with their travel carbon footprint. There are many carbon calculators online that allow travellers to estimate the carbon emissions generated by their journey; try resurgence.org/resources/carbon-calculator.html. Many airlines and booking sites off er travellers the option of offsetting the impact of greenhouse gas emissions by contributing to climate-friendly initiatives around the world. We continue to offset the carbon footprint of all Lonely Planet staff travel, while recognising this is a mitigation more than a solution.

Emirati Cuisine

Indulge in Emirati cuisine at the Sheikh Mohammed Centre for Cultural Understanding, a local nonprofit in Dubai's Al Fahidi Historic District dedicated to showcasing Emirati culture, traditions and hospitality.

Unesco Marvels

Visit the Al Ain Oasis, a Unesco World Heritage Site known for the ancient form of irrigation known as *falaj*. There are two central aflaj systems that bring water from the mountains and underground wadis.

Take a wildlife safari at Sir Bani Yas Island, home to over 17,000 animals in the UAE's largest wildlife reserve. Expect to spot cheetahs, Arabian oryx, gazelles, giraffes, flamingoes, grey herons and more.

Look for local ingredients. ERTH Restaurant (erthrestaurant.ae) in Abu Dhabi uses locally grown produce from farms across the UAE to craft its menu – a contemporary take on Emirati cuisine.

CULTURAL CRUISES

Cruise along Dubai Creek in a traditional dhow. Once the ship of choice for local fishermen, today, dhows are being repurposed to host nightly dinner cruises down the Dubai Creek and Dubai Marina.

OFF-SEASON TRAVEL

Travelling during the off-season, which runs approximately from April to October, means fewer crowds, cheaper flights and accommodation. Expect a more local experience as well.

Desert Reserve

Spend time in the Dubai Desert Conservation Reserve to immerse in the country's Bedouin heritage and culture. Located just 30 minutes from Downtown Dubai, the sprawling reserve is home to over 200 flora and fauna, including the Arabian oryx, caracal and sand fox.

Dolphins

The UAE Dolphin Project is dedicated to conserving and documenting the UAE's dolphin population. Consider volunteering during one of their public events or to do marine fieldwork throughout the year. Find out more at uaedolphinproject.org.

Green Iftars

Dig in during Green Ramadan where participating hotels across the UAE focus on composting excess food waste from nightly *iftar* dinners, grow their own fruits and vegetables, source sustainable ingredients and donate leftover food to the local food bank.

Join a Frying Pan Adventures food tour led by longtime local Dubai residents. You'll walk through Old Dubai and taste popular street foods from some of the city's oldest communities.

Discover the ancient Emirati arts of *Al-Sadu* (weaving), *khoos* (date palm weaving; pictured) and *talli* (decorative embroidery) at the House of Artisans within Qasr Al Hosn in Abu Dhabi.

WALKABLE NEIGHBOURHOODS

The Heart of Sharjah (heartofsharjah.ae) aims to create a walkable neighbourhood and revitalise traditional Emirati culture and architecture.

40

The Global Sustainability Index ranks the UAE in 40th place worldwide. While the country falls behind on climate action, it offers low-cost solar energy and is currently a significant investor in renewable energy projects.

RESOURCES

UAE Ministry of Climate Change & Environment (moccae.gov.ae) The country's official environmental agency.

Emirates Nature-WWF (emiratesnaturewwf.ae) Local nature nonprofit in association with WWF, offering volunteering opportunities.

Sheikh Mohammed Centre for Cultural Understanding (cultures.ae) Local nonprofit dedicated to understanding culture and customs in the UAE.

Health & Safe Travel

Anti-LGBTIQ+ Laws

Homosexuality is a criminal offence in the UAE that can result in prison sentences, hefty fines and deportation. Discretion is highly advised regarding public displays of affection – kissing and fondling are an offence – for both LGBTIQ+ and heterosexual travellers. Cross-dressing is also illegal and can incur fines and a minimum of six months of jail time.

RESOURCES

Government restrictions make it difficult for NGOs working on LGBTIQ+ issues to operate officially in the UAE. If you need help, contact your country's nearest embassy. Bloggers Stefan and Sebastien of Nomadic Boys have several helpful articles on gay life in the UAE (nomadicboys.com/gay-life-in-dubai/). A worthwhile watch is *Only Men Go to the Grave* by Emirati filmmaker Abdallah Al Kaabi.

Hotels

Same-sex couples that share a hotel room while visiting the UAE may be considered friends or travellers on a budget-friendly holiday. While no one will check, the expectation is to have separate beds, such as one king bed and a twin or two queen beds.

THE CONCEPT OF TASAMUH

The UAE embraces the Arab concept *tasamuh*, or mutual tolerance for its diverse population. Embracing cultural diversity here means accepting the nuances in sexual and gender behaviours that would mean something else altogether in the West. For example, it's not uncommon to see men walking hand in hand or kissing on the cheeks – these are signs of friendship and not an indication of sexual orientation. Emirati men sometimes greet friends with a 'nose kiss'. There's even a Ministry of Tolerance & Coexistence (tolerance.gov.ae) dedicated to promoting these values.

BARS & CLUBBING

Despite the inherent risks that exist for local LGBTIQ+ individuals, both Abu Dhabi and Dubai have underground queer social scenes. However, foreign travellers may find accessing them a challenge, as events typically spread via word-of-mouth or discreetly through social media.

Sites & Apps

LGBTIQ+ websites and dating apps like Grindr are officially blocked. Online retailers like Amazon restrict the sale of LGBTIQ+-related items.

DRUGS & PRESCRIPTION MEDICINES

Prescriptions are required for all medicines brought into the country. It's also good to have a doctor's note that outlines your need to take it. Certain medicines are considered controlled drugs and require prior approval from the UAE's Ministry of Health for personal use – check with the UAE embassy in your country for an updated list.

Extreme Heat

Temperatures continue to rise across the UAE each summer. It's not uncommon to see temperatures approach 50°C (122°F) during the day with 95% humidity. As a result, most activities move indoors – alfresco dining is simply impossible – where there's air-conditioning. If you decide to brave the outdoors, stay hydrated, wear sunscreen and avoid direct sunlight.

Road Accidents

Driving in the UAE is not without its risks. Common causes of road accidents include tailgating, reckless driving and speeding, for which hefty fines and penalties exist. Most roads in Dubai and Abu Dhabi are well maintained and often feature state-of-the-art cameras – so always make sure you follow the speed limit when driving.

TAP WATER

While bottled water is the popular go-to for most UAE residents, tap water is perfectly safe to drink.

DRIVE SAFELY

Roundabout
Travel in direction of the arrow

Minimum speed on freeway
Do not drive any slower

Give way to pedestrians
Pedestrians have the right of way

Watch out for camels
Slow down and do not honk your horn

Health Insurance

Hospitals in Dubai and Abu Dhabi uphold high standards. In order to avoid hefty medical bills, purchase travel insurance (it's mandatory for any trip) that also includes health coverage for the duration of your visit. Also make sure that the policy also includes repatriation to your home country in case of emergencies. In Abu Dhabi, emergency treatment is free.

LEGAL MATTERS

Don't let the UAE's glitz and glam fool you, because not everything goes here – and ignorance is no defence. The country is tolerant and open up to a point; go beyond that and you could face some of the strictest penalties. Read up on Dubai's Code of Conduct (dmcc.ae/application/files/5914/8465/5175/TheDubaiCodeOfConduct-Eng.pdf) to prevent yourself from getting into any unnecessary trouble during your trip.

Language

Arabic is the official language of the United Arab Emirates (UAE), but English is widely understood. The Arabic variety spoken in the UAE (and provided in this section) is known as Gulf Arabic.

Basics

Hello. اهلا و سهلا. *ah·lan was ah·lan*
Goodbye. مع السلامة. *ma' sa·laa·ma*
Yes./No. نعم./لا. *na·'am/la*
Please.
من فضلك. *min fad·lak* (m)
من فضلِك. *min fad·lik* (f)
Thank you. شكران. *shuk·ran*
Excuse me.
اسمح. *is·mah* (m)
اسمحي لي. *is·mah·ee lee* (f)
Sorry. مع الاسف. *ma' al·as·af*
What's your name? اش اسمَك/اسمِك؟ *aash is·mak/is·mik (m/f)*
My name is ... اسمي ... *is·mee ...*
Do you speak English?
تتكلم انجليزية؟ *tit·kal·am in·glee·zee·ya* (m)
تتكلمي انجليزية؟ *tit·ka·la·mee in·glee·zee·ya* (f)
I don't understand مو فاهم. *moo faa·him*

Directions

Where's the ...? من وين ...؟ *min wayn ...*
What's the address?
ما العنوان؟ *ma il·'un·waan*
Could you please write it down?
لو سمحت اكتبه لي؟ *law sa·maht ik·ti·boo lee* (m)
لو سمحت اكتبيه لي؟ *law sa·maht ik·ti·bee lee* (f)
Can you show me (on the map)?
لو سمحت وريني *law sa·maht wa·ree·nee*
(علخريطة؟) *('al·kha·ree·ta)*

Signs

Entrance مدخل
Exit خروج
Open مفتوح
Closed مقفول
Information معلومات
Prohibited ممنوع
Toilets المرحاض
Men رجال
Women نساء

Time

What time is it? الساعة كم؟ *i·saa·a' kam*
It's (two) o'clock. الساعة (ثنتين). *i·saa·a' (thin·tayn)*
Half past (two). الساعة (ثنتين) و نس. *i·saa·a' (thin·tayn) wa nus*
yesterday ... البارح ... *il·baa·rih ...*
tomorrow ... باكر ... *baa·chir ...*
morning صباح *sa·baah*
afternoon بعد الظهر *ba'd a·thuhr*
evening مساء *mi·saa*

Emergencies

Help!
مساعد *moo·saa·'id (m)*
مساعدة! *moo·saa·'id·a (f)*
Go away! ابعد!/ابعدي! *ib·'ad/ ib·'ad·ee (m/f)*
Call ...!
تصل على ...! *ti·sil 'a·la ...* (m)
تصلي على ...! *ti·si·lee 'a·la ...* (f)
a doctor طبيب *ta·beeb*
the police الشرطة *i·shur·ta*

NUMBERS

1
دحاو ١
waa·hid

2
نينثا ٢
ith·nayn

3
ةثالث ٣
tha·laa·tha

4
عبرا ٤
ar·ba'

5
ةسمخ ٥
kham·sa

6
ةتس ٦
si·ta

7
عبس ٧
sa·ba'

8
ةينامث ٨
tha·maan·ya

9
ةعست ٩
tis·a'

10
ةرشع ١٠
'ash·ar·a

DONATIONS TO ENGLISH

Numerous – including alcohol, assassin, candle, coffee, cotton, jar, syrup

Introduction to Arabic

Muslims say that Arabic is the most perfect language of all, as it's the language in which the Quran was revealed. Religious beliefs aside, the international status of Arabic is impressive: it's one of the world's 10 most widely spoken languages, with over 300 million speakers.

Arabic is spoken as the first language across the Middle East and North Africa and is widely used as a second language throughout the Islamic world. It has official status in 25 countries, the Arab League and the African Union, and it's one of the six official languages of the United Nations.

Gulf Arabic is spoken in the UAE, while Egyptian, Levantine and Tunisian Arabic are other spoken varieties that cover broad parts of the Middle East.

DISTINCTIVE SOUNDS

The **gh** is a guttural sound (like the Parisian French 'r'), **r** is rolled, and **kh** sounds like the 'ch' in the Scottish *loch*

Pronunciation

Stress usually falls on the first syllable of a word or the one with a long vowel. The symbol ' is pronounced like the pause in the middle of 'uh-oh'.

MSA

Modern Standard Arabic or MSA is the modernised version of Classical Arabic, used in schools, administration and the media – the official lingua franca of the Arab world.

WHO SPEAKS MODERN STANDARD ARABIC?

Modern Standard Arabic is spoken across Northern Africa, the Arabian Peninsula and parts of the Middle East – however, not all dialects are mutually intelligible.

313 million Speakers of Arabic in the world

11 million Speakers of Gulf Arabic

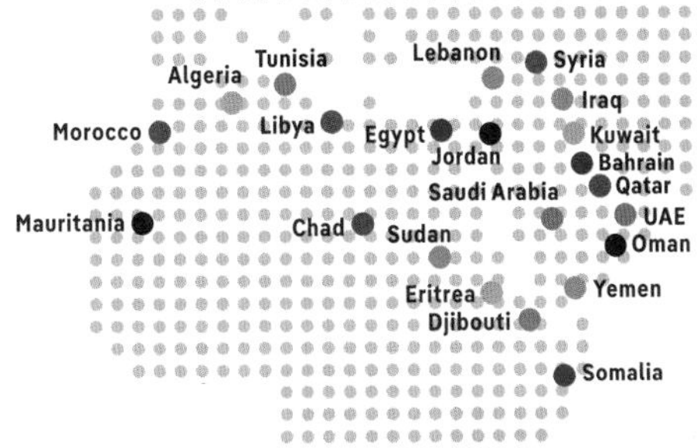

Travelling to the UAE During Ramadan

Extended daylight fasting and vibrant nightly Iftar feasts reshape societal rhythms in the UAE during the holy month of Ramadan. It's not uncommon for life to slow down during the day. In the evenings, socialisation surges well into the night as people gather over communal meals and shared plates.

IMPORTANT DATES

- **Eid Al Fitr** This marks the end of Ramadan.
- **Eid Al Adha** This marks the pilgrimage to Mecca.
- **Islamic New Year** Also known as Hiri New Year, marked by the crescent moon.
- **Prophet Muhammad's Birthday** Also known as Mawlid al-Nabi; it's celebrated on the 12th day of the third month in the Islamic calendar.

What is Ramadan?

Ramadan is a deeply spiritual time for Muslims in the UAE. As the holiest month of the Muslim year – it falls during the ninth month of the Islamic calendar; the exact start date changes annually based on the sighting of the crescent moon – Ramadan marks a period of fasting from dawn to dusk, piety, charitable acts and the purification of a person's mind, body and soul. Eid Al Fitr celebrates the end of Ramadan.

Iftar Dinners

Iftar is the big feast served at sunset for Muslims to break their day's fast. *Iftar* dinners in the UAE tend to be hearty affairs with large spreads featuring everything from local Emirati dishes like *machboos* (a spiced meat and rice casserole) and *harees* (a wheat porridge-like stew with meat) to a selection of popular Middle Eastern meze like vine leaves, fatayer, kibbeh and grilled meats.

Restaurants & Bars

During Ramadan, bars in Dubai serve alcohol and remain open throughout the day. Most clubs, however, tend to close for the month. You also won't find any live music or DJs during this period. In 2021 the Dubai and Abu Dhabi governments further relaxed the rules during Ramadan for restaurants – they are now no longer required to cover their shopfronts with curtains or put up screens during fasting hours.

RULES TO REMEMBER

It's not mandatory for non-Muslims to fast during Ramadan.

Avoid eating, drinking (including water), chewing gum or smoking in public during daylight hours.

No loud music or dancing in public.

Dress modestly; ie cover your shoulders and knees, and avoid showing cleavage or wearing any revealing clothing during the month.

TRAVEL DURING EID

Eid Al Adha, which marks the pilgrimage of Muslims to Mecca, is a popular time for travel in the region. Dubai sees an influx of travellers from nearby Gulf Cooperation Council (GCC) countries, including Saudi Arabia and Qatar, while residents opt to travel overseas during the long break. If you find yourself travelling to the UAE during Eid, it's best to book in advance and arrive early, as delays at the airport are to be expected, especially on weekends.

Jumeirah Grand Mosque (p95), Dubai

HOW TO... Visit a Mosque

Though the scale of grand mosques can seem intimidating to first-time visitors, stepping inside offers an unparalleled view into Emirati culture and traditions. Both the Sheikh Zayed Grand Mosque (p156) in Abu Dhabi and Jumeirah Grand Mosque (p95) in Dubai allow non-Muslims the opportunity to marvel at Islamic architecture from the inside. It's the chance to interact with local worshippers and understand the intricacies of Islam, the UAE's official religion.

When to Visit

Sunni Muslims make up the majority of the local population in Dubai and Abu Dhabi. As a result, prayer occurs five times a day – the position of the sun determines the timings, and the *azan* (Muslim call to prayer) signals worshippers when it's time to pray. While most mosques stay open throughout the day, the best time for non-Muslims to visit is outside these five prayer times. Some mosques even have special visiting hours for tours. Jumeirah Mosque, for example, offers two daily tours from Saturday to Thursday; the first begins at 10am and the second at 2pm.

Clothing

The mosque is a sacred place of worship for Muslims and dressing modestly is key when visiting. Long, loose-fitting clothes – ankle-length skirts, trousers and long sleeves, plus a headscarf for women – are preferable attire for both men and women. That means no shorts, skirts (unless ankle-length), sleeveless shirts, graphic tees, or transparent or tight clothing. Most mosques offer traditional clothing (*kandouras* and hooded *abayas*) during your visit. Shoes must be removed before entering the mosque.

Entering the Mosque

There are separate prayer areas for men and women and separate entrances for both. Very often, the main entrance leads to the men's prayer hall. Larger mosques like the Sheikh Zayed Grand Mosque allow women to enter the main prayer hall during tours scheduled in between prayer times.

It's customary for Muslims to step into the mosque with their right foot first; on exit, it's the left foot that leaves first.

Photography 101

You're welcome to take pictures of the mosque's facade and interiors, but avoid capturing worshippers during ablution or prayer time.

AL FAROOQ OMAR BIN AL KHATTAB MOSQUE

Named after Umar bin Al Khattab, a close friend and counsellor to the Prophet Muhammad, this was one of the first mosques to open its doors to non-Muslims in the UAE. Originally built in 1986, the mosque (p94) was rebuilt entirely in 2011 after being demolished the year prior. Twice-daily tours focus on the stunning art and architecture of the mosque – which takes inspiration from Istanbul's famed Blue Mosque and Moroccan and Andalusian art. There's also an Islamic centre with an extensive library where visitors can learn more about Muslim culture, art and science.

JAMES JIAO/SHUTTERSTOCK ©

Bedouin desert camp experience

HOW TO... Visit the Desert

No visit to the UAE is complete without spending some time in the sand – after all, more than 80% of the country's land area is desert. Swathes of arid desert landscape stretch from the Arabian Gulf to the Empty Quarter and the gravel plains bordering the rugged Hajjar mountains in the east. Whether you want to experience the thrilling sport of dune bashing, stare at the starry night sky or get a taste of Bedouin hospitality, here's how to get the most out of your desert adventure.

Solo vs Group Tour

Unless you have experience driving and navigating in the desert, a group tour is the best option for first-timers who want to visit the desert. Group tours also offer more in terms of activities, including sandboarding, quad tours, barbecues and overnight camping. A popular company for desert safaris in Dubai is Platinum Heritage Tours (platinum-heritage.com).

Best Time to Visit

November to April remains the best time to visit the desert as temperatures during the day are mild, and cool and breezy at night. Always check the weather forecast for sandstorms before you head out into the desert – they tend to occur more frequently as winter changes into spring.

What to Wear

Depending on the time of year, the weather in the desert can change drastically compared to the city. Loose-fitting clothing, a scarf (to protect from the sun, sand and wind) and sandals are recommended from May to October. Dressing in layers and closed shoes is highly recommended when visiting from November to April – temperatures tend to drop as soon as the sun sets in the winter.

Adventure Sport Insurance

If you plan to partake in thrilling activities like ATVing or sandboarding while in the desert, checking whether your travel insurance covers adventure sports is a good idea.

DUNE BASHING

Dune bashing is a popular adventure sport in the UAE. On weekends, you'll often find residents hurrying down the Dubai–Hatta road, past rush-hour traffic, into the desert to ride sand dunes like 'Big Red', a stunning red swathe of desert home to one of the area's biggest dunes. They manoeuvre their 4WD vehicles at high speeds over towering sand dunes, producing an adrenaline-fuelled roller=coaster experience. If you don't have experience driving off-road in the desert, consider booking a desert safari package – many tour companies in the UAE also include dune bashing as an activity.

SABINO PARENTE/SHUTTERSTOCK ©

Dune bashing

GEEPAS
جيباس
to advertise : 04 391 32 23
113

THE DUBAI & ABU DHABI

STORYBOOK

Our writers delve deep into different aspects of life in Dubai and Abu Dhabi

A History of Dubai & Abu Dhabi in 15 Places

A grand saga of ebb and flow.

Christabel Lobo

p218

Street Food & the City

Street food serves as the UAE's unofficial universal language.

Christabel Lobo

p222

Building Narratives

The UAE's architectural panorama presents a kaleidoscope of styles.

Christabel Lobo

p224

Pearls, Petrol & Progress

The tale of the UAE's economy weaves from pearl-rich depths to the heights of trade, tourism and innovation.

Christabel Lobo

p226

The Canvas of a Nation

The UAE's art and culture scene serves as its vibrant heartbeat.

Christabel Lobo

p228

Dubai Creek (p57)

A HISTORY OF DUBAI & ABU DHABI IN 15 PLACES

The tale of Dubai and Abu Dhabi is a grand saga of ebb and flow: of wandering Bedouin tribes; of pearl divers and their treasures; of bustling trading hubs. This narrative is a temporal voyage that commences with ancient settlements and culminates in the metropolitan marvels we witness today. By Christabel Lobo

THE FOUNDING FATHER of the UAE, Sheikh Zayed bin Sultan Al Nahyan, once said that history is nothing but a continuous chain of events, connecting the future with its past and present. 'He who does not know his past cannot make the best of his present and future.'

The country's fertile lands have long enticed its residents and visitors, from foreign traders bargaining for silks, metals and spices in the bustling souks to pearl divers braving the ocean depths in the 20th century and ambitious rulers envisioning an oasis amid the stark desert landscape.

Emiratis have long celebrated their past with pride, often emphasising their rapid ascent from nomadic Bedouin culture to a beacon of modernity while thoughtfully navigating the implications. Even today, as the country is poised on the precipice of evolution, it remains tethered to its humble roots as institutions, entrepreneurs and artists collaborate to present a holistic portrayal of the nation's journey from simple pearling hamlets to thriving global epicentres of commerce and tourism.

1. Jebel Hafit Tombs

BACK TO THE BRONZE AGE

Situated at the base of Jebel Hafit mountain are a collection of over 500 beehive-shaped tombs dating back to the Bronze Age. The striking domes feature a narrow keyhole-like entryway into the interior burial chamber. Also uncovered in the tombs were jewellery, shells, precious stones like agate and carnelian, copper objects, pottery and fish vertebrae.

The first discovery happened in the early 1950s by Danish archaeologists at the request of Sheikh Shakhbut bin Sultan, then-ruler of Abu Dhabi. The findings helped put the UAE on the map, giving experts a more complex look at the development of life and the importance of sea trade in the Arabian Peninsula more than 5000 years ago.

For more on Jebel Hafit, see page 218

2. Jumeirah Archaeological Ruins

AN ANCIENT ROUTE UNCOVERED

The UAE may be a young country, but Jumeirah's archaeological site shows visitors that life continued to exist in the region for millennia. Clearly visible in the background of this site is Dubai's iconic skyline.

It perfectly contrasts the archaeological ruins – remnants of an ancient Islamic settlement that include five houses, a mosque, a marketplace and caravansary along a trade route between Mesopotamia, Oman and the Far East – that date back to the Abbasid Dynasty. The visitors centre provides a closer look at the excavation findings, from copper coins and glazed pottery to stone tools and gold ornaments.

For more on Jumeirah Archaeological Ruins, see page 94

3. Rub' al Khali – the Empty Quarter

EXPLORE THE UNEXPLORED DESERT

As the world's biggest stretch of sand, the Rub' al Khali or Empty Quarter extends into Yemen, Oman, Saudi Arabia and the UAE. With an estimated half of the Sahara's sand volume, it's among Earth's least explored regions. Historically, its harsh climate deterred permanent settlement, yet nomadic Bedouin tribes occasionally navigated its expanse. Only in the early 20th century, through explorers like Bertram Thomas and Wilfred Thesiger, did it unveil its mysteries to the broader world. Today, a short drive south from the capital reveals its breathtaking dunes, some towering at 250m – a testament to natural grandeur and human resilience.

For more on the Empty Quarter, see page 181

4. Qasr Al Hosn

WHERE CULTURE MEETS HISTORY

For a glimpse of life in Abu Dhabi before oil, head downtown to the heart of the city where its oldest surviving stone structure, Qasr Al Hosn, still stands. Initially constructed in the 1760s as a watchtower to protect the island's invaluable freshwater source, it expanded into a fort before evolving into the royal residence for the Al Nahyan family until 1966.

Qasr Al Hosn, or the White Fort, reopened in 2018 as a museum and cultural hub after a substantial decade-long restoration that carefully restored the outer palace's striking vernacular design – a mechanism for naturally cooling building interiors without the need for air-conditioning.

For more on Qasr Al Hosn, see page 130

Qasr Al Hosn (p130)

ELENA BEE/SHUTTERSTOCK ©

5. Dubai Creek

THE ECONOMIC EPICENTRE

Often considered to be the heart and soul of the city, Dubai Creek contributed to the area's economic development long before the formation of the seven emirates. One of the Creek's earliest references is in the 16th-century travelogue of Gasparo Balbi, a Venetian merchant who travelled to the Gulf for its thriving pearling industry.

Fast forward a few centuries, and the Creek became an essential port for Dubai's pearl diving, fishing, trading and boat-building industries. Abras, the cheapest form of transport in the UAE, continue to ferry passengers between Bur Dubai and Deira. In 2016, the Dubai Water Canal developed the Creek even further by extending it inland and looping it back to the sea.

For more on Dubai Creek, see page 57

6. Abu Dhabi Corniche

SANDY SHORES & CITYSCAPES

Once a sandy shoreline lined with fishing boats and palm-frond barasti huts, Abu Dhabi's Corniche is a stark contrast from its humble beginnings. Located along the capital's northwestern shore, the scenic 8km promenade epitomises modernity and luxury. Towering skyscrapers, chic hotels and refined restaurants serve as its backdrop, resulting from years of expansion and upgrades to the area.

After a 2014 massive upgrade, the Corniche now boasts immaculate beaches, beautifully landscaped gardens, abundant seating, and a walkway for leisurely strolls, biking and taking in the sights. It reflects Abu Dhabi's growth, celebrating the city's past, present and future.

For more on Abu Dhabi Corniche, see page 134

7. Al Ain Palace Museum

TRADITIONAL VERNACULAR ARCHITECTURE

It's hard to imagine the UAE before all the staggering skylines and glitz and glamour, but Al Ain Palace Museum serves as the perfect example of life before the discovery of oil. Built in the 1930s, the building encapsulates over eight decades of the nation's history – and also insights into even earlier eras. This was originally the residence of the UAE's founding father and first president, Sheikh Zayed bin Sultan Al Nahyan, who lived in the palace until the late 1960s before moving to Abu Dhabi. The restored cinnamon-coloured structures, which now function as a living museum, are some of the best representations of traditional vernacular architecture and feature indigenous building materials like adobe and palm tree roofs.

For more on Al Ain, see page 184

8. Al Fahidi Historical Neighbourhood

LIFE BEFORE THE SEVEN EMIRATES

Al Fahidi's Historical Neighbourhood is a perfectly preserved capsule of Dubai's rich past. Also known as Al Bastakiya, this secluded, pedestrian-only enclave sits along Dubai Creek and offers a look at the local lifestyle from the mid-19th century until the formation of the Emirates in 1971. Restored sand-coloured buildings made from coral, stone, palm fronds, sandalwood and teak wood feature characteristic barjeel (wind towers), flanking the neighbourhood's narrow, meandering alleyways.

An extensive renovation in the 1980s transformed the area into what it is today: a hub of museums, art galleries and cultural exhibits. It's a testament to Dubai's persistent commitment to preserving its rich heritage in an ever-evolving metropolis.

For more on Al Fahidi, see page 66

9. Etihad Museum

THE BIRTHPLACE OF A NATION

The Etihad Museum, located at the very site of the Union House in Dubai, where the UAE was founded in 1971, encapsulates a monumental moment in the country's history. Here, the founding fathers signed the constitution to unite the Trucial States into a single nation. The grounds house a carefully restored Union House and striking modern museum building, with a curved roof resembling a sheet of paper and seven columns signifying the pens used to sign the declaration.

For more on the Etihad Museum, see page 94

10. Burj Al Arab & Burj Khalifa

WELCOME TO NEW DUBAI

The Burj Al Arab and Burj Khalifa are prominent symbols in the city skyline, best representing Dubai's growth and transformation into a thriving 21st-century global hub for trade, finance, transport, architecture and tourism. Opened in 1999, the iconic Burj Al Arab hotel, with its ultraluxe interiors and self-proclaimed seven-star service, showcases the city's insatiable attraction for opulence. Fast forward to a decade later, and the Dubai skyline welcomed its most prized architectural asset – the world's tallest building – Burj Khalifa.

For more on Burj Khalifa, see page 78

11. Ras Al Khor Wildlife Sanctuary

DESERT WETLANDS AND CONSERVATION

The juxtaposition of the sanctuary's wildlife against the backdrop of Dubai's famed skyline and roaring highways makes it a unique attraction. Founded in 1985 and declared a Ramsar site in 2007, Ras Al Khor Wildlife Sanctuary remains a critical habitat for more than 170 species of birds, most notably the pink greater flamingo that take centre stage in the winter.

Despite Dubai's encroaching modernity, the sanctuary continues to remain an essential stopover point for birds migrating along the East African–West Asian Flyway. There are three bird hides (platforms) and binoculars for visitors to observe the wildlife without disturbing them.

For more on Ras Al Khor Wildlife Sanctuary, see page 87

12. Dubai Mall

A CULTURE OF CONVENIENCE

In a country known for many firsts, from the world's tallest building to the constructed palm islands, the UAE's numerous malls stand out. They're not just spaces where you can shop for department store clothes or dine in fast-casual food courts; instead, most malls here also have

Flamingoes, Ras Al Khor Wildlife Sanctuary (p87)

supermarkets, pharmacies, banks, restaurants and movie theatres. And in the case of Dubai Mall, there's also a 10-million-litre indoor aquarium and an Olympic-sized ice rink. In the summertime, it becomes a refuge from the harsh sun and humidity outdoors; during Ramadan, extended late-night hours go well past midnight to accommodate those fasting.

For more on Dubai Mall, see page 38

13. Saadiyat Island

AN ISLAND OF ART AND CULTURE

Saadiyat Island's transformation from a small fishing hamlet to global cultural hub helped put Abu Dhabi at the forefront of discussions of modernity in the UAE. Manarat Al Saadiyat, which opened in 2009, serves as an immersive arts space for the local community.

Architectural masterpieces like the Louvre Abu Dhabi – designed by architect Jean Nouvel – seamlessly integrate into Saadiyat's coastline with a floating geometric dome that has since become a popular sanctuary for rest and reflection. With the future Guggenheim and Zayed National Museum set to open in 2025, the island epitomises a dynamic intersection of culture, architecture and visionary development.

For more on Saadiyat Island see page 162

14. Hatta Mountain Reserve

A NATURAL WONDER

Don't let the UAE's arid desert landscape fool you: it's also home to some stunning ecological havens like the Hatta Mountain Reserve. Set in the Hajar Mountains just 135km southeast of downtown Dubai, the area dates back centuries – petroglyphs depicting animals, people and ancient scripts go back 3000 years. Declared a nature reserve in 2014, the mountainous terrain is rich in native flora and fauna, as well as wildlife like the Arabian tahr, spiny mouse and sand cat. Approximately one-third of the UAE's arthropods can be found here. Farming remains a mainstay in Hatta, with more than 550 farms growing everything from dates and citrus to wild figs and millets.

For more on Hatta Mountain Reserve, see page 185

15. Abu Dhabi Mangroves

VANGUARDS OF BIODIVERSITY

Adept at tackling the effects of climate change and providing a safe habitat for local wildlife, dense mangrove forests dot Abu Dhabi's coastal areas – there are approximately 70 sq km of mangrove ecosystems in the emirate.

Found within the confines of the city is Mangrove National Park, a serene 19-sq-km forest that's home to sea turtles, dugongs, dolphins and over 60 different species of birds, including flamingos and herons. In 2020, Jubail Mangrove Park opened with ranger-led nature tours along its three expansive boardwalks – a kayak tour through the forest provides a more immersive experience.

For more on Abu Dhabi Mangroves, see page 159

STREET FOOD & THE CITY

Street food serves as the UAE's unofficial universal language, providing a sense of community and connection to the more than 200 nationalities that call the country home. By Christabel Lobo

IT'S NO SURPRISE that food and community are inextricably linked in the UAE. From the very first waves of South Asian and European expats in the mid-20th century to the country's diverse 9.28 million residents today, food has served as an important social connector, imparting international spices and flavours into the local cuisine and creating a sense of permanence in a highly impermanent country.

With expats making up more than three-quarters of the population, the UAE has become a truly cosmopolitan community, transforming Dubai and Abu Dhabi into gastronomic hubs for global nomads to gather and experiment.

It is here at the crossroads of three continents where cultures collide and coalesce, giving rise to unique foodways that are just as diverse as its people.

Uniquely UAE

The best way to explore the UAE's distinctive culture is to connect with its soul. And in the case of Dubai and Abu Dhabi, that means heading into the heart

Clockwise from top left: Spice Souq (p51), Dubai; Bur Dubai Souq (p70); shawarma seller; karak chai

of the city to get a taste of its vibrant street-food culture.

Cafeterias across both cities showcase delicacies from neighbouring Gulf states like Oman all the way east to India and the Philippines, providing a window into the multicultural tapestry of its residents. Predominantly run as takeaway-only spots – a testament to the country's love of convenience culture – these no-frills spaces are staffed by South Indians (mainly Keralites) who can just as easily switch from Arabic to Hindi and English to Urdu and even Russian.

An order of an egg sandwich, Emirati *rigag* (wafer-thin flatbread) or flaky, Kerala-style *parotta* stuffed with cheese and a crumbled packet of Chips Oman crisps can end up being so much more than just a filling budget-friendly snack. The star of the show is Chips Oman, a ubiquitous 40-year-old brand of Omani potato chips known for its signature flavour profile – it's slightly hot, slightly tangy and slightly salty – crunch and accompanying dose of nostalgia.

Take a bite into any iteration of this cult-favourite dish, which can run you as little as Dhs5, and you'll discover the smorgasbord of life here – it may be part Indian-part Omani-part Emirati, but one thing's for certain: it's a homegrown staple.

The Ancient Spice Route

Archaeological ruins in the UAE help paint a picture of life in the region prior to the discovery of oil and union of the seven emirates. In Jumeirah, remnants of a caravan stop dating back to the Abbasid dynasty indicate a long-distance trade route passed through the city, linking the thriving civilisations of Mesopotamia (modern-day Iraq) with the Far East.

Frankincense, pottery and copper moved east, away from the Arabian economies, while silk and spices travelled west from China and Southeast Asia, often via the Indian subcontinent. Merchants didn't always just pass by; many settled here, bringing with them cooking techniques and ingredients that eventually began to shape and infuse the local cuisine.

The influence of this centuries-old exchange can be tasted in popular cafeteria dishes today – spices like cardamom, coriander seeds, cumin, cinnamon, nutmeg, cloves and saffron are now considered integral flavours in Emirati cuisine thanks to a lengthy history of trade in local ports.

For a taste of the subtle process of diffusion in local food culture from different parts of the world, order a plate of *chebab* – a small serving from the popular Abu Dhabi chain Luqaimat and Chebab will cost just Dhs11. This is the Emirati version of pancakes, made from a pourable yeast batter and seasoned with cardamom and turmeric from the subcontinent and saffron from Iran. You'll often find it served for breakfast or during Ramadan with *dibs* (date syrup), cheese and honey.

Karak Chai Culture

Often dubbed the country's 'unofficial national drink', karak chai is a staple in the daily diet of Emiratis and expatriates alike. This sweet and creamy cardamom-infused tea traces its origins to the South Asian masala chai, arriving in the UAE with Indian emigrants during the 1960s oil boom.

Today, tiny tea shops dot neighbourhoods across the seven emirates, with experienced *chaiwallas* preparing their highly sought-after concoctions, a blend of tea, evaporated milk, sugar and a secret mix of spices – the word 'karak' translates to strong or hard in Hindi.

Enjoyed all throughout the day, this steaming hot cup is a surprising social unifier – you'll often find co-workers grabbing this cheap, Dhs1 staple before work in the morning or young friends enjoying a late-night meet-up sipping on glasses of freshly brewed karak from the comfort of their cars.

Much like its street-food counterparts, karak chai has become a quintessential part of the country's culture, highlighting how the UAE's street-food scene has absorbed culinary influences from its sizeable expatriate population. The streets are a culinary kaleidoscope, showcasing a mix of global flavours, from shawarma stands and Filipino panaderias to Indian *chaiwallas* and Lebanese bakeries.

And, in a country that's known for its luxe fine-dining restaurants and extravagant gold-foil-wrapped dishes, street food serves as much more than just a budget snack or drink. It's a delicious echo of the smorgasbord of life here in the UAE.

BUILDING NARRATIVES

The UAE's architectural panorama presents a kaleidoscope of styles, underscoring the country's rapid growth and transition. By Christabel Lobo

LOOK BEYOND THE country's newly minted architecture – that includes some of the world's tallest skyscrapers, sweeping superhighways and cutting-edge airports – and you'll discover a diverse range of architectural styles, each serving as a perfect metaphor for the UAE's rapid pace of growth since its founding in 1971.

1960s Winds of Change

A visit to Al Ain Palace in Abu Dhabi transports visitors straight to the country's pre-petrol era – oil was first discovered in the capital in 1958. Dating back to the 1930s, this adobe-style building is an excellent example of local building techniques, with palm-tree roofing, central courtyards and characteristic *barjeel* (wind towers) that provided a natural form of air-conditioning during the desert's harsh summer months.

Apart from tribal sheikhs and wealthy merchants, most people in Abu Dhabi lived in *barasti* houses made from palm fronds. Fresh water and electricity were nonexistent. However, with newfound wealth from oil revenues and the start of Sheikh Zayed bin Sultan Al Nahyan's rule, Abu Dhabi's economy flourished – more schools opened, banks were established, and hotels and housing were built.

The rapid modernisation during this decade brought with it an influx of immigrants from Asia, Europe, Africa and the surrounding Arab world, who came to develop the city's masterplans and infrastructure.

Local rulers enlisted foreign architects and planners to design buildings in the country that symbolised modernity and prosperity. The result was a mix of functional concrete structures that drew on international design trends of the time and bespoke projects that represented a nascent national identity.

By the end of the 1960s, city skylines in both Dubai and Abu Dhabi began to transform, setting the stage for the high-rise towers and iconic structures that the country is known for today.

1970s Moderism

By the time the 1970s rolled around, foreign architects and construction companies had set up shop in the UAE. Modernist and international styles of architecture

 Top left: Al Ain Palace; Top right: Museum of the Future (p80), Dubai

quickly began to replace traditional ones. As a result, building codes changed, heralding the emergence of multistory concrete buildings in both Dubai and Abu Dhabi.

Government buildings, housing developments and commercial buildings were all designed with modernist facades that featured geometric forms with crisp angles and simple designs. A landmark example from that time period, and also one of Sheikh Zayed Rd's earliest skyscrapers, is the Dubai World Trade Centre.

Advent of Regional Modernism

During the '80s, UAE architecture went through an interesting phase. Local laws established mid-decade mandated that building designs must include some form of Arabic and Islamic elements.

Intricate arabesque motifs, calligraphy, domes and symmetrical archways started to get incorporated into contemporary structures, creating a unique regional Modernist style that continued on for decades – iconic structures like the Sheikh Zayed Grand Mosque and the Emirates Palace exemplify this architectural synthesis.

This conscious effort by the government to establish a unique national identity in the country – one that paid homage to its Islamic roots, while continuing to highlight the nation's hyper rate of modernisation – led to a distinct style that is characteristic of architecture in the UAE today.

Futuristic Facades

Inscribed into the facade of the Museum of the Future are the words of Sheikh Mohammed bin Rashid Al Maktoum, ruler of Dubai: 'the future belongs to those who can imagine it, design it and execute it'. The concept of an ultra-modern architectural marvel is not foreign to Dubai and the UAE at large. Since the city's meteoric rise from a modest pearl-diving hamlet to a global metropolis, it has continuously pushed boundaries.

The Museum of the Future exemplifies this audacious spirit. Resembling an avant-garde sculpture, the building's striking torus shape stands out on Sheikh Zayed Rd, symbolising Dubai's vision as a global innovation hub.

Drive south to Saadiyat Island in Abu Dhabi, and you'll be met with even more architectural icons designed – and in some case still under construction – by renowned international architects like Jean Nouvel and Frank Gehry. Opened in 2017, the Louvre Abu Dhabi combines modern architectural techniques with Arabic cultural motifs – its signature feature is the latticed dome, inspired by the interlaced palm leaves traditionally used in Emirati roofing.

Upcoming unveilings include the Guggenheim museum by Frank Gehry, and the Zayed National Museum by British architectural firm Foster + Partners, both scheduled to open in 2025, as well as the Abu Dhabi Performing Arts Centre by Zaha Hadid Architects.

Need for Preservation

The allure of a city resides in its architectural plurality, and both Dubai and Abu Dhabi have their fair share. But the country's quick ascension from desert to global hub has triggered drastic shifts in its architectural landscape, where the old is razed to make way for the new.

In order to preserve the UAE's rich architectural heritage, Emirati urban typologist Hussain AlMoosawi has been photographing the country's distinctive facades since 2013. His Instagram (@hugraphy) serves as a visual grid of symmetry, inviting viewers to discover the surprising diversity of architectural styles that exist in buildings across the UAE – oftentimes within the same block.

An essential step to keeping a city's culture, history and memories alive for generations to come, preservation helps restore the balance between abandonment and rejuvenation. In 2016, Abu Dhabi passed the Cultural Heritage Law to safeguard the city's architectural and urban spaces.

Remarkably, architecture serves as an unexpected yet eloquent narrator of the UAE's history, encapsulating its rapid growth and transformation. The diverse range of structures and styles, from restored traditional vernacular buildings in old Dubai to towering futuristic skyscrapers, reveals a nation balancing reverence for its past with a daring vision for the future.

PEARLS, PETROL & PROGRESS

The tale of the UAE's economy weaves from pearl-rich depths to petroleum-swept dunes and its current economic landscape as a global hub of trade, tourism and innovation. By Christabel Lobo

ARCHAEOLOGICAL FINDS TELL us that despite the country's young age and size, the United Arab Emirates has played an essential role in the course of history. A thriving pearling industry that started more than 7000 years ago and the 20th-century oil boom were just precursors of the successful economic developments to follow.

Navigating a historical landscape entwined with deeply held social, political and cultural complexities is complex. But the UAE has managed to do so quite successfully, emerging with an unparalleled standard of living and economic stability in today's Middle East.

The Pearl Trade

Evidence dating close to 8000 years ago testifies to the enduring legacy of the region's pearl diving trade. The large-scale trading of pearls originated in Mesopotamia and flourished for millennia, with the area exporting pearls far and wide, from Imperial Rome all the way east to India and China.

The pearl trade emerged as the economic backbone for many coastal communities in the Gulf in the 19th and early 20th

Below left: Dubai oil refinery; Below right: Fisherman looking for pearls

centuries. Abu Dhabi and Dubai both saw significant development as a result, with the latter's pioneering ruler, Sheikh Maktoum bin Hasher Al Maktoum, turning the city into a duty-free port – an enticing tax-free offer for Indian and Persian merchants, who, still today, remain keepers of Dubai Creek and its surrounding souqs.

Pearling was a tough, seasonal job that relied on the cooperation of weather and sea. The months of June to September provided optimal temperatures and calm waters, marking what was known as *Ghous Al Kabir,* or the big dive. Pearl diving crews would set off for sea in wooden dhows at the break of dawn for months at a time. Interspersed throughout the rest of the year were shorter, one-month stints of pearling, specifically in October and November.

Diving for pearls was nothing short of perilous; divers were only equipped with *fettam* (nose clips traditionally made from sheep bone or turtle shell) and *dean,* a woven bag tied around their necks to hold the collected oysters. A rope, known as *zubail,* had a stone weight and would be tied to the diver's legs to help sink them to the sea bed.

Their prized catch, luminescent pearls, were renowned for their size and lustre. According to Saif Marzooq al-Shamlan's 1970s memoir, *Pearling in the Arabian Gulf,* 1912 was a 'Year of Superabundance' when dhows would return from each trip with hundreds of pearls – a principal export for most of the region.

By the early 1930s, however, the pearl trade took a hit, collapsing on the heels of the Great Depression and the advent of Japanese cultured pearls – by 1935, Japan was producing approximately 10 million pearls per year. Once-bustling pearling centres turned into ghost towns, leading to a profound impact on local life in the region.

Discovery of Oil

The Trucial States, as they were commonly called at the time, began their explorations for oil throughout the Emirates. In 1960, the first commercial oil field was discovered in Abu Dhabi. Six years later, Dubai followed suit, turning the soon-to-be country's luck around. Newfound wealth from oil exports was not just used to modernise the emirates; it also served as a significant factor in the federation's formation in 1971.

For the next two decades, the country focused on building new infrastructure, investing in education and developing other critical sectors of the economy. This swift development on the heels of discovering oil helped solidify the UAE's status as one of the wealthiest countries globally.

Today, the UAE has the sixth-largest oil reserves and the seventh-largest reserves of natural gas in the world – approximately 96% of its oil fields lie in the emirate of Abu Dhabi. But sustained slumps in oil prices, coupled with Russia's war with Ukraine and the ongoing climate crisis, indicate the growing need for diversification in the country's sources of wealth.

Economic Diversification

The 21st-century push towards economic diversification led to a complete transformation of the UAE's economy. Gone were the days of its sole reliance on oil as a source of wealth. Instead, the country implemented strategic plans to foster growth in sectors like tourism, real estate, manufacturing and finance. Dubai's diversification strategy was particularly admirable, and a testament to its ruler, Sheikh Mohammed bin Rashid Al Maktoum's vision. Its non-oil sectors are thriving today, accounting for over 95% of the city's GDP.

As the country moves towards its future, renewable energy and sustainable technology are new economic focal points, aligning with the global shift towards greener economies. Initiatives like smart city projects, digital transformation and the development of the tech workforce are vital in helping the UAE on its path to becoming an internationally recognised tech hub.

Further hopes to transform the economy were unveiled with the country's 'We the UAE 2031' vision launch in 2022. Doubling its GDP to Dhs3 trillion is a top priority for the next decade, along with increasing the rate of non-oil exports, foreign trade and tourism. On the UAE's 50th anniversary, the country's vice president, Sheikh Mohammed bin Rashid Al Maktoum, couldn't help but remind residents that while 'building a state, a home, a united people, a homeland for all' may have started out as just a dream, today, the country stands proud, rivalling some of the world's top nations.

THE CANVAS OF A NATION

The UAE's art and culture scene serves as its vibrant heartbeat, echoing the everyday life of a transient and diverse population through the themes of identity, nomadism and impermanence. By Christabel Lobo

ART HAS ALWAYS played a central role in life in the United Arab Emirates, going back centuries. From the discovery of ancient petroglyphs in the expansive Hajar mountain range to the contemporary cultural hub blossoming on Abu Dhabi's Saadiyat Island, the nation's unique art is a testament to its transient and ever-shifting demographic.

Today, art galleries like the Third Line and Carbon 12 in Dubai's vibrant Alserkal Avenue, along with Manarat Al Saadiyat and Warehouse421 in Abu Dhabi, continue to redefine what it means to create art and be an artist in the UAE.

Folk Art

The Trucial States functioned primarily as a tribal society in the 19th and early 20th centuries. While Western art forms may not have been commonplace, the region did have its own unique forms of artistic expression, deeply interwoven with rich cultural traditions and everyday life.

The practice of oral tradition was highly valued throughout the emirates and served as the primary way of storytelling and passing on historical events from one generation to the next. Nabati poetry, in particular, played an essential role in conveying emotions, preserving heritage and social commentary in the region.

Traditional folk dance and music, such as *ayyalah* and *al-harbiya,* were important forms of artistic expression, often incorporating singing and poetry. When it came to visual arts, it was crafts like weaving, pottery and metalwork that took centre stage.

Contemporary Art

By the 20th century, traditional art forms started to intersect with global art movements, giving rise to a blend of styles that touched on the notions of identity – both self and national – impermanence and nomadism.

Exhibit brochures of pioneering UAE artists in the 20th-century indicate that photography, painting and sculpture were the primary traditional artistic mediums of choice. Art shows, which were few and far between, often occurred in private

 Top left: Sharjah Biennial; Top right: Manarat Al Saadiyat (p169)

residences and other ephemeral creative spaces.

However, it wasn't until a decade later that art initiatives started to gain momentum, first with the formation of the Emirates Fine Arts Society in 1980 and then the Sharjah Biennial in 1993.

Pioneering contemporary artists like Hassan Sharif began exploring themes tied to their changing realities, from societal shifts due to urbanisation and the effects of the oil boom on the UAE's emerging identity after achieving independence in 1971.

Fast forward to 2023, and the turn of the millennia's technological advances have wholeheartedly been adopted by 21st-century artists in the region; you'll find emerging local artists like the Al Najjar brothers, Talal and Ziad, seamlessly coalesce traditional mediums with digital ones in their works.

Sharjah

Often seen as the cultural heart of the UAE, Sharjah's Biennial has been attracting international artists and visitors since first launching three decades ago. Spearheaded by the Sharjah Art Foundation, the Biennial showcases the work of artists and curators from around the world.

Through the years, its editions have seen a shift from traditional arts to more contemporary expressions, including everything from gallery exhibits and art installations to theatrical performances and film screenings, challenging the notions of identity and culture in the 21st century.

Dubai

Dubai's creative landscape transformed in 2008 with the opening of Tashkeel, a multi-disciplinary art and design incubator. The brainchild of Her Highness Lateefa bint Maktoum bin Rashid Al Maktoum, Tashkeel pushed the boundaries of what it meant to create art and be an artist in the UAE. It was the first mixed-gender, open-access art centre that not only promoted a sense of belonging in Dubai's emerging creative community but also provided a space where artistic resources abounded.

Head 20 minutes south of downtown Dubai and you'll wind up in Al Quoz, a gritty industrial neighbourhood that houses the city's renowned artistic and cultural hub: Alserkal Avenue. This 4600-sq-metre cultural quarter features artists' studios, homegrown businesses and art galleries showcasing regional and international artists, including two that played a significant role in developing the city's contemporary art scene: the Third Line and Carbon 12. Situated in the heart of Al Quoz for close to two decades, they've helped dynamise the UAE art scene by offering platforms for discourse, creativity and cross-cultural exchange.

Beyond these burgeoning culture hubs are spaces like Bayt Al Mamzar, where art drives community and vice versa. Opened in 2021 by Emirati brothers and patrons of the local arts scene, Khalid and Gaith Abdulla, this beautifully restored one-storey house in Al Mamzar – it was once their grandmother's home – serves two main functions. First, it exists as an evolving community arts space, complete with a gallery, co-working space, library and artist studios. And second, the restored facade and interiors exude a nostalgic appeal that's now much harder to find in the skyscrapers and glitz of New Dubai.

Abu Dhabi

No longer confined to traditional forms, art in the UAE embodies the nation's forward-looking spirit and embraces a global, inclusive vision. The up-and-coming arts offerings on Abu Dhabi's Saadiyat Island perfectly represent this progressive transformation.

The first art and cultural space to open in Saadiyat's Cultural District was Manarat Al Saadiyat in 2009. Translating to 'place of enlightenment', this expansive space is all about cultivating and sustaining a creative artists' community in the nation's capital through year-round curated art exhibits, performances, film screenings and workshops.

From the preservation of Bedouin folk art to the showcasing of avant-garde art installations, the spectrum of artistic expression in the UAE unveils a nation balancing its respect for culture and heritage with a progressive outlook, shaping its creative future.

INDEX

A

Abrahamic Family House 165
abras 57-8
Abu Dhabi 128-35, 136-45, 146-51, 152-61, 162-71, **132**, **138**, **148**, **154**, **164**, **174**
  accommodation 133, 134, 139, 144-5, 150, 161, 169, 178, 201
  activities 134, 144, 159, 160-1, 171, 178
  art 229
  drinking 150, 160, 170, 177, 178
  food 133, 134, 142, 143, 144, 145, 148, 149, 150, 155, 160, 161, 167, 171, 177
  itineraries 24-5
  shopping 133, 134, 148, 168, 170
  sights 130-1, 134, 139, 140-1, 142, 143, 145, 155, 156-7, 158-9, 160-1, 165, 166-7, 169-70, 175, 176, 177-8
  spas 178
Abu Dhabi Children's Library 131
Abu Dhabi Corniche 25, 134, 144-5, 219
Abu Dhabi Falcon Hospital 159
Abu Dhabi Heritage Village 143
Abu Dhabi Island 152
Abu Dhabi Mangroves 221
accessible travel 205
accommodation 200-1, *see also individual locations*
activities, *see* outdoor activities
aflaj 183
Ain Dubai observation wheel 107, 115
airports 57, 196
Ajman 192
Al Ahmadiya School 51
Al Ain 183
Al Ain Palace 220, 224
Al Fahidi Fort 66
Al Fahidi Historical Neighbourhood 66, 220
Al Ghurair Centre 52
Al Hisn 193
Al Hosn 130-1
Al Hudayriyat Island 160-1
Al Jaddaf 68
Al Jahili Fort 184
Al Mamzar Beach Park 55
Al Marmoom Desert Conservation Reserve 122-3
Al Maryah Island 146-50
Al Mina 162
Al Qudra Lake 122
Al Quoz 97
Al Rafisah Dam 188
Al Reem Island 146-50
Al Seef Dubai 67
Al Zahiyah 146-50
alcohol 33
amusement parks, *see* theme parks
apartments 200
apps 43
aquariums
  Lost Chambers 108
  National Aquarium Abu Dhabi 161
Arabic 210-11
archaeological sites
  Jebel Hafit Tombs 218
  Jumeirah Archaeological Ruins 218
architecture 224-5
art 6-7, 228-9
  Abu Dhabi 177, 229
  Dubai 86, 99-100, 229
art galleries, *see* museums & galleries
Atlantis, The Palm Dubai 108

B

beach clubs 9, 114-15, 170
beach resorts 200
beaches 9
  Abu Dhabi Beach 134
  A'l Bahar 145
  Al Hudayriyat Beach 160
  Al Sahil Beach 145
  Corniche Beach 144-5
  Jumeirah Public Beach 91
  Khor Fakkan Beach 190
  Kite Beach 91
  Marsana Beach 160
  Palm West Beach 105
  Sunset Beach 99
  Yas Beach 175
Bedouin people 122-3, 143, 218
bird-watching
  Abu Dhabi Falcon Hospital 159
  Abu Dhabi Mangroves 221
  Al Ain Oasis 183
  Al Marmoom Desert Conservation Reserve 122
  Al Zorah Nature Reserve 192
  Eastern Mangrove National Park 159
  Mushrif National Park 59
  Ras Al Khor Wildlife Sanctuary 87, 220
Bluewaters Island 107
boat trips 57-8
books 29
border crossings 196
Breakwater area 136-45, **138**
brunch 113, 144, 203
Bur Dubai 61-73, **62**, **63**
  accommodation 66, 67, 201
  drinking 69, 73
  food 64, 67, 69, 70, 71
  itineraries 22
  shopping 68, 69, 73
  sights 62-3, 64-5, 66-7, 68
Bur Dubai Grand Mosque 62
Burj Al Arab 92, 220
Burj Khalifa 78-9, 220
bus travel 197
business hours 33

camel milk ice cream 31
camels 87
camping 186
canoeing, *see* kayaking
car travel 197, 209
children, travel with 16-17, 86, 204
Children's City 52
cinemas 55
climate 26-7, 209
clothing 73, 187, 205
coffee 32-3, 72-3, 97, 203
comedy 35
Conrad Abu Dhabi Etihad Towers 142
Conrad Spa 144
costs 198
credit cards 198
Cultural Foundation 131

dangers, *see* emergencies, safe travel
dates 181
day trips 180-93
  Al Ain 183
  Al Rafisah Dam 188
  Al Zorah Nature Reserve 192
  Fujairah 191
  Hatta 185-8
  Jebel Hafit 184
  Jebel Jais 191
  Khor Fakkan 189-90
  Liwa Oasis 181-2
  Qasr Al Sarab 182-3
  Sharjah 193
Deira 49-59, **50**, **56**
  accommodation 59, 201
  activities 59
  food 54, 57, 59
  shopping 50, 51, 52, 54
  sights 57-9
Deira Clocktower 52

Map Pages **000**

Deira Corniche 58
Deira Old Souq 51
Deira Waterfront Market 54
desert 13, 214
deserts
 Al Marmoom Desert Conservation Reserve 122-3
 Dubai Desert Conservation Reserve 101, 207
 Qasr Al Sarab 182-3
 Rub' al Khali 181, 219
disabilities, travellers with 205
diving 99
Downtown Dubai 75-87, **76**
 accommodation 79, 80, *see also individual locations*
 activities 81, 82
 entertainment 80, 83, 86-7
 food 77, 81, 86
 itineraries 22
 shopping 79
 sights 77, 78-9, 81, 82, 85-6
 walking tours 84, **84**
drinking 32-3, 202-3, *see also individual locations*, nightclubs 33
drinks 223
driving 197, 209
drugs 209
Dubai Balloon 106
Dubai Creek 57, 219
Dubai Creek Resort and Golf Club 54
Dubai Desert Conservation Reserve 101, 207
Dubai Design District 82
Dubai Fountain 79
Dubai Frame 65
Dubai Garden Glow 68
Dubai Gold Souq 50
Dubai Islands 55
Dubai Mall 38-9, 79, 84, 85, 220-1, **84**
Dubai Marina & Palm Jumeirah 103-15, **104**, **111**
 accommodation 105, 108, 109, 201
 activities 107, 109, 114-15
 drinking 104, 107, 110, 115
 food 104, 108, 109, 110, 113, 115
 itineraries 23, 112
 shopping 104, 106
 sights 105, 106, 107, 110
Dubai Opera 80
Dubai Water Canal 77, 85
dune bashing 214

E

Eastern Mangrove National Park 159
economy 226-7
Eid Al Adha 212
Eid Al Fitr 27, 212
electricity 199
emergencies, *see also* safe travel
 language 210
 services 199
Emirates Palace Mandarin Oriental 139
entertainment 34-5, *see also individual locations*
etiquette 38, 165, 187, 202
 mosques 213
events, *see* festivals & events, sporting events
Expo City Dubai 120

family travel 16-17, 86, 204
festivals & events 27, *see also* sporting events
 Abu Dhabi Art Fair 169
 Eid Al Adha 27, 212
 Eid Al Fitr 27, 212
 Islamic New Year 212
 Liwa International Festival 182
 Ramadan 27, 212
 Sharjah Biennial 193, 229
 Sharjah Light Festival 193
films 29
flamingoes 192
food 30-1, 112, 202-3, *see also individual locations*
 fine dining 40-3, 115
 Michelin guide 40, 43
 street food 222-3
 sustainability 41
Founder's Memorial 139
free experiences 18-19

galleries, *see* museums & galleries
gardens, *see* parks & gardens
gay travellers 208
gold 50, 133
golf
 Dubai Creek Resort and Golf Club 54
 Saadiyat Beach Golf Club 171
 Yas Links 178
Gulf Arabic 210-11

Hadid, Zaha 80
hammams 10, 171
 Spa at W Abu Dhabi Yas Island 178
Hatta 185-8
Hatta Fort 187
Hatta Heritage Village 187
health 208-9
highlights 6-21
hiking 27
 Al Rabi Tower Trail 189
 Al Rafisah 188
 Hatta Mountain Reserve 185-6, 221
 Jebel Jais 191
history 226-7
holidays 199
horse racing 87
horseback-riding 59
hostels 200
hotels 200

Iftar 212
insurance 209
internet resources 207
Iridium Spa 171
Islam 212-13
itineraries, *see also individual locations*
 Abu Dhabi 24-5
 Dubai 22-3

Jebel Hafit 184, 218
Jebel Hafit Desert Park 184
Jebel Jais 191
Jumeirah 89-101, **90**, **93**
 accommodation 92, 96, 98, 99, 201
 activities 91, 92, 99
 drinking 92, 97
 food 92, 95, 96, 97
 itineraries 23
 shopping 91, 96, 97
 sights 94-5, 97, 98
Jumeirah Archeological Ruins 94
Jumeirah Beach Residence 111
Jumeirah Emirates Towers 77

karak chai 160, 223
Karama Market 68
kayaking
 Al Rafisah Dam 188
 Al Zorah Nature Reserve 192
 Hatta Dam 187
Khor Fakkan 189-90

language 29, 210-11
legal matters 209
 alcohol 33
 LGBTIQ+ travellers 208
lesbian travellers 208
LGBTIQ+ travellers 208
live music 35
Liwa Oasis 181-2
Louvre Abu Dhabi 166-7
Love Lake Dubai 122

Madha 188
Madinat Jumeirah 90
malls, *see* shopping malls
Mamsha Al Saadiyat 170
mangroves 13, 159, 170, 221
Marina Breakwater 143
markets, *see also* souqs
 Dates Market 168
 Fruit & Vegetable Market 168
 Jumeirah Fish Market 95
 Karama Market 68
 New Fish Market 168
 Time Out Market 39, 77
massage 10, 144
medical services 209
Meydan 87
Mina Seyahi 109
Mina Zayed 162, 168, 170
mobile phones 196
money 198
Moon Lake 122
Moses Ben Maimon Synagogue 165
mosques 213
 Al Bidya Mosque 191
 Al Farooq Omar Bin Al Khattab Mosque 213
 Al Farooq Omar Mosque 94
 Bur Dubai Grand Mosque 62
 Eminence Ahmed El-Tayeb Mosque 165

mosques *continued*
Jumeirah Grand Mosque 95
Sheikh Zayed Grand Mosque 152, 156-7
movies 29
Museum of the Future 80, 225
museums & galleries 228-9 421 170
Akkas Visual Art 66
Al Ain Palace Museum 220
Al Eslah School Museum 193
Al Marsam Al Hor 131
Al Shindagha Museum 63
Alserkal Ave 97
Art Connections 66
Artbooth Gallery 161
Coffee Museum 72
Cultural Foundation 131
DIFC sculpture park 99
Etihad Modern Art Gallery 145
Etihad Museum 94, 220
Hatta Honeybee Garden and Discovery Center 188
Hisn Khor Fakkan 189
Indigo Dubai Downtown 86
Jameel Arts Centre 68
Louvre Abu Dhabi 166-7
Madame Tussauds 107
Manarat Al Saadiyat 169-70
MB&F M.A.D Gallery 86
Museum of the Future 80, 225
Museum of the Poet Al Oqaili 53
Naif Museum 53
Opera Gallery 86
Perfume House 63
Sharjah Art Museum 193
Sharjah Calligraphy Museum 193
Sharjah Heritage Museum 193
Sharjah Museum of Islamic Civilization 193
Sheikh Mohammed Centre for Cultural Understanding 67

Map Pages **000**

Theatre of Digital Art 98
Women's Museum at Bait Al Banat 53
XVA Gallery 66

Nahwa 188
Najd Al Maqsar Heritage Village 188
National Bank of Dubai 59
national parks & reserves
Al Marmoom Desert Conservation Reserve 122-3
Al Zorah Nature Reserve 192
Dubai Desert Conservation Reserve 207
Eastern Mangrove National Park 159
Hatta Mountain Reserve 185-6, 221
Jebel Hafit Desert Park 184
Mushrif National Park 59
Qasr Al Sarab Protected Area 182
Ras Al Khor Wildlife Sanctuary 87, 220

oil industry 227
opening hours 199
oud 51, 63
outdoor activities 8, 13, 214, *see also individual activities*
Al Rafisah Dam 188
Hatta 185-7

Palm Jumeirah, *see* Dubai Marina & Palm Jumeirah
Palm Jumeirah Monorail 112
Palm West Beach 105
parks & gardens 12, *see also* national parks & reserves
Al Ittihad Park 110
Al Jahli Park 184
Al Mamzar Beach Park 55
Al Wadi Park 184
Botanic Garden 155
Burj Park 82
Butterfly Garden 87
Dubai Public Parks 55
Formal Park 134
Green Mubazzarah Park 184
Green Planet 83
Hatta Honeybee Garden and Discovery Center 188
Jubail Mangrove Park 170
Lake Park 134
Umm Al Emarat Park 155
Zabeel Park 65
pearl-diving 143, 227
pearl trade 226-7
Perfume Souq 51
planning
clothes 28
Dubai basics 28-9
etiquette 28
Play DXB 82
podcasts 29
Portuguese Fort 190
public holidays 199
public transport 196, 197, 205

Qasr Al Hosn 130-1, 219
Qasr Al Sarab 182-3
Qasr Al Sarab Protected Area 182
Qasr Al Watan 140-1
QE2 65

Ramadan 27, 212
responsible travel 206-7
religion 212-13, *see also* Islam, mosques
ridesharing 197
road accidents 209
roller-coasters 119, 175, 176
Rub' al Khali 181, 219

Saadiyat Island 162, 169, 170, 171, 221, **164**
safe travel 208-9
Sharjah 193, 229
Sheikh Mohammed bin Rashid Boulevard 81
Sheikh Saeed Al Maktoum House 64
Sheikh Zayed Grand Mosque 152, 156-7
shisha 202
shopping 36-7, *see also individual locations,* markets, shopping malls, souqs
shopping malls
Al Ghurair Centre 52
Dubai Mall 38-9, 79, 84, 85, 220-1, **84**
Galleria Al Maryah Island 148
Madinat Zayed Shopping & Gold Centre 133
Mall of the Emirates 36, 91
Mercato Shopping Mall 96
Nakheel Mall 104
Outlet Village 121
The Beach, JBR 111
Wafi Mall 69
sky-diving 107
Sky Views 81
smoking 199
snorkelling 99
souqs 36, *see also* markets
Bur Dubai Souq 70
Carpet Souk 168
Deira Old Souq 51
Dubai Gold Souq 50
Old Souq (Khor Fakkan) 189
Perfume Souq 51
Souk Al Bahar 77
Souq Madinat Jumeira 90
Spice Souq 51
World Trade Center Souk 134
South Dubai 117-23, **118**
accommodation 119, 120, 121, 122
food 121
shopping 121
sights 119, 120, 122-3
souvenirs 37, 72
spas 100-1
Iridium Spa 171
Spa at W Abu Dhabi Yas Island 178
Spice Souq 51
spices 223
sporting events 27, 34-5
Abu Dhabi Grand Prix 27, 176
Dubai Desert Classic European Tour 27
Dubai Duty Free Tennis Championships 27
Dubai World Cup 27, 87
St Francis Church 165
sustainability 41, 206, 207

tailors 73
taxes 198

taxis 197
telephone services 196
television 29
theatre 35
theme parks 14-15
  Dubai Garden Glow 68
  Dubai Parks and Resorts 119
  Ferrari World Abu Dhabi 176
  Legoland Dubai 119
  Motiongate Dubai 119
  Neon Galaxy 119
  SeaWorld Abu Dhabi 177-8
  Warner Bros World Abu Dhab 175
Time Out Market 39, 77
tipping 198
tours 214, *see also* walking tours
travel seasons 26-7, 214
travel to/from Abu Dhabi 196
travel to/from Dubai 196
travel within Abu Dhabi 197
travel within Dubai 197

under-the-radar experiences 20-1
Unesco World Heritage Cultural Sites
  Al Ain Oasis 183
  Jebel Hafit Desert Park 184

vegetarian travellers 31
visas 196

Wafi City 69
Wahat Al Karama 158
walking, *see* hiking
walking tours
  Dubai 71-2
  Dubai Mall 84, **84**
water parks 14
  AquaDhabi 145
  Aquaventure 108
  Wild Wadi Waterpark 92
  Yas Waterworld 175
weather 26-7, 209
websites 207
weights & measures 199
wellness 10-11
wildlife-watching, *see also* bird-watching
  Al Marmoom Desert Conservation Reserve 122-3
  Ras Al Khor Wildlife Sanctuary 87, 220
World Islands 98
World Trade Center Souk 134

Yas Island 172-9, **174**
  itineraries 24
Yas Marina Circuit 176

zip-lining 59, 160, 187, 191

"To cool off on a hot summer day there's nothing like a rose namlet, a fizzy beverage that was popular in the UAE in the 1970s."

NATASHA AMAR

"Seeing the plethora of flora and fauna that thrive in Abu Dhabi's unique mangroves is nothing short of remarkable."

CHRISTABEL LOBO

"The best dirham I've ever spent is on an abra boat crossing on Dubai Creek. It's the cheapest and most charming way to travel."

SARAH HEDLEY HYMERS

"The first time I spent a night under the stars in the Arabian desert, I knew I'd found my happy place."

HAYLEY SKIRKA

LEFT: SERGII FIGURNYI/SHUTTERSTOCK ©, RIGHT: ALI A SULIMAN/SHUTTERSTOCK ©

Mapping data sources:
© Lonely Planet
© OpenStreetMap http://openstreetmap.org/copyright

THIS BOOK

Destination Editor Zara Sekhavati

Production Editors Joel Cotterell, Kate James

Book Designer Virginia Moreno

Cartographer Valentina Kremenchutskaya

Assisting Editors Peter Cruttenden, Andrea Dobbin

Assisting Book Designer Mazzy Prinsep

Cover Researcher Hannah Blackie

Thanks Ronan Abayawickrema, Sofie Anderson, Andrea Dobbin, Karen Henderson, Ania Lenihan, Darren O'Connell

Paper in this book is certified against the Forest Stewardship Council™ standards. FSC™ promotes environmentally responsible, socially beneficial and economically viable management of the world's forests.

Published by Lonely Planet Global Limited
CRN 554153
11th edition – Mar 2024
ISBN 978 1 83869 728 0

10 9 8 7 6 5 4 3 2 1
Printed in Malaysia